JIHADISM, TERROR AND RIVALRIES

IN THE MIDDLE EAST

ISIS, HEZBOLLAHIS AND TALIBAN

HOSHANG NORAIEE

Contents

List of illustrations

Acknowledgements

This project was developed out of my research on the spread of militant Islam among Sunnis in Iran, who were influenced by the events in Afghanistan and Pakistan. My original interest was in radical Deobandi sectarian conflicts in Pakistan and Afghanistan. Later, particularly in the context of the Arab Spring, my curiosity in this area merged with the consequential developments in the greater Middle East and North Africa. The rise of ISIS/IS and jihad in the whole Middle East and North Africa opened new opportunities for further rivalries to emerge between Iran and Saudi Arabia on the one hand, and Sunni jihadists and Hezbollah on the other. The Taliban was also a big jihadist player, but it was mostly concentrated in Afghanistan and Pakistan. In Iran, the Sunni issue was not new but raised further questions about the possibility of the emergence and spread of sectarian conflicts in Iran, particularly along the border regions in south-eastern Iran. Since the project was developed overtime it emerged as a collection of essays, with a reasonable degree of cohesion.

I would like to thank many anonymous people who kindly answered my questions through telephone calls, social media messaging, or just in personal conversations. Since many of them are in Iran, they prefer to be kept anonymous.

I would also like to thank Habib Seyedzadeh for providing me with some good advice on designing the cover of the book.

My thanks also goes to my proofreader and editor Ivan Veller, who worked very hard to prepare the script for presentation. However, I am responsible for any remaining mistakes in this book.

Most of all, I would like to express my gratitude to my wife, Lihua, and our son, Dara, both of whom – even while also needing my own support – patiently gave me time to work on this project.

Abstract

As the hopeful promise of the Arab Spring has devolved into the cold-hearted backlash of the Arab Winter, the greater Middle East has become engulfed with unprecedented level of violence, chaos and insecurity. Reasons for the avalanche-like juggernaut of asymmetric and proxy wars have been widely and often strictly defined in terms of religious ideological conflicts in Islamic/jihadist form. Yet the manifestation of such conflicts tends to mirror deep-seated problems and concerns which merit investigation. Such investigations are needed because still, from Afghanistan to North Africa and even beyond, surprisingly few immediately-prospective, realistically-compelling solutions have yet to visibly emerge. In religious terms, the problems are not limited to "fundamentalist" Sunni jihadists, nor are they particular to the Taliban, al-Qaeda, or the Islamic State (ISIS, IS). Similar issues arise in conjunction with the radicalism of Shia Hezbollah forces which themselves, in turn, continue to be associated with hard-line elements within the Islamic Republic of Iran. At the political level, these conflicts should be understood in the broader context of rivalries and conflicts among regional powers such as Saudi Arabia and Islamic Republic of Iran. At the social level, injustice, inequality, economic deprivation, along with the absence of well-developed institutions of civil society, have made the whole region dangerously vulnerable to the 'metathesis of radicalism' given the jihadists' absolutist claims of delivering certainty, truth, and justice. This book, which methodologically incorporates both primary and mostly secondary sources, is designed to investigate immediate (though often-overlooked) agents of the problem. It is focused on the strategies and ideologies of ISIS, Taliban, and Hezbollah's forces, along with the vulnerabilities of the Iranian political system and its challenges in addressing the internal causes of these deep-rooted problems (rather than viewing the problem merely as an external threat). The adoption of cooperative, rather than sectarian, policies by all parties in both Shia and Sunni countries is essential for the building and strengthening of a cohesive civil society, and this is vital for weakening extremisms in the whole region.

INTRODUCTION

Introduction

The nature of wars, particularly since the end of the Cold War, has transformed. According to Mary Kaldor, we are now facing 'new wars'.[1] However some other overlapping concepts such as asymmetric wars, intra-state wars, civil wars, and ethnic wars (etc.) have also been widely used to explain this phenomenon.[2] The concept of 'new wars' can be explained on the grounds of competing perspectives: either as essential and intrinsic factors of ethnic and religious divisions, in line with Huntington's argument in *Clash of Civilizations*; or as contingent factors of social, political, and economic conditions as argued by Kaldor in *New and Old Wars*.

This heat of conflict, which first began in the greater Middle East (including Afghanistan, Pakistan, and other central Asian countries), has reached many corners of the world. The nature of these wars is not different from 'new wars'. In other words, these conflicts are not classical, symmetric, or inter-estate wars as defined by Clauswitzian terms; nor are they governed by the Geneva Convention.[3] In intra-state wars, countries do not fight with each other, and there are no established definitions clearly delineating enemy combatants from civilians. There is no distinct front line, leaving states to confront invisible enemies that have little to no commitment to conventional rules.

Asymmetric wars have always existed, but the dimensions of current wars have reached an alarming level and have preoccupied politicians and military strategists alike. Previously, the dominant types of asymmetric wars in the world could be demarcated as Latin-American-type leftist and Marxist guerrilla wars or as armed national liberation movements. These types of wars erupted after World War II and nearly diminished after the end of the Cold War in the 1990s. However, towards the end of the 20th century, a new type of asymmetric war appeared. Ethnic nationalists, as well as radical jihadists, emerged on the political scene.

Jihadist movements, as illustrated by al-Qaeda (on 9/11) and now by ISIS[4], who applied violent actions, similar to secular anarchist and Jacobinist revolutionary movements.[5] Their method of preaching violence is a common feature of their revolutionaries and is used as the dominant method for finding identity, changing society, and achieving salvation. As Frantz Fanon states in his famous book *The Wretched of the Earth*, that violence, for revolutionaries, is essential for defining and consolidating identity and fighting for freedom from the oppressors.

Jihad ('struggle'), in the language of jihadists such as Sayyid Qutb, has a similar meaning. What makes their operational strategy very different from most previous secular radical guerrilla wars is their extensive use of suicide bombings, indiscriminate massacres, and deliberate collateral damage. The Tigers Tamils, before the jihadists, were also known to extensively use suicide bombings against the Sinhalese Regime in Sri Lanka.[6] The jihadists' spectacular actions of horror and destruction are designed to put themselves 'on the map' and showcase themselves on a global network of worldwide screens. Similar to the terrorist character Mr. Verloc as depicted by Joseph Conrad in his classic novel *The Secret Agent*, they make strategic use of an unbelievable extent of seemingly irrational yet calculated actions carefully designed to capture worldwide attention.[7]

The brutality may seem random. However, there is a common historical thread here. After the end of the Cold War, ethnic nationalist and leftist groups in many countries used similar methods of indiscriminate massacre and collateral damage. The ethnic wars in the Balkans, the Tutsi massacres by Hutsis in Rwanda, and the violence in Somalia, Sudan, Liberia, Sierra Leone, Nigeria, Afghanistan, Sri Lanka, Iraq, Syria, Pakistan and Libya are all examples of similarly disastrous events. Security forces, particularly within failed or dictatorial states (such as Peru, Pakistan, and Sri Lanka)[8], have exercised 'dirty war' on their own citizens and used indiscriminate and extra-legal attacks against their opponents, many of whom have been 'disappeared'.[9] The use of hidden wars of terror by dictatorial governments, particularly in Latin America, occurred even prior to the end of the Cold War (e.g. within Argentina during Pinochet's rule).

Today, asymmetric wars have become even more complex and dangerous than before because now, many of them are associated with proxy wars – situations where other countries enter/or support conflicts against each other but do not directly engage each other and even strongly deny their involvement in the proxy wars themselves. Iran, Saudi Arabia, Iraq, UAE, Syria, Yemen, Pakistan, Afghanistan, India, Turkey, Russia, and also the US, UK, France, and other countries have all – to a greater or lesser extent – been involved in such complex proxy wars in the Middle East.[10]

A further layer of complexity is added when one member of a group of allies supports insurgent groups against other allied members for their own sectional or national interests. For example, Pakistan is allied with the US—but it is also involved in supporting the Taliban in Afghanistan. Saudi Arabia and Turkey are also allied with the US, but have been involved in supporting radical Islamists in Syria. Of course, these supporting actions may not always be a direct and deliberate policy of these governments. They may simply be planned at a lower level by security forces and implemented through different channels, such as business or religious channels.

The reasons for the rise of violent jihadists (even non-jihadists) cannot be explained only at the macro level, such as through national or religious factors or even through social and economic deprivations. Nevertheless, social and economic insecurities at this level are indeed crucial factors in understanding the atrocities committed by radical jihadists, whose acts should be viewed in a wider global context. Zigmunt Bawman explains in *Liquid Times* that the end of the Cold War and the globalisation process are associated with rapid change and dislocation of traditional authorities.[11] Beck has also conceptualized, the new societies as 'risk societies'" typified by systemic problems.[12] These problems include the failure of many regions and states, the privatization of security forces, and easy access to the means and resources for violence. Huntington and Lewis's orientalist approach views Al-Qaida and ISIS, and other Salafi jihadists, as representative of a 'civilization'. By contrast, Eric Hobsbawm argues that they are "symptoms, not significant historic agents".[13] Furthermore, they may reflect the most painful and disheartening aspects of uncertainty in a runaway globalising society.[14]

Naji: nature and strategy of jihad

To have a better picture of ISIS's operational strategies and ideology, it may be useful to look at some aspects of the ideas developed by Abu Bakar Naji.[15] However relevant they remain, Naji's ideas were developed on the experiences of Egyptian radical jihadists and al-Qaeda, rather than the new jihadists that emerged during the US occupation of Iraq.

Abu Bakar Naji explains in *Management of Savagery* that Salafist jihadist ideology is based on the concept of '*Tawhid wa Jihad*' (monotheism and jihad). Salafi jihadists are seen as distinctive from all other Islamic movements, particularly mainstream and variant branches of the Muslim Brotherhood, who are viewed as unreliable and worthy of suspicion. The radical ideologue Sayyid Qutb has been an important source of inspiration and knowledge for Salafi jihadists and is considered to be a martyr—yet ironically, many have either partially or entirely rejected him.

For Naji, jihad is an offensive and extremely complex process that focuses on utilizing extreme forms of violence and massacres. For him, jihad goes through different stages in order to reach the state of a Caliphate. It employs chaos and fear to harass and exhaust its enemies and their supporters. This use of 'vexation and exhaustion' is the most violent aspect of this phase, which is aimed at creating maximum instability. It is also associated with attracting a high level of publicity by committing seemingly indiscriminate attacks and beheadings. At the same time, it aims to polarise people into opposing camps of 'believers' and 'non-believers'. This further gives rise to questioning the ability and power of 'apostate' rulers and discrediting them among the Muslims—who are, according to Naji, intrinsically searching for salvation (by joining the real jihadists).

Naji explains that through this insecurity and chaos, a phase he calls the 'management of savagery' appears. In this phase, certain constructive measures are taken, and further training for jihad starts in mujahidin-controlled on territory (*Dar ul Islam*). Note that by this stage, the mujahidin already control territory. One might assume their end goal has been achieved. However, this home base is seen, by jihadists, as a staging ground for waging more jihad rather than less. From there, the road is cleared for further progress to be made in terms of restoring and then expanding the caliphate. From this point of view, the caliphate is a glorified ideal—a borderless empire to be claimed both from within (by societal purification) and from without (by territorial expansion).

Naji attacks reformists and sheikhs who argue for defensive and peaceful solutions designed to promote national unity and stability above all else. Refuting them, Naji argues:

> If you fight the desert and the city until they perish, that is of less significance than them setting up a Taghut [an apostate rebel reprobate] upon the earth

who rules contrary to the sharia of Islam with which Allah sent His Messenger (peace and blessings be upon him) [cf. page 44: "If you fight the desert and the city until no one in them remains, this is better than a Taghut being appointed who rules contrary to the sharia of Islam"].[16]

If utter annihilation of the entire *"ummah"* in jihad is seen as preferable to apostate governance, then the destruction of non-Muslims – and the annihilation of stability and peace in 'apostate' territories – is even a bigger aim of these jihadists than many realise. Naji praises all destructive operations, even if they cannot achieve such a level as the 9/11 operation, as an ideal level for him, did.

Naji believes that the stability and security of the rule of infidels (non-Muslims) and apostates (former Muslims) ought to be destroyed:

> Some imagine—by their unique reasoning—that jihad against the invading enemy is only at the beginning of the arrival of this enemy with his forces. But if this enemy settles and his goal is achieved, among the harmful things (that result) is the corruption of that stability and security in which the people live! In reality, the only benefit to be had is in the destruction of that stability, for if the infidel or the apostate settles and rules some country, he will begin to work toward dislodging the people from their religion. Let the reader consider Chechnya now and Chechnya a quarter-century ago when there were people living in security and the infidel ruler stripped it of its religion.[17]

If the points made by Naji are to be put together, terror is for him an absolute necessity and an essential strategy. This is very similar to what revolutionary anarchist Johannes Most believed. Townshend has quoted him as saying:

1. Outrageous violence will seize public imagination;
2. its audience can thus be awakened to political issues;
3. violence is inherently empowering and is (as the later anticolonial writer Frantz Fanon put it "a cleansing force";
4. systematic violence can threaten the state and impel it into delegitimizing reactions;
5. violence can destabilise the social order and threaten social breakdown;
6. ultimately, the people will reject the government and turn to "terrorists".[18]

Naji has not hidden that his ideas on the process of war and organisation had (ironically) been influenced by Western management theorists as well as by Latin American guerrilla war strategists, though he strongly rejects their secular political and ideological approaches.

Naji has used cost-benefit analysis to indicate the sources of weaknesses, rivalries, and conflicts among the regimes of secularists and unbelievers, as well as to highlight the strengths of jihadists who, according to him, have no material concerns. For the jihadists, destruction of 'the other' has been associated with the destruction of symbols related to others' identities. The destruction of historical monuments and related shrines, mosques, and historic places such as Bamiyan by the Taliban, or Almyra and Christian churches and Sufi shrines and mosques by ISIS, are elements of a 'total war' designed to destroy others' identities and existence.

A particularly important characteristic of the jihadists is the idea that jihad is a permanent and an offensive principle whereas peace is merely seen as a short-term cessation of hostilities and an interim goal, rather than an end. It is doubtful that committedly *takfirist*, Salafist jihadist groups such as ISIS could be easily persuaded to implement a permanent peace. However, the use of what could be called a 'tactical peace treaty' (as a tactical weapon) is acceptable for the radical Muslim Brotherhood ideologue Sayyid Qutb. For Qutb, peace treaties and contracts are just part of a temporary "peaceful time of preparation" for "open warfare" in the process of waging "eternal" jihad:

> [T]his struggle is not a temporary phase but an eternal state—an eternal state as truth and falsehood cannot coexist on the earth. Whenever Islam stood up with the universal declaration that Allah's Lordship should be established over the entire earth and that men should free from servitude to other men, the usurpers of Allah's Authority on earth have struck out against it fiercely and have never tolerated it. It becomes incumbent upon Islam to strike back and release man throughout the earth from the grip of these usurpers. The eternal struggle for freedom of man will continue until the religion is purified for Allah.[19]

The problem is not just about the clear ideological desires these jihadists have about 'the other'. More than that, the problems are about the existence of appropriate social, political, and economic conditions in which jihadists grow and spread, both globally and nationally.

The turbulent region

The growth and spread of the radical jihadists in the Middle East are obvious phenomena which occurred after the US's hasty and mostly unilateral invasion of Iraq. The post-Saddam-Hussein era became a prosperous time for the growth of jihadist sectarian conflicts. This has been viewed as a clear indication of the failure of the "war on terror" policy started by George W. Bush and supported by Tony Blair after the 9/11 incident. By removing traditional forms of political authorities in the context of lack of alternative and legitimate institutions and forces, instability and chaos easily fed the radical jihadists, who were always looking for such a condition in which they can easily growth. With the high costs of resistance taking its toll, the wave of jihadist activities tended to be weaker by 2011. However, having started to grow during the Arab Spring, it again reached its peak with the continuation of civil war in Syria. Now ISIS has turned into a formidable force which has challenged not only all states in the Middle East and North Africa but also some others, particularly Western countries.

At the national level, particularly in the Middle East, there are many problems including a limited capacity for making political reforms, for tackling corruption, and for improving economic conditions for the majority of the population. At the regional level, severe competitions between different countries – most notably between Iran and Saudi Arabia – have created fertile ground for radicals to grow and for sectarian conflicts to erupt.

From the beginning of the anti-Assad protests, the Islamic Republic of Iran (IRI) systematically and full-heartedly supported Bashar al Assad's government. To a large extent, this intervention reflected competition between regional powers – particularly between Iran and Saudi Arabia. In the process of deepening the conflict (helped by the reluctance of Assad to reform the system and to compromise), radical jihadist groups – including ISIS – rapidly grew. These militants also benefitted from (even if not directly) resources sent by foreign governments – particularly Turkey, Saudi Arabia, and Qatar – to strengthen all opposition groups involved in fighting against the Assad regime. By means of their support,

Arab countries intended to weaken Iran. The Turkish government, in particular, turned a blind eye towards ISIS activities in order to weaken or destroy PKK alliances across the border in Syria.

Turkish policy created a wave of anger all over the world.[20] Turkey has now undertaken quite an active policy against ISIS, but has continued to attack Kurdish forces – such as the PKK – and to weaken the Kurds' close allies in Syria, the People's Defense Units (YPG). This has happened, despite this fact that the Kurdish forces are supported by the US, and have demonstrated their potential to play a vigorous and decisive role in opposing ISIS, as was shown in Kobani.

It has also been suggested, by some commentators, that the radical Islamists and jihadists (at least when the US was in Iraq, and at the earlier phase of the Arab Spring in Syria) were supported by both Iran and Syria. This policy was adopted to undermine the US's power on the one hand, and to justify their own claims about the nature of their opponents on the other.[21]

In spite of all the efforts made by international alliances to tackle the issue of ISIS, and in spite of the spread of rivalries among the Islamists and radical jihadists, ISIS has not shown much sign of weakness. According to Cockburn, the size of land occupied by ISIS is larger than Great Britain.[22] ISIS has also formed *velayats* (provinces) in many other Muslim countries. ISIS has also widened its alliance with other radical jihadists or ex-al-Qaeda forces. While ISIS has retreated in some areas, it has started bigger attacks in some other directions, has occupied new territories, and continues to recruit and train more forces.

Gaining and controlling a specific territory may be by far less significance than rapidly spreading ISIS organisations to many other parts of the world. New evidence shows that the 'received wisdom' of the well-established idea in strategic planning of making too much of a distinction between whether an enemy happens to be a 'far enemy' or a 'near enemy' is (in this context) quite simplistic because for jihadists, these are extremely interconnected strategies. They have a principally global strategy, as far as they believe in offensive jihad and consider Ummah beyond any national entity. Practically, this means they may make use of a unified, holistic strategy rather than a zone-based or nationally-oriented one. Conquering land may not be a goal of their strategy at the earlier phase of jihad. Yet ISIS has never pursued a 'near enemy' as their long-term strategy, and later developments have shown that ISIS has had, and still has, far more international ambitions even than al-Qaeda does.

Caliphate territory (as *Dar ul Islam*) is, for ISIS, extremely important to defend. Yet at this stage of jihad, it may not be considered as an ultimate goal. Ideologically, for jihadists, territorial occupation for building a 'nation-state' is different from the realisation of the "Sovereignty of Allah" in *Dar al-Islam*. These are seen as two completely different and inconsistent things. So tactically, they can retreat, if necessary, to spread their messages and capture other territories for the same purpose. It is believed to be an integral part of jihad/war to "test" the faith and strength of jihadists during training. For ISIS, in an ideological sense, defeat in war does not exactly mean losing land since they do not recognise the concept of 'land' and 'defeat' in secular terms. This ideologically-determined strategy may lose its meaning at a certain phase of engagement in political/territorial consolidation, but that has not happened yet. Still, they may argue that by spreading jihad worldwide and by sending their messages all over the world, they have won the battle.

The Iranian Islamic Republic, from the time it was established in 1979, has tried to present itself as a source of inspiration for the Islamisation of politics and society by "exporting Islamic revolution". It has supported an "Islamic awakening" and has encouraged insurgencies against secular and non-compliant governments. But Sunni clerics and governments in Sunni Islamic countries have been very suspicious about the Shia version of Iranian Islamism. Thus, it was much easier for Ayatollah Khomeini to encourage and support Shia populations – who were likely to be under pressure and suffering marginalisation and discrimination in Sunni-dominant countries – to absorb the messages of the Iranian revolution and build their own radical organisations. These Shia groups appeared as the main Iranian agents of exporting revolution. This created a context for more "fundamentalist", anti-Shia groups to strengthen their positions in more organised ways and to enter sectarian conflicts, particularly in Pakistan with its large Shia population. Sipah-e-Sahaba Pakistan and Lashkar-e-Jhangvi in Pakistan, along with certain factions of the Afghani mujahidin and later the Taliban, reflected this anti-Shia trend. The Taliban emerged as the biggest threat against the Iranian Shia on the eastern border with Afghanistan. Storming the Iranian consulate in Mazar-e Sharif in 1998 and killing 8 or so Iranian diplomats, or attacking and killing Hazarahs, are some examples.

The Islamic Republic of Iran, as was made clear in Mecca-related events in 1980, had shown its very hostile attitude towards secular regimes in the Middle East and towards the Saudi Arabian regime, as a close allied of the US, in particular. In the context of the Afghanistan wars against the Soviet Union, Saudi Arabia – with its huge resources – undertook an active role to export its own version of Sunni-Wahhabi Islam to compete with the version of Shia Islam promulgated by the Iranian regime. This has had a long-term effect on the whole Middle Eastern region and related Islamic countries, as radicalism among Sunnis has been influenced by Wahhabi-Salafi puritanical ideas. ISIS – which has emerged in this turbulent conditions of rivalries, wars, and conflicts – is now a force to be reckoned with. Following Zarqawi's ideological blueprint, ISIS has become a far greater threat against Shias and the Iranian regime than the Taliban ever was. It is a significant threat against the regime in Saudi Arabia, too.

Organising, training, and sending fanatical Shia militias from different countries to combat ISIS in Syria and Iraq by means of the Sepah-e Qods (Quds Force), the cross-border branch of the Sepah Pasdaran (Iranian Revolutionary Guard Corps, or IRGC), and Iranian security forces has heightened tensions between Shia and Sunnis further and has helped increase polarisation of the population (as ISIS wishes). This was a basis for the warning by Masoud Barzani, a top Kurdish security official from Iraqi Kurdistan, regarding the danger posed by Shia militias in Iraq.

The spread of ISIS in the Middle East – and in particular, its formation of active cells surrounding Iran – needs more attention. ISIS has already moved from Iraq towards Iran's border. ISIS threatens not only Shias but also Sunni Kurds in Iqlim-e Kurdistan. ISIS has attacked Shia mosques in Kuwait, Yemen, Saudi Arabia, Bahrain, and even Bangladesh. Further targeting in other Gulf countries such as UAE could be far more disastrous for the economy of the whole area than ever before. Moreover, ISIS has moved into Pakistan and Afghanistan and has established *Velayat-e Khorasan*.[23] ISIS has recruited forces from the Tajiks and Uzbeks as well as the Chechens.[24] This seems to be a way of besieging Iran in a very-well-calculated manner. In this way, ISIS not only tries to persuade the Sunnis in Iran to rise, but also puts more pressure on the Iranian forces in Syria, Iraq, and Lebanon.

The apocalyptic elements of the conflict have increased regional volatility and danger. From both sides, Sunni jihadists – particularly ISIS on the one hand, and radical Shia militias on the other (with fighters coming from other countries such as Lebanon, Iraq, Iran, Afghanistan, and Pakistan) – have intensified sectarian conflicts by framing them in apocalyptic terms. ISIS believe that they are fighting against prophesied enemies and are preparing conditions for the ummah-unifying emergence of the Mahdi (Messiah) at Dabiq, as a starting point for a global rule of 'real' Muslims. For Sunni jihadists, the Shias and their allies are the ones who are part of the anti-Mahdi forces of evil. For Shia radicals, who expect that the Twelfth Imam (also called the Mahdi) would appear to spread justice all over the world, Salafi jihadists and all anti-Assad forces are anti-Mahdi, or enemies of the Twelfth Imam.

Part of ISIS's project in besieging Iran, may be related to put direct pressure on Iran by influencing Sunni minorities along the western, eastern, and southeastern borders of Iran. In this regard, the Sunnis along the southeastern borders of Iran are likely to be the main target of recruitment. For instance, Sistan and Baluchestan Province, a marginal area bordering Afghanistan and Pakistan. Because of the weakness of secular political traditions in this area, as well as widespread dissatisfaction among the populace, a considerable section of the Sunni population may show sympathy to ISIS. There are already Sunni militia groups who support Sharia-based Islamic Sunni rule and who consider themselves to be jihadist activists. They have been closely influenced both by Taliban and by other Sunni jihadists within Pakistan and Arab countries. The jihadists in the area – Jondollah (now it is mainly succeeded by Jaish-e Adl) and Ansar-e Forqan, for instance – have exercised suicide bombings, deliberate collateral damage, and indiscriminate massacres against Shia and Iranian security forces. Since a combination of religious issues and ethnic grievances against the government is closely tied in this area, the appeal for generating pushback against the Iranian Shia government is quite high.

The issue of ISIS is currently so dominant on the international and regional scene that attention to both al-Qaeda and the Taliban have, to a large extent, moved to backstage. Recently, the Taliban has been facing severe challenges from ISIS inside Afghanistan. The Taliban has also faced a split during last few months after Mullah Omar's death became known. The significance of the Taliban in terms of both their radicalisation of jihadist forces in the area and their severe competition with ISIS requires more consideration. The Taliban, although not an international threat, is likely to remain as a destabilising force in the region for many years to come.

Al-Qaeda has been weakened by rivalries and riven by its severe conflicts with ISIS. But it still has its international networks all over the world; and it wields a strong armed force in Syria, where it still controls some land. Lessening the attention paid to al-Qaida may only give them more space to strengthen their organisation in preparation for further attacks in future—particularly due to their hope that ISIS will lose its current influence and power.

Structure of the Book

This book has five sections which cover various topics including ISIS, the Taliban, the Islamic Republic of Iran, and the militant Sunnis in southeastern Iran. These sections originally were developed as separate essays. Apart from the Introduction as Section 1 other sections are organised in the following way.

In **section 2**, the Taliban and ISIS will be compared with regard to their main differences in terms of their theocratic approach, political ideology, political strategies, and operational strategies. In same section, the conflicts between jihadists will also be explored.

In **section 3**, the myth and reality of ISIS's threat to the Islamic Republic of Iran (IRI) will be examined. Section two will discuss some similarities extant in the political ideologies of both ISIS and IRI. But it will argue that the anti-Shia approach by ISIS, in the political context of the existing conflicts in which Iran is an active supporter of the Iraqi and Syrian governments, has become a great threat to Iran and can create some significant problems in certain parts of Iran.

In **section 4**, the focus will be on the social and political conditions in southeastern Iran, where radical Sunni groups such as Jondollah and Jaish al-Adl have been challenging the Iranian regime and, to some extent, have been showing sympathy to Sunni global jihadists.

Section 5 will be the overall conclusion.

References

Bauman, Zygmunt. *Liquid Times: Living in an Age of Uncertainty.* Cambridge: Polity Press, 2007.

Beck, Ulrich. "Living Your Own Life in a Runaway World: Individualisation, Globalisation and Politics". Ed. Hutton, Will, and Anthony Giddens. *On the Edge: Living with Global Capitalism.* London: Jonathan Cape, 2000. 164-174.

Browning, Christopher. *International Security: A Very Short Introduction.* Oxford: Oxford UP, 2013.

Cockburn, Patrick. *The Rise of Islamic State: ISIS and the New Sunni Revolution.* New York: Verso, 2014.

Conrad, Joseph. *The Secret Agent.* 1907. Amazon Createspace, 2010.

Fanon, Frantz. *The Wretched of the Earth.* 1963. Trans. Richard Philcox, 2004 (New York: Grove Press, 2004). 9 Mar. 2016 <https://books.google.com/books?id=-XGKFJq4ec-cC&vq>.

Giddens, Anthony. *Runaway World: How Globalisation is Reshaping Our Lives.* London: Profile Books, 1999.

Gray, John. *Al Qaeda and What It Means to Be Modern.* Chatham: Faber & Faber, 2003.

Hobsbawm, Eric. *Globalisation, Democracy and Terrorism.* London: Abacus, 2007.

Idiz, Semih. "Is Turkey Really Committed to Fighting IS?" *Al-Monitor* 28 July 2015. 18 Dec. 2015 <http://www. al-monitor.com/pulse/originals/2015/07/turkey-syria-pkk-kurds-dilute-efforts-against-isis.html>.

Kaldor, Mary. *New and Old Wars: Organized Violence in a Global Era.* 3rd ed. Stanford: Stanford UP, 2013.

Naji, Abu Bakar. *The Management of Savagery: The Most Critical Stage Through Which the Umma Will Pass.* Trans. William McCants, John M. Olin Institute for Strategic Studies, 2006. [Cambridge]: Harvard U., 2006.

Qutb, Sayyid. *Ma'alim fi-l-Tariq* [Milestones]. Delhi: Islamic Book Service, 2002.

Stern, Jessica, and J. M. Berger. *ISIS: The State of Terror.* London: William Collins, 2015.

Townshend, Charles. *Terrorism: A Very Short Introduction.* 2nd ed. Oxford: Oxford UP, 2011.

Weiss, Michael, and Hassan Hassan. *ISIS: Inside the Army of Terror.* New York: Regan Arts, 2015.

Endnotes

1 Mary Kaldor, *New and Old Wars: Organized Violence in a Global Era,* 3rd ed. (Stanford: Stanford UP, 2013).

Christopher Browning, *International Security: A Very Short Introduction* (Oxford: Oxford UP, 2013) 47-62.

3 Carl von Clausewitz (1780-1831) was a prominent Prussian Enlightenment theorist whose book *On War* has been an influential classic work on symmetric wars.

4 The Islamic State (commonly known as 'ISIS') has also been referred to as 'IS', 'ISIL', and in Arabic and Farsi languages) 'Dae'sh'. But here, we have mainly used the term 'ISIS', given its usage as the most popular abbreviation.

5 Eric Hobsbawm, *Globalisation, Democracy and the Terrorism* (London: Abacus, 2007) 121-136. See also Gray, John, *Al Qaeda and What It Means to Be Modern* (Chatham: Faber & Faber, 2003).

See pages 38 and 64 of Frantz Fanon, *The Wretched of the Earth,* 1963, trans. Richard Philcox, 2004 (New York: Grove Press, 2004), 9 Mar. 2016 <https://books.google.com/books ?id=-XGKFJq4eccC&vq>.

6 Hobsbawm 121-137.

7 Joseph Conrad, *The Secret Agent*, 1907 (Amazon Createspace, 2010).

8 According to Hobsbawm 146, the CIA (in 2004) had identified 50 regions where the titular governments of the states in question had little to no governing control over their own security forces.

9 Hobsbawm 121-137.

10 See Michael Weiss and Hassan Hassan, *ISIS: Inside the Army of Terror* (New York: Regan Arts, 2015). See also Cockburn, Patrick, *The Rise of Islamic State: ISIS and the New Sunni Revolution* (London: Verso, 2014).

11 Zygmunt Bauman, *Liquid Times: Living in an Age of Uncertainty* (Cambridge: Polity Press, 2007).

12 Ulrich Beck, "Living Your Own Life in a Runaway World: Individualisation, Globalisation and Politics", *On the Edge: Living with Global Capitalism*, ed. Will Hutton and Anthony Giddens (London: Jonathan Cape, 2000) 164-174.

13 Hobsbawm 136-137.

14 Anthony Giddens, *Runaway World: How Globalisation is Reshaping Our Lives* (London: Profile Books, 1999).

15 Abu Bakar Naji, *The Management of Savagery: The Most Critical Stage Through Which the Umma Will Pass*, trans. William McCants, John M. Olin Institute for Strategic Studies ([Cambridge]: Harvard U., 2006).

16 Naji 104.

17 Naji 257.

18 Charles Townshend, *Terrorism: A Very Short Introduction*, 2nd ed. (Oxford: Oxford UP, 2011) 14. See also Fanon 51 ("violence is a cleansing force").

19 Sayyid Qutb, *Ma'alim fi-l-Tariq* [Milestones] (Delhi: Islamic Book Service, 2002) 65.

20 Semih Idiz, "Is Turkey Really Committed to Fighting IS?" *Al-Monitor* 28 July 2015, 18 Dec. 2015, <http://www.al-monitor.com/pulse/originals/2015/07/turkey -syria-pkk- kurds-dilute-efforts-against-isis.html#>.

21 Weiss and Hassan (2015) show that, for example, the Assad Government had (in different ways) supported the radical Islamists both inside Syria after the eruption of the Arab Spring, while also either supporting or ignoring their actions on the Iraqi border in attacking US forces. See also Jessica Stern and J. M. Berger, *ISIS: The State of Terror* (London: William Collins, 2015).

22 Cockburn 27.

23 Citing *The Encyclopaedia of Islam* (1979), Wikipedia indicates that "'In...early Islamic times, the term 'Khurassan' frequently had a much wider denotation, covering [not only an area in the Persian northeast but] also parts of Central Asia and Afghanistan; early Islamic usage often regarded everywhere east of western Persia...as being included in a vast... region of Khurasan, which might even extend to the Indus Valley and Sind'". Thus the choice of this name may hint at the scope of the Islamic State's vision and intended aims.

24 Stern and Berger 179-198.

لا إله إلا الله

الله
رسول
محمد

SECTION 2

THE TALIBAN, ISIS, AND DISARRAY AMONG JIHADISTS

ISIS Flag

Abstract

The emergence of the Islamic State (ISIS) – a starting point for building a caliphate – has led to much human catastrophe, not only in that area but in many other parts of the world including Europe—and yet there is no prospect of seeing an immediate end to this problem. In many respects, the ISIS issue may seem to be a phenomenon similar to the Taliban in Afghanistan; but there are many differences, both from ideological and strategic points of view, between these two movements. The outbreak of violent conflict inside Afghanistan between these two forces reflects, to a great extent, their deep ideological differences. Disarray among jihadists and prospects for further tensions among them, particularly between radical Salafists such as al-Qaeda and ISIS, is another issue which needs further exploration.

Key words: ISIS, the Taliban, Salafi, Sunni, Shia, jihadi, takfir, Islam, al-Qaeda, Deobandi, Afghanistan, Iraq, Syria, caliphate.

2.1: Introduction

A tragedy that is unfolding in Iraq and Syria has already developed into an unprecedented crisis and has spread beyond the region and taken on a global dimension. Policies based on religious and ethnic divisions have fuelled sectarian conflicts. These divisions developed in the context of the occupation of Iraq by America and her allies through what they called the "war on terror". In Iraq, where civil society was underdeveloped and growth and consolidation of civil rights was poor, sudden collapse of formal authority – particularly the deliberate disintegration of the army – created a new context for widening social divisions and strengthening ethnic and religious fragmentations, which are contemporarily constructed as people's most accessible collective identities. Prior to the occupation of Iraq by the US and her allies, there was hardly any jihadist political force. However, during the occupation of Iraq, jihadist activities rapidly started to spread and grow. From there, Abu Mus'ab al-Zarqawi led the establishment of the first international branch of al-Qaeda—al-Qaeda in Iraq (which later became the Islamic State of Iraq), an organization which planted the political and ideological seeds of a sustainable, radical jihadi movement.

However, with great effort and by much expenditure of 'blood and treasure' (including distribution of resources to allies) on the part of the US and her allies, towards the end of the occupation of Iraq this problem had, to a great extent, been brought under control. The formation of a united council of Sunni tribes – the Anbar Salvation Council, leaders of the National Front for the Salvation of Iraq, also known as the Sahwa (Awakening) Movement – was a crucial step in fighting and weakening al-Qaeda in Iraq. By 2009, the Sahwa Movement had mobilised over 100,000 tribesmen in Anbar Province.[1]

The sectarian policies adopted by Nouri al-Maliki's government quickly opened up the dividing boundaries much further, and created fertile ground for growing the current bleeding tensions. There was deep discontent of the Sunnis in Iraq, as well as widespread corruption and incompetency among the bureaucratic and security forces of the Maliki government. This made it very easy for ISIS, as an extremist Salafist jihadist group, to come back after a few years and take the control of such a large area both in Iraq and in Syria—an area which is now bigger than the UK.[2]

Because of Maliki's discriminatory and alienating policies, many of the same tribal militias who had once defeated al-Qaida in al-Anbar joined ISIS. The authoritarian nature of the Maliki government, to some extent, was based on its bigger brother, the Islamic Republic of Iran. Comparable to ISIS's approach, two decades earlier, the Taliban – as another Sunni "fundamentalist" group – emerged in Afghanistan, where it ruled the "Islamic Emirate of Afghanistan" and sheltered al-Qaeda as it organized and trained radical global jihadists.

The Taliban emerged in the context of spreading conflict, corruption, and insecurity, which had become more widespread during the rule of the mujahidin in the early 1990s. The Taliban, as a brutal force, rapidly seized power in the mid-1990s as an alternative to mujahidin-Islamist groups. But the Taliban was a Pashtun force located in Afghanistan—situated just within the margin of the Middle East and yet outside the zone of core Islamic culture and language of the Arabic Middle East. The Taliban attracted the attention of the international community; however, it was mainly given publicity for its strict policies against women's education, demolition of historical heritage sites, and sheltering of al-Qaeda leaders. Otherwise, the Taliban remained as a local power rather than as an internationally influential force. Even some time after having been removed from power by the US and her allies, for some years the Taliban remained in a very defensive position. Gradually, though, it emerged as a powerful force again—this time not only in Afghanistan but also in Pakistan.

Since then, they have used comparatively more effective measures than previously to attack both the governments of (the then) President Hamid Karzai and (now) President Mohammad Ashraf Ghani Ahmadzai, and to attack the foreign forces in Afghanistan, using suicide attacks and spreading their messages by using social media.

As jihadi movements, the Taliban and ISIS – for the sake of implementing their own versions of the Islamic agenda – both succeeded in establishing their own governments through application of the most extreme forms of violence.

While they share some similarities in terms of actions and aims, they have fundamental differences in terms of their origins and social bases, along with their religious and political ideologies as well as their political and operational strategies.

To gain better insights into their differences, it may be appropriate to look at some similarities between the Taliban and ISIS.

Similarities

First of all, both the Taliban and the Islamic State (ISIS, IS, or ISIL) are political movements. For this reason, to a great extent, much of the rhetoric they use arguably cannot precisely reflect their main objectives. They have taken many practical measures employed for the sake of gaining, strengthening, or consolidating their power.

The nature of both movements' organisations and associated states can be described in terms of a strong desire for total control of the society through strict authoritarianism, oppression, and the destruction of pluralistic cultural and historical diversity. In discussions of totalitarianism, their organisations have been described by analysts as being "totalistic" in nature (Robert Jay Lifton), in language of Erving Goffman[3] as being "total institution[s]" or "total domination", as Hannah Arendt had argued.[4] However, this totalitarian approach is – by far – more systematic and cohesive in ISIS than in the Taliban.

Both the Taliban and the Islamic State are, in general, Sunni Muslims. Both are anti-American and anti-Western in nature. Both believe in using extreme forms of violence and waging jihad against secularism and secular states. Both are fanatical jihadi martyrdom-seekers; and now, both are extensively using suicide attacks as a key weapon in their operations. Both are anti-Shia, but at a completely new level; and they are against any religious denomination different from their own specific form of Sunni Islam. Shias are considered by both as being heretics (*beda'ati*) and apostates (*moshrek*)— rejectionist (*rafida*) and non-believers (*kafir*). With an anti-Semitic approach, they also consider Shias as being "Jewish" in dress, accuse them of giving Islam a bad name, and regard them as being the main enemy and/or as an enemy's 'fifth column' within Islamic societies. Abu Mus'ab al-Zarqawi, the architect of the strategies now being followed by ISIS, has very clearly waged a war against Shias opposed even by al-Zawahiri.[5] However, the anti-Shia approach of the Taliban, which was influenced by Deobandi and fanatical mullahs in Afghanistan, is – to a lesser extent – systematic and cohesive.

The hostile attitude harboured by the Taliban towards Hazara Shias in Afghanistan – and now, Pakistan (as expressed by both the Pakistani Taliban and by their allies such as Lashkar-e Jhangvi) – is, to some extent, similar to the anti-Shia approach of al-Zarqawi. ISIS's current actions against Iraqi Shias is a good example of this. Under Taliban rule, hostility towards other religions, such as Sikhs and Hindus, forced them to either flee Afghanistan or to stay and pay extra tribute (*jizya*) and carry specific marks of identification to be distinguishable from their Muslim 'superiors'. Blowing up the famous Buddha statues in the World Heritage site at Bamiyan in March 2001[6] was a clear expression of anger, hatred, and intransigence by the Taliban towards not only Buddhists and any form of Buddhist identity, but also towards all other religions and religious forms of cultural heritage.[7] Now, ISIS's approach towards Yazidis, Armenian Christians, and other Christian minorities is similar or even harsher than what the Taliban did with non-Muslim minorities.[8] There were very shocking reports that ISIS jihadists, – similar to what Boko Haram had done with Christians in Nigeria[9] – kidnapped Yazidi women as plunder and forced them to convert to Islam and marry jihadists, or forced them into slavery—putting them for sale on the market.[10] They have also committed violent and discriminatory acts against Christians and Jews—despite the fact that in Islam, such groups are considered to be minority owners of the Abrahamic heritage, being 'People of the Book'. Destruction of ancient relics in Palmyra, Syria, and the execution of a well-known archaeologist of the site, has been widely reported.[11]

Both ISIS and the Taliban do not even hesitate to destroy Islamic holy places such as mosques, schools, shrines, and other places of worship belonging to Sufis and Shiites or even to Sunni opponents. To justify their actions, they frequently mention the destruction of the Masjid al-Dirar. Masjid al-Dirar was a Medinian mosque destroyed by Mohammad, who considered it as a place for conspiracy of the hypocrites against Islam.[12] On the basis of this analogy, radical jihadists including the Taliban have frequently attacked and destroyed mosques and killed Sunni religious figures in Afghanistan. Therefore, it should not be so surprising when they try to justify their attacks on the Christians, Buddhists, and Jews along with their places of worship such as churches, temples, and synagogues.

Both the Taliban and ISIS have similarly pursued particularly harsh policies to enforce self-approved guidelines governing religious rituals and ceremonies. It is known that the Taliban have closed down and even ruined photo shops, off-license alcoholic drink shops, cinemas, theatres, cassettes, and televisions.[13] The Taliban had even 'hung' video cassettes and televisions on trees. According to the Taliban's rules, men had to have graspable beards; and it was said that police of the "promotion of virtue and prevention of vice" had stopped and measured men's beards, which were not to be shorter than a certain size.[14] Flogging, the stoning of women, and public beheadings have been some of the other brutal actions used by both the Taliban and ISIS.

These indicate that both the Taliban and the Islamic State enforce strict *sharia* rules in daily life, and in similar ways. But since the main focal point of this article is on differences between both groups, we now turn to those differences in more detail.

In Section 2.2, important differences between radical Salafists (particularly ISIS and the Deobandi Taliban) in terms of their social bases, along with their ideological, political and operational strategies, will be examined. In Section 2.3, the current disarray among radical jihadists, particularly among Salafists, will be explained.

2.2: The Taliban and ISIS—both brutal but different

Social and political roots

In terms of roots and social bases, there are fundamental differences between the Taliban and ISIS. The Taliban has its roots among the rural mullahs who fought as mujahidin during the occupation of Afghanistan by the USSR, and many of them had experienced life in Afghan refugee camps in Pakistan. These mullahs had played a crucial role in mobilizing seminary *talibs* (students), mainly from Deobandi madrassas in Pakistan. They built their social bases among Afghan emigrants, particularly madrassas' students (*talibs*), and among Pashtuns in rural areas who were very discontent with the oppression of mujahidin warlords after the Russians had left and the mujahidin had seized power. Vulnerable Afghans, who were suffering from insecurity and chaos amidst the conflicts between Islamists of the Jamia'at-e Islami and Hezb-e Islami parties in Afghanistan, found they had little to no option but to turn to the Taliban as their only viable choice. The Tali-

Taliban website http://shahamat-farsi.com/?p=16065

Figure 2-1 Mullah Omar

ban were benefiting from the support of the Pakistani security forces (the ISI), while they also received financial support from the Gulf countries, particularly Saudi Arabia.[15] But in general, the Taliban developed into a broad-based social movement rather than into a vanguard organisation.

ISIS, by contrast, has acted as a vanguard organisation. Their leaders mainly come from Salafist-educated Arabs, the majority of whom have little relation with traditional madrassas.[16] Their social base is built among the urban poor and a sizeable section of the middle class (particularly those of the diaspora) suffering from insecurity and alienation in the globalising era. They have attracted a considerable number of Western-educated Muslim jihadists. For example, some estimate that about 3,000 jihadists have come from the West to join radical jihadi organisations in Syria and Iraq.[17] Furthermore, there are also many jihadists who have joined ISIS from other Middle Eastern and North African countries as well as central Asian ones. More specifically, a sense of deprivation and discrimination among the Sunnis in Iraq under Maliki's government, facilitated the conditions for ISIS to take advantage and gain some sympathy among certain sections of the Sunni population in Iraq. Continuation of conflict in Syria, particularly in the context of the corruption of moderate opponent organisations such as the Free Syrian Army (FSA), has helped all radical jihadists, particularly ISIS, to gain ground.

However, both the Taliban and ISIS are strongly patriarchal and have very strict attitudes towards women. The discrimination and marginalisation of women is actually accepted as intrinsic parts of the values they defend. The Taliban and ISIS both deny women any employment in public sector, – possibly apart from enforcement activities by the religious police for the so-called "promotion of virtue and prevention of vice" – and even banned them from going to non-religious schools and participating in the battlefields of jihad.[18] At the same time, the roles given to women are different under each. In contrast to the Taliban, ISIS actively invites Muslim jihadist women from any part of world to join ISIS and persuades them to participate in activities publicly validated and recognised by ISIS male leaders. It is estimated that about 10-15% of jihadists from Western countries have been women.[19]

Ideology

There are fundamental differences between the Taliban and ISIS in terms of religious and political ideology. The Taliban's ideology is based on a hybrid of Deobandi-Hanafi religious views mixed with Pashtun ethnic and tribal customs. In the context of brutal conflicts and of the failure of mainstream Islamists, such as Burhanuddin Rabbani and Ahmad Shah

Massoud on the one hand, and Gulbuddin Hekmatyar on the other, these views took on further political orientation.[20] Deobandism was originally developed as an educational approach in 1860s India. Its intent was multiple, but more importantly to purify Hanafi traditions in India from the influence of both mysticism and Hinduism; and to restructure traditional organisations to be more effective, in the face of the spread of modern, secular judicial and educational systems of British colonial power, than the traditional Hanafism existed at that time.[21]

Deobandism reformed Hanafism (to some extent) through the influence of the comparatively more restrictive ideas, as introduced by Shah Waliullah Muhaddith Dehlavi (1703-1762) and his son Shah Abdul Aziz Dehlavi (1745-1823), to combat and weaken the influence of Sufism and customary Hindu traditions.[22] For example, in comparison with traditional Hanafist approaches, Deobandi Ulama pursued a harsher approach towards such forms of entertainment as music, singing, and dancing. They were also harsher on spiritual Islam – particularly Sufi rituals, donations, and offerings in the name of saints. They ruined many existing saints' shrines (viewing them as signs of polytheism), and in many places physically attacked pilgrims who were visiting these saints' shrines. They showed more intolerance regarding women's visibility in public and women's dress code. Meanwhile, unlike the Deobandi jihadist groups, a large section of the Deobandi religious authorities have remained traditional or quietist, and have adopted a very conservative approach towards politics.

Since the mid-nineteenth century, Deobandis have managed to establish a vast network of madrassas in the Indian subcontinent. Likewise, the majority of madrassas within Pakistan (estimated to be over 20,000 registered schools, plus many more unregistered ones) are Deobandi.[23] Inside Pakistan, the number of these schools dramatically increased during the rule of General Muhammad Zia-ul-Haq and during the fighting of the mujahidin in Afghanistan. These madrassas, being financially supported – particularly by the rich in Gulf countries and elsewhere – provided the students with free lodging and food. So in providing free accommodation and board, these institutions were highly attractive places to which Afghani refugees and homeless people could send their children. In the process, many Deobandi religious authorities became more radical than before and played a significant role in training Taliban jihadists.[24]

The name of 'Taliban' was taken from the students (*talibs*) who mainly studied in Deobandi madrassas in Pakistan, as well as in more traditional Hanafi madrassas based in rural Afghanistan. The term 'Taliban' was originally used, as a derogatory title (like 'school boys,' meaning 'in need of being educated'), by experienced warlord mujahidin fighters to belittle the Talibs as though, they were incompetent fighters. Nevertheless, with the emergence of the Taliban, the BBC World Service began using the term 'Taliban' which became the popularly accepted name for the whole movement.[25] The measures that the militant Deobandis adopted were very harsh, but they were never developed into a systematic and totalitarian set of ideological and political rules as has been done by the Wahhabi- Salafists.

Deobandi Pashtun clerics in Pakistan such as Maulana Sami ul Haq and Maulana Fazal-ur-Rehman, both of whom are leaders of two competing branches of Jamiat Ulema-e-Islam, have been mentioned as mentors of Mullah Omar and of other Taliban leaders. Both of these leading clerics have their own networks of affiliated schools, which have played an important role in training Talibs and Taliban leaders.[26] But after the removal of the Taliban government, the Taliban have succeeded in spreading all over Pakistan, particularly in the Pashtun areas, and gaining support of many more Deobandi clerics and madrassas.

ISIS's ideology is based on Salafism.[27] Salafism is, in general, a Sunni approach; but to a large extent, it is independent from the four traditional Sunni schools of jurisprudence (*madhhab*): Hanafi, Shafi'i, Maliki, and Hanbali. In their historical context, they refer to Ibn Taymiyyah (1263-1328) and Muhammad ibn Abd al-Wahhab (1703-1792), who were both radical anti-Shia figures from the Hanbali school of jurisprudence. These connections make them close to the then-new version of Hanbalism, a version that is now known as Wahhabism. However, Salafists are not Wahhabis and consider themselves to be 'non-imitators' because they do not follow any specific school of thought and instead argue for direct reference to the Quran and the *hadith* (tradition) for understanding "true" Islam.

This way of referencing the Quran and the *hadith* is an individualistic method and does not confer any special authority to clerics. It is also noticeable that Salafist ideology is entangled with aristocratic and Arab-centric elements. For example, Muhammad Nasiruddin al-Albani's radical followers such as al-Jama'a al-Salafiyya al-Muhtasiba (JSM) in Saudi Arabia believed that caliphs, emirs, and other Muslim leaders should be from the Quraysh.[28] By so doing, they literally excommunicated the Saudi ruling class.[29] They also accorded a special place to Arabs, who are considered to be unique in their deep understanding of the Quran due to their knowledge of the Quran's language. They believe that this provides radical Salafists with a degree of (or, shall we say, a sense of) superiority and makes them a source of inspiration for non-Arabs.[30]

Salafists' search for Islamic purity has, in reality, ended in an approach both eclectic and fragile. According to Abu

Mus'ab al-Suri (a key strategist among jihadists), ideological sources drawn upon by jihadi Salafists are varied and include the organisational programme of Sayyid Qutb. Sources also include Ibn Taymmia and the Salfiyya school of ideas—particularly the thesis of 'loyalty and disavowal' (loyalty to Islam and Muslims, and disavowal of other religions and non-Muslims). Salafists have also been influenced by the Wahhabis' jurisprudential and doctrinal legacy, and they have absorbed some basic elements of the Muslim Brotherhood.[31]

In a similar way, but in a geographical sense, Reuven Paz, believes that ideological influences can be categorised into three branches. The first branch is the Egyptian branch of Sayyid Qutb and includes Sayyid Imam al-Sharif, Dr. Fadl, and the radical fathers of Egyptian jihad and al-Jama'a al-Islamiyya in the 1970s. The second branch is the Saudi Arabian neo-Wahhabism led by Shaykh Abd al-Aziz ibn Baz and his disciples. The third branch is the ideology of Palestinian scholars, in particular the trio of radicals comprised of Abdullah Yusuf Azzam, Omar Abu Qatada al-Filistini, and (most importantly) Abu Muhammad al-Maqdisi—who was a mentor of al-Zarqawi.[32] These figures had a key role in the development of *takfirism*.[33]

From his early contemporaries to current Salafist ideologues, Abu Muhammad al-Maqdisi (1959-) has had, and continues to have, an important role among the community of Salafist jihadists. Al-Maqdisi is a radical Palestinian-Jordanian Salafist known for his theory of *al-wala' wa-l-bara'* (loyalty to Islam and 'denial' of non-Muslims). The meaning of this concept of 'denial' can be clarified by the following quotation from al-Maqdisi who addresses the jihadists:

> It is compulsory for you (*fa-l-wajib 'alayka*) – if you want Paradise – to disbelieve in him (the modern-day *taghut)*, disavow him and his servants and his friends

(*awlialiya'ihi*) and to hate them (*tubghidulhum*) and to make them detestable (*tubghghiduhum*) for your children and your family, to work and wage *jihad* (*tujahidu*) all of your life for his destruction and his annulment (*min ajl hadmihi wa-ibtalihi*) and that you do not give up [that you will not] be satisfied or happy unless [there is] the rule of God the Most High and his legislation alone. Otherwise there is hell. Hell![34]

As result of sectarian ideological influence, the Taliban and ISIS have many differences regarding religious observances. For example, they differ regarding the ways to perform prayers or over how to hold wakes or other funereal ceremonies. Salafists who are very close to Wahhabis in this area of practice reject the practices of the Taliban. Salafists rarely join the collective prayers shared by Hanafi Sunnis, or attend Hanafis' mosques. However, these types of differences may not be very strong between moderate politically motivated approaches. But for many ordinary Sunnis, these kinds of differences seem very strange and may have a negative impact on how Salafist jihadi behaviour is perceived.

Political strategy

Both the Taliban and ISIS have shared the same general goal of establishing an Islamic state whether in the form of a caliphate or as a transitional or provincial form of Islamic emirate, but none of them has set forth a clear set of systematic ideas regarding the place and function of the modern state in the globalising world. Politically, Salafist jihadists and even the Taliban have had a different view of 'state' and statecraft than either quietists or Islamists such as the Muslim Brotherhood or Jama'at-e-Islami. Traditional methods of governance have been observed as being practised by Taliban ministers who only keep the form of modern institutions (ministries) without the substance of modern, cohesive bureaucratic functions.[35] Initially, the Taliban did not even have any clear political ambition to seize power at the national level, and instead simply emerged as an armed group formed to protect local people from the pressure of gangs associated with mujahidin warlords.[36]

For many Salafist jihadists – Naji, for example – a state and its associated modern institutions are universal moulds— neutral forms to be filled, by the jihadists, with Islamic values according to the rules of *sharia*.[37] An important impact of this perspective is the jihadists' apparent inability to create a long-term, efficient, and clear economic strategy sustainably functional in the global context. Ad-hoc measures designed to create a degree of security and an Islamic egalitarian society, may – for many Muslims at certain times – be attractive. However, ISIS's heavy reliance on coercive measures for the elimination of all kinds of opposition – along with its removal of the nationally-defined power structure – makes strategic governance very difficult for ISIS, as Caris and Samuel have aptly observed.[38]

The Taliban, led by Mullah Omar, rapidly proceeded to successfully capture the largest part of Afghanistan and establish the Islamic Emirate of Afghanistan. Mullah Omar considered himself as the Emir or Emir al-Momenin (Commander of the Faithful) of the Emirate of Afghanistan—possibly in the hope that in future, his province would join the land of the caliphate. In spite of sheltering al-Qaeda, however, the Taliban had no clear and open ambition to organise an international, global jihad (whether directly or by inviting Muslims to immigrate to Afghanistan).

In contrast to the Taliban, ISIS seriously regards their territory as being Darul Islam (House of Islam), a caliphate and a starting point for waging international jihad. Since it is Darul Islam, the 'real' Muslims are invited to migrate there, to support it, and to get training for international jihad to expand their land further by facilitating the conditions for liberating 'occupied' Muslim territories and even moving beyond to non-Muslim lands. For Salafi jihadists, all Muslim lands – not just Israel, or Afghanistan – are considered to be occupied because they are not ruled by a caliph and so-called 'real' Muslims, but remain under the control of apostates or *taghuts*.

By inviting Muslims to immigrate to the Islamic State, Abu Muhammad al-Adnani (Taha Subhi Falaha), Syrian emir and the official spokesperson for ISIS, has stated:

> Come, oh Muslims, to your honour—to your victory. By Allah, if you disbelieve in democracy, secularism, nationalism, as well as all the other garbage and ideas from the West, and rush to your religion and creed, then by Allah, you will own the earth[—]and the East and West will submit to you. This is the promise of Allah to you. This is the promise of Allah to you.[39]

Al-Adnani has also announced: "The proclamation of the caliphate means that every Muslim has the duty to pledge allegiance to the new caliph of Muslims or otherwise die the death [sic.] of the time of jahiliyya. The proclamation of the caliphate invalidates the legitimacy of all other Islamic emirates."[40]

Not only is this an exclusionary approach, it is also an expansionist strategy that can be seen in a map circulated among ISIS supporters. This map shows they have both the desire and the will to remove many borders...not only in the Middle East, central Asia, and Asia proper, but also in Europe including Andalusia and the Balkans, according to the timetable of a 5-year plan. Some other aspects of this strategy has been declared by Abu Mohammad al-Adnani who has also stated that "The legality of all emirates, groups, states and organizations becomes null by the expansion of the caliph's authority and the arrival of its troops to their areas".[41]

This perspective influences jihadists' tactics and geopolitical strategies. To understand how they define their enemies geopolitically will be the focus of further examination in the next part.

Near and far enemies

As was mentioned earlier, the Taliban had (and has) remained a local movement in the Pashtun areas of Afghanistan and Pakistan. In their jihad, they gave (and give) priority to close and immediate enemies—that is, what has been seen as a 'near enemy'. For the Taliban, priority is given to those enemies who are immediate and close, such as the secular regime in power and their direct supporters including the ISAF and the US forces in Afghanistan.[42] So far, they have not had an active strategy to export Talibanism to other countries, and they have also not attempted, at least from what is publicly known at this time, to create a task force designed to target America or Europe by conducting operations within their enemies' own land. The activities in which they have been engaged have, of course, spread to neighbouring countries—particularly Pakistan. Their close allies in Pakistan include Sipah-e Sahaba Pakistan, Lashkar-e Jhangvi, and Jaish-e-Mohammed, as well as Tehrik-i Taliban Pakistan (the Pakistani Taliban Movement) (TTP).

The history of ISIS cannot be separated from the al-Qaeda network in terms of their adoption of a set of radical strategies against the West. But ever since Abu Mus'ab al-Zarqawi (1966-2006) established Jama'at al-Tawhid wal-jihad, the then-al-Qaeda-related organisation in Iraq, more attention was gradually paid to the 'near enemy' to a degree previously absent in the strategy of mainstream al-Qaeda. ISIS, as the closest follower of al-Zarqawi's legacy, seemed – by conquering and holding territory – to be an even stronger supporter of the 'near enemy' policy than the original supporters of this idea. Yet this dichotomous and heuristic approach in defining the strategy of al-Qaeda and Salafist jihadists may be misleading in that it is based on short-term activities. The existence of interchanged, combined, or hybridized strategies among these groups seems to be a comparatively sounder description. Now ISIS is using a combined strategy of engagement both with far and near enemies—as well as capturing and holding land and then retreating and preparing for attack somewhere else (see, for example, their further engagement in Libya).

Among those earlier radicals in Egypt who inherited Sayyid Qutb's legacy and later joined al-Qaeda (with some having joined al-Qaeda at an even earlier stage of their own activities), their strategic focus was less on the 'far enemy' and more on the 'near enemy.'[43] Regional and local affiliates such as al-Nosrah in Syria may also focus more on local enemies (those directly targeted on the battlefield) and national enemies (those who run the country as a whole) than on the international focus of headquarters leadership. But this does not mean that al-Qaeda as a whole has currently abandoned the 'far enemy' strategy of making plans to attack American and European peoples in their own countries.[44] For example, at the same time as they have engaged in Syrian activities and had land under their control, al-Qaeda has been strengthening the Khorasan group in Syria.

Differing perspectives on how one defines what constitutes jihad also affects the meaning of 'enemy' along with the methods and courses of action to be taken by jihadists. A permanent and offensive jihad, for instance, has different requirements and consequences than a defensive one (a principle defined by Naji and Qutb). For Salafist jihadists, jihad is an offensive and permanent principle, while the Taliban does not understand it in the same way.

The Islamic State's strategy is in line with the thinking of other radical jihadi strategists in al-Qaeda such as Abu Yahya al-Libi[45], who believed that war between Islam and the infidels is a permanent war and that neither will stop until one side is totally vanquished.[46] Al-Libi very clearly did not trust many Muslims in the *ummah* and said that the only way to secure victory is by creating "rivers of blood of martyrs, high mountains of torn organs, and souls carried forward by the zealotry of religion[—]searching for martyrdom and running towards the broad gardens of paradise".[47]

Abu Yahya al-Libi believed that "We should fight all the infidels, whether apostates or crusaders, nationals or foreigners, Arabs or non-Arabs, whether their names are 'Abd al- -Aziz Boutaflika', 'Abdallah ibn Abdal-Aziz', 'Abdallh ibn al-Husayn', Mu'mmar Qadhafi or George Bush, Tony Blair, [Nicolas] Sarkozy or [Ehud] Olmert" (Arabic spelling included; bracketed text added).[48] Enemies, in his view, are both national and international; however, he has elsewhere stated his belief that the enemies from inside are more dangerous than are foreign crusaders.

This was a logic which was also supported by al-Jama'a al-Islamiyya in Egypt, which put emphasis on the 'near enemy': "No doubt that he who prefers man-made positive laws to the laws of the God is a *kafir*"—adding that "as it is not allowed for a *kafir* to rule over Muslims (*la wilaya li-kafir 'ala muslim*), it is a duty to depose the rulers of our country".[49] So *kafirs* are not only foreigners but even secular rulers as well—Anwar Sadat, for example. This only serves to indicate that for radical jihadists, in principle, there is no strong demarcation between 'near' and 'far' enemies.

▓ Organisational and operational strategies

In terms of organisation and operational strategies, radical jihadists both from al-Qaida networks and now from ISIS have pursued Abu Bakar Naji's thesis of the 'management of savagery' (although not in all respects—see Naji, for example, regarding the Asharis).[50] They have also used a decentralised strategy of global dispersal of organisations into leaderless groups, a thesis forwarded and developed by Mus'ab al-Suri. It is not very clear if the Taliban has ever used a systematic approach to its operation in a way that Naji had instructed; but suicide bombings and the idea of intentionally inflicting collateral damage were some operational points similar to those al-Qaeda networks had followed. What remains clear, however, is that al-Suri had a very close relationship with the Taliban and had expressed his allegiance with Mullah Omar—but that the Taliban could only use al-Suri's thesis of leaderless and dispersed organisation on a limited scale, rather than widely in a global context.[51] Since the Taliban has been a mass movement, based on traditional values, it has not found it necessary to use strict forms of leadership and structured forms of modern organisation and leadership.

The Taliban and ISIS can also be differentiated in terms of their distinctive methodological approaches towards publicizing their operations. The attitude of the Taliban towards using visual media (using TV and pictures, for example) had been very limited or completely negative when they were in power; but now, they have changed their approach. By contrast, ISIS has always been extremely keen on using media to convey their message more effectively to a worldwide, global audience. They have been skilfully using social media and internet platforms such as email, Facebook, Twitter, YouTube, and real-time weblogs to communicate with each other, spread their messages, and recruit jihadists from all over the world.[52] This is, in part, related to there being comparatively

ABNA24.com (http://modafeon.blog.ir)

Figure 2-2 Al-Qaeda Jihadists in Syria

more computer-literate urban supporters among the ranks of ISIS jihadists. The Taliban movement is likely to have far fewer computer-literate people, and to have less access to internet facilities, particularly in rural areas of Afghanistan and poor suburban areas of Pakistan, than does ISIS.

In operational terms, ISIS can be categorised as an extremist organisation in the tradition of al-Qaeda. ISIS employs actions similar to those of al-Zarqawi. Al-Zarqawi, as emir of the al-Qaeda Branch in Iraq (AQI) till his death by the Americans in 2006, continued to create tensions between his organization and that of mainstream al-Qaida (particularly al-Zawahiri).[53] This tension with al-Zawahiri intensified under the leadership of Abu Bakr al-Baghdadi, who considered himself as the main follower of al-Zarqawi in Iraq and Syria.

Therefore, it comes as no surprise to see that the potentially volatile sectarian elements of Salafist-Takfirist perspectives have developed into the kinds of predictable conflicts we now find erupting between radical jihadists, not only in Syria and Iraq but also in all other parts of the world.

2.3: War among the radical jihadists

▨ Takfirism and the Taliban

Since the Salafists consider their own method to be the only method or the most authentic one, they act as an elite force and claim to have in-depth and direct knowledge of the texts. On the basis of their understanding of the Arabic texts, which admittedly does require a high level of Arabic-language knowledge, the Salafist leaders have a tendency to consider themselves as the only knowledgeable scholars on Islam. Thus, being Arab is seen as an important privilege and a kind of superiority over others.

Since radical Salafists reject conventional boundaries drawn by the traditional schools of jurisprudence and consider most of these schools as being polluted by non-Islamic rituals, and since they deprecate clerical authorities, they are likely to enter into conflicts both with other schools' followers and (even) with those Salafists who do not follow them. This is a highly conflictual approach—one which easily encourages and is enhanced by declarations of *takfir* (excommunication).

Abu Mus'ab al-Suri, a top figure in al-Qaeda and a famous Salafist jihadi strategist who had a critical view of the radical Salafists, believes that Salafists are the most conflict prone of all. He argues that they are a sect at war with "nearly every other revivalist school, [...] in particular the reformist schools (*al-madaris al-islahiyya*), the Sufis, the *tablighi* movement (jama'at al-Tabligh wa-l-Da'wa [Tablighi Jamaat]), [and] most official clerics and imams, as well as the clerics of the four schools of jurisprudence".[54]

For example, even al-Suri – who argued for a softer approach – was excommunicated (*takfir*). He was even called "James Bond" by supporters of his ex-colleague, Abu Qatada, the famous hard-line cleric, at that time based in London.

This difference in perspective reportedly developed into friction between certain Taliban members and many al-Qaeda officers. Salafists, particularly the radical jihadists, had a very negative view of the Taliban. According to al-Suri, the Arab Salafists were arrogant and considered Taliban members and other Afghans to be superstitious, deviant, backward, and primitive. The radical Salafists even believed that the Taliban were unbelievers and that it was thus not the duty of a Salafist jihadi to fight for them or even alongside them. Radical Salafists even believed that Afghans who were killed in fighting between the Northern Alliance and the Taliban, regardless of which side they were on, would all be going straight to hell.[55]

Radical Salafist jihadists considered Afghanistan to be merely a safe haven rather than as a starting point for the caliphate.[56] Radical Salafists had even criticised bin Laden for having paid allegiance to Mullah Omar. Abu Mus'ab al-Suri, who defended the Taliban and was faithful to Mullah Omar, had written:

> One of the astonishing things I must mention in this context is a statement made by one of those extremist Salafist Jihadists. He told me in[,] in one of our conversations that "jihad must be under the Salafist banner; its leadership, programme, and religious rulings must also be Salafist; and everything should be subjected to proof [in accordance with Salafist methodology]. If we should accept that non-Salafists participate with us in jihad, we only do so because we need them. However, they should not have any leadership role at all. We should lead them like a herd of cows to perform their duty of jihad". I could not really understand how we are going to participate in jihad with our brethren in religion and faith if we should deal with them as [if they were] a herd of cows [....]![57]

Mullah Omar, despite being the Emir of the Islamic Emirate of Afghanistan and host (a role traditionally deserving of respect and gratitude) to a whole army of Salafist jihadists, was – in their eyes – nothing more than any number of tribal, Pashtun mullahs who were likewise not immune from the mockery of the hard-line Salafists. For the hard-line Arab Salafists, Mullah Omar could not be "*Amir al-mu'menin* [Commander of the Muslims]", but merely one of the "herd of cows" like any other Taliban member.

The emergence of ISIS/IS against al-Qaeda

For radical jihadists such as Abu Jarir al-Shamali, a former associate of al-Zarqawi, Islamic rules were absent in territories controlled by the Taliban and al-Qaeda in 2014. Al-Shamali wrote in the sixth issue of *Dabiq* that after his release from an Iranian jail, he visited South Waziristan where he had expected to find that Taliban and al-Qaeda mujahidin had enforced *sharia* and created an Islamic society in the areas under their control. But upon going there, he found it very regrettable that the tribal rules were still in place, children were attending secular schools, women were intermingling with men, and Islamabad still had much control—while still, "cronies" of al-Zawahiri were carrying his private and secret messages from there.[58] This criticism by ISIS leaders over perception of Islamic rules reflected a huge credibility gap and lack of mutual trust between ISIS and al-Qaeda, which erupted into open conflict. But the roots of this hostility goes back to the disputes which had appeared between al-Zarqawi and al-Zawahiri in Iraq.

The disagreements/arguments between al-Zawahiri and al-Zarqawi were mainly over operational priorities—priorities which could (according to al-Zawahiri) lead to alienating Sunnis and ignoring the main enemies (i.e. the US and her allies).

Al-Zarqawi's extremist anti-Shia policies were criticised by al-Zawahiri in his July 2005 letter to al-Qaeda. In that letter, al-Zarqawi explained his anti-Shia tactic in this way: "Targetting and striking their [the Shiite population's] religious, political, and military symbols will make them show their rage against the Sunnis and bear their inner vengeance. If we succeed in dragging them into a sectarian war, this will awaken the sleepy Sunnis who are fearful of destruction and death".[59] This policy was very much similar to Naji's instructions regarding "the power of vexation and exhaustion". But for Naji, the Shias are not seen as a target, as he even argued that co-existence and cooperation with Asharis might sometimes be necessary.[60]

Al-Zawahiri was against al-Zarqawi's policy of indiscriminately massacring Shias; while he rejected Shias, he considered them to be ignorant and thus in need of further guidance. Al-Zawahiri, in the same July 2005 letter, criticised al-Zarqawi's actions in killing ordinary Shiites as unreasonably brutal which were unnecessary and diverting media focus away from the main enemy—the American crusaders. He also believed that these actions were creating unnecessary conflicts within Iran, where more than 100 prisoners, many of them from the leadership of al-Qaeda, were being held in custody.[61]

With the emergence of ISIS as a strong force in Syria, and then in Iraq, ISIS persistently suppressed or abandoned non-compliant jihadist opponents inside territories they controlled. In this way, they tried to totally monopolise power and impose order by supressing other political forces and insecurity-creating agents. Doing so in the midst of chaos and insecurity would facilitate their ability to implement policies without much resistance, as they did in Raqqa province in Syria.[62] After gaining more territories in Iraq, particularly capturing Mosul, ISIS announced the establishment of a caliphate (an

Islamic empire), and clearly adopted a strategy of expanding their territory to further consolidate the caliphate.

Abu Bakr al-Baghdadi, leader of ISIS, declared himself the Muslim's caliph—and following this, ISIS asked all Muslims to pledge allegiance to Abu Bakr al-Baghdadi as the caliph of all the world's Muslims. This was a claim to a new level of authority unmatched even among al-Qaeda's broad network; and as such, this claim was a serious challenge against the authority of al-Qaeda. This strategy exploded into a source of further conflict and disarray among all other jihadists—particularly Salafists who now had to decide whether to break their previous pledge of allegiance (*baia'a*) to al-Qaeda and offer homage to Abu-Bakr al-Baghdadi instead, or whether to reconfirm their *baia'a* and continue to support al-Zawahiri while incurring the wrath of al-Qaeda for doing so. The consequences for refuting the demand for allegiance to the self-styled "Caliph" al-Baghdadi were severe, and such people were considered as being rebellious – even treasonous – against the Islamic State.

As a result of ISIS clashes, kidnappings, and even executions of some senior members of al-Nosrah Front (an affiliate of al-Qaeda), al-Qaeda commander Ayman al-Zawahiri publically disowned ISIS.[63] ISIS's clashes have not been limited to al-Nosrah Front, but have included many other moderate and radical jihadi organisations in Syria—particularly in Raqqa, where ISIS gained full control. For example, on 9 September 2014, at least 50 people – including Hassan Aboud, commander of the Salafist group of Ahrar al-Sham, were killed in a devastating car bomb blast. Ahrar al-Sham's supporters accused ISIS of being responsible for this killing.[64]

Since then, in Syria, clashes between ISIS and Ahrar al-Sham as well as Jaish-al-Islam, which is supported by Saudi Arabia, on the one hand, and with Jebha-al-Nosrah on the other, have intensified even further. For example, there has been evidence that a week after ISIS's beheading of 11 members of Jaish-al Islam (plus an al-Nosrah Front member), Jaish-al-Islam beheaded 18 members of ISIS in revenge.[65]

Announcement of the formation of the caliphate (ISIS) by Abu Bakr al-Baghdadi created a firestorm of controversy among radical jihadi groups all over the world and rapidly devolved into much disarray among their ranks. Abu Bakr al-Baghdadi's decision has been condemned by many radical jihadi groups – for example, by the al-Nosrah Front and by eight other radical groups in Syria.[66] The prominent jihadi ideologue Sheikh Mohammad al-Maqdisi has also seen ISIS as being a "deviant group" acting against *sharia* and against Islam.[67]

When al-Maqdisi had tried to mediate between ISIS and al-Qaeda, ISIS had rejected mediation. ISIS had justified their actions by accusing al-Qaeda, led by al-Zawahiri, as being deviant from the path of jihad.[68] In same way, Abu Qatada, being another prominent Salafist jihadi ideologue and close friend of al-Maqdisi, not only rejected ISIS's caliphate claim as meaningless[69], but even said they were "like a mafia group".[70] Because of their very critical positions against the caliphate announcement and against Abu Bakr al-Baghdadi's rule, both prominent ideologues were rebuked by ISIS's media as being "stooges" of the West and as being part of a conspiracy against the caliphate. The sixth issue of ISIS's magazine, *Dabiq*, in English, had published a full-page picture of al-Maqdisi and Abu Qatada, labelled as "misleading scholars" who should be avoided more than the devil himself.[71] In line with similar condemnations by other critics of caliphate-builders, Harith bin Ghazi al-Nazari, a top official cleric and supporter of Al-Qaeda in the Arabian Peninsula (AQAP), harshly condemned al-Baghdadi for his announcement of the caliphate and for dividing jihadists.[72]

In an open letter to al-Baghdadi, 126 Islamic scholars (seconded by 49 subsequent signatories) from different countries have harshly criticized ISIS (See Appendix 1).; and in a 2015 fatwa, over 1,000 Indian Islamic scholars – including muftis and imams – have called ISIS's actions "absolutely inhuman" and its Khilafat Rule "accursed".[73] According to al-Yaqoubi (a Syrian Islamic scholar and outspoken opponent of the Assad regime), ISIS has not hesitated to kill many Sunni clerics who oppose them in different countries, including in (but not limited to) territories they control.[74] Al-Yaqoubi has strongly criticised ISIS as well as al-Qaeda, and has even issued a *fatwa* that fighting against ISIS and "killing them" is an Islamic "obligation".[75]

ISIS has also been condemned by Saudi Arabia's top official clerics, who have stated that "Terrorism has nothing to do with Islam, which is innocent of deviant ideology ... [terrorism] is nothing more than corruption and criminality rejected by Islamic sharia law and common sense". They also announced that any Muslim who thinks that jihad (which means 'struggle') means joining a terrorist group "is ignorant and has gone astray". The kingdom's grand mufti, Sheikh Abdul-Aziz al-Sheikh, has said that under *sharia* law, terrorists merit the punishment of execution followed by the public display of the body as a deterrent.[76]

New policies adopted by the ISIS seriously challenged al-Qaeda at different levels of leadership and strategies, particularly in respect to the importance of occupying and controlling the territories. Now, it seems that the al-Nosrah Front is seriously competing with ISIS and has adopted a relatively conciliatory approach with other Syrian Salafi organisations in order to strengthen their position in Syria and play a hegemonic role in fighting against Bashar al-Assad. This, rather than moving to Iraq or openly linking their local jihad to global jihad, has been their approach. Possibly, their release of the 45 Fijian, UN peacekeepers taken hostage in the Golan

Heights is a reflection of their softer side, perhaps in consideration of factors relevant in order to maintain their alliance with other jihadists in Syria.[77]

ISIS is spreading further

ISIS has appeared as a tough force, not only in its occupation and control of land but also in its emergence as a well-organised power dedicated to undertaking global jihad and to spreading terror on a large scale. In line with its strategy of creating disruption and chaos to maximise a sense of fear and horror among its 'enemies' along with the subsequent phase of a "Management of Savagery" (as was formulated by Abu Bakar Naji), ISIS has extensively undertaken suicide attacks, terror attacks, and beheadings.[78] The large-scale attacks in Paris on 13 November 2015[79] and the mid-air shooting down of a Russian passenger jet on 31 October 2015[80] were internationally significant events. These events exposed that, in quite a short period, ISIS had built – far more effectively than al-Qaeda –well-organised cells with proven ability to strike terror into the very heart of Western societies.

But at the same time, they have not confined their activities to within organised and guided cells alone. They have even, with effect, incited and used headless groups and 'lone wolves'—a method of attack taken from strategies developed by Abu Mus'ab al-Suri after the US attack on Afghanistan and implementation of strict security measures in different countries, particularly in the West. In September 2014, Abu Mohammad al-Adnani, spokesperson for ISIS, incited their supporters to kill disbelievers particularly those who support France and America in attacking ISIS)—

> [whether] civilian or military, particularly from all who have participated in air strikes and supported

them, and particularly French and American ones.
He said, "If you are not able to find an IED or a bullet,
then single out the disbelieving American or any of
his allies. Smash his head with a rock, or slaughter
him with a knife, or run him over with your car, or
throw him down from a high place, or choke him, or
poison him...If you are unable to do so, then burn
his home, car, or business. Or destroy his crops. If
you are unable to do so, then spit in his face.[81]

In spite of all the strong internal criticisms by jihadist dissent-
ers and Islamic scholars, ISIS has gained much support among
the radical jihadists in the Middle East, the Greater Middle
East (Pakistan and Afghanistan, for instance), and North Africa (for example, a section of the Algerian jihadist branch of
AQIM). Some members of the Libyan branch of Ansar al-Sharia Libya defected to ISIS Libya. However, ISIS Libya itself is
very active and influential. Likewise, sections of the Tunisian
branch of Ansar al-Sharia, and the Egyptian Ansar al-Bayt
al-Maqdis (Ansar Jerusalem), have supported and become affiliated with ISIS (e.g. the conversion of most of Ansar Jerusalem to 'ISIL—Sinai Province').[82] Abu Sayyaf in the Philippines
and some other groups associated with al-Qaeda in the Arabian Peninsula (AQAP) also offered allegiance to ISIS.[83] This
has created a degree of confusion among some other jihadists, some of whom have advised al-Qaida and ISIS to find a
peaceful solution. For example, such a suggestion came from
Boko Haram, under the leadership of Abubakar Shekau—but
they announced their own caliphate.[84] The evidence indicates
that divisions and conflicts among the main radical jihadists
have reached an unprecedented level and are likely to continue even further.[85]

ISIS has widely targeted Shia Muslims in a strategic effort
to polarize societies—such polarization being an important

intended product of the tactics of disruption and vexation, in consequence of distinguishing between good and bad Muslims, or between real Muslims and infidels. This has happened not only in Syria and Iraq, but also within many other countries. They have attacked Shia shrines, mosques, and communities to facilitate this polarisation by provoking Shias to react against Sunnis. For example, ISIS has attacked Shias in Lebanon[86], Bahrain[87], Kuwait[88], Saudi Arabia[89], Yemen[90], and Bangladesh.[91]

Since the Taliban was an important part of this chapter, we now look at the events following the emergence of ISIS in Afghanistan.

ISIS challenges the Taliban inside Afghanistan

ISIS, having started its operation in Afghanistan and Pakistan, has established a new *velayt* (province)—that of Khorasan. (The wider historical meaning of 'Khorasan' is much larger than the Khorasan province within Iran proper.) This new geographical area of their activities (Afghanistan, Pakistan, and central Asia) means an increase in intensification of continued rivalry against both al-Qaeda and the Taliban and has gone beyond the earlier era of some al-Qaeda Salafist radicals' verbal belittling of the Taliban (as mentioned earlier). ISIS's activities in Afghanistan have, from the beginning, been marked by bloody and severe conflict with the Taliban. According to credible reports, ISIS has accused Taliban members of being Pakistani ISI agents. According to Harun Najafizada (a BBC reporter in Kabul), for instance, ISIS supporters in Nangarhar Province had, in June 2015, beheaded 10 members of the Taliban. ISIS also killed other Taliban by detonating bombs under their feet as yet another brutal method of execution. While the Taliban's leadership have rejected al-Baghdadi's caliphate and have warned ISIS against meddling in jihad within Afghanistan, Moulvi Abdul-Rahim Muslimdust – an ex-Guantana-mo-Bay prisoner and ex-supporter of the Taliban – has openly announced his allegiance to al-Baghdadi.[92] ISIS is strongly relying on foreigner jihadists, estimated to be about 7,000, particularly from central Asia. They have also proven themselves capable of attracting some dissatisfied members of the Taliban. Heavy reliance on foreign fighters by ISIS, however, risks intensifying the conflicts with Afghans in Afghanistan. Such measures might not lead to much popular support, considering the different religious setting, stronger traditional and tribal relations among, the Taliban in the context of Afghanistan in comparison to ISIS in Arabic countries, for instance.[93]

ABNA24.com (http://modafeon.blog.ir)

Figure 2-3 An ISIS Jihadist

ISIS in Afghanistan has taken advantage of the internal conflicts within the Taliban—splits and divisions which started after the death of Mullah Omar (mainly over choosing of a successor). The Taliban's new leader, Mullah Akhtar Mansur, was not unanimously accepted by the Taliban's senior figures. Some powerful Taliban commanders such as mullahs Mansoor

Dadullah, Hasan Akhond, Abdul Razzaq, and Jalil did not offer their allegiance to Mullah Akhtar Mansur. Later on, they established their own separate organisation and chose Mullah Muhammad Rasul as their leader. Clashes between the newly-established Taliban and the mainstream Taliban from which they split have also been reported. At an earlier stage, even Mullah Omar's own brother (Mullah Abdul Mannan) and son (Mullah Yakub) had both rejected the leadership of Mullah Akhtar Mansur—but now, they have forged a compromise.[94]

Under existing tribal, social, and religious conditions within Afghanistan, internal conflicts have begun erupting within ISIS from an early stage, according to some reports. Moulvi Muslimdust, the commander of ISIS in Afghanistan, withdrew his allegiance to Hafiz Saeed as the leader (emir) of ISIS in Khorasan province. Muslimdust announced that Hafiz Saeed had acted in an un-Islamic way by having insulted, arrested, and killed people.[95] This internal rivalry indicate some serious problems ISIS is facing in the Afghanistan.

2.4: Conclusion

While many similarities exist between the Taliban and Salafist jihadists – particularly regarding their exercise of the strict rules of *sharia* in daily life – one can conclude, on the basis of the evidence provided, that fundamental differences exist between both movements—particularly between the Taliban and ISIS. Ideologically, ISIS has roots in radical Salafist-takfirist ideas, whereas the Taliban has been inspired by a mix of Deobandi traditions together with tribal and Pashtun ethnic values. The Taliban has apparently had no expansionist policy, whereas ISIS has pursued a policy of removing the existing national borders of neighbouring countries to establish an expanded caliphate for the *ummah* whenever they have the opportunity and power to do so.

ISIS has developed from within al-Qaeda networks and, being more extreme than mainstream al-Qaeda, represents a more radical approach among Salafist jihadists. From the earliest stage of al-Qaeda's activities, as indicated by its policies within Afghanistan and Sudan, and among the Taliban, it seems that rather than following one single unified strategy, al-Qaeda's top cadres of leaders have formed and shaped a variety of different political and operational strategies. These differed concerning the value of building a bloc of political alliances among other Muslims, particularly among local Muslims. Within al-Qaeda, in comparison to standard organisational policy, softer and gentler approaches by al-Zawahiri and others, such as those proposed by al-Suri with regards to the Taliban, emphasised promoting quite conciliatory relations with other Sunni Muslims. By contrast, more hard-line ideological approaches by al-Zarqawi and others, such as the Salafist's view of the Taliban as being a mere herd of cows, promoted harsh engagement with non-Muslims and secular political enemies or even Muslims with any religious beliefs different from their own. Such inherently self-conflictual, sectarian approaches within al-Qaeda led to the adoption by ISIS of a harsh takfirist (excommunicative) policy, not only towards non-Muslims but also towards those whom they considered to be 'false' Muslims. This inconsistency reflected the weight of isolationist takfirist ideology against more politically-oriented calculations among ideologues and strategists in the al-Qaeda network.

ISIS, both ideologically and strategically, is much more sophisticated than the Taliban. Tactically, it is also far more aggressive and brutal in its application of force. This is in keeping with the brutal nature of its expansionist strategy, which has the potential to lead to a great deal of further tension and disaster in the whole region. The logic of takfir and the tendency to narrow the boundary of 'Muslim-ness' has been taken by ISIS to mean treating any form of human authority which they cannot bring under their own control as if it were polytheist and subject to a harsh *fatwa* to justify starting a war against them. This policy might temporarily gain ground among radical discontents. However, in the long term, takfirism can seriously undermine any process of sustainable governance. Applying violence and coercion as a rightful, necessary, and dominant means of destroying all political and religious opponents – including Shias, Yazidis, Christians, Kurds, non-compliant or belligerent tribes, and Sunnis alike – indicates that ISIS has a limited capacity for building a hegemonic state, even among Muslims. The Taliban, in general, has had comparatively more flexibility in dealing with tribal values and Sunni groups—although compared with ISIS, it has had fewer people with the knowledge and skill to provide standard state services.

The evidence shows that ISIS continues to challenge other Salafist jihadists as well as the Taliban, as it likely will for some years in future. But the dimension of conflict goes beyond this, and ISIS continues to threaten the existing political regimes and boundaries in the world of Islam, particularly in the Middle East. Furthermore, ISIS has no intention to abandon its 'far enemy' policy and sectarian anti-Shia approach. To gain greater insight as to the true dimensions of the threat posed by ISIS, the next section will examine the problem in relation to the Islamic Republic of Iran being both a Shia-dominated regime and an active supporter of ISIS's enemies, such as Bashar al-Assad of Syria, Iraqi government, and Hezbollah in Lebanon.

References

"27 killed in ISIS attack on Kuwait mosque". *Al-Arabiya* [English]. 26 June 2015. 1 Dec. 2015 <http://english.alarabiya.net/en/News/middle-east/2015/06/26/Explosion-hits-mosque-in-Kuwait-during-Friday-prayers-.html>.

Al-Daameh, Mohamed. "Abu Qatada, Maqdisi can unify Islamist ranks against ISIS: experts". *Aawsat.* 27 Sept. 2014. 23 Oct. 2014 <http://www.aawsat.net/2014/09/article55336996>.

Ali, Suleiman Abdallah. "ISIS announces Islamic caliphate; changes name". Ed./Trans. Pascale El-Khoury. *Al-Monitor.* 26 June 2014. 30 June 2014 <http://www.al-monitor.com/pulse/ar/security/2014/06/iraq-syria-isis-announcement-islamic-caliphate-name-change.html>.

Al-Yaqoubi, Shaykh Muhammad. *Refuting ISIS: A Rebuttal of Its Religious and Ideological Foundations*. USA: Sacred Knowledge, 2015.

Arendt, Hannah. *The Origins of Totalitarianism*. London: HBJ, 1975.

"Beruz-e ekhtelaf mian-e farmandeh-e Daesh dar Afghanistan ba rahbare mantaqeh-ei in gruh [Eruption of differences between ISIS commander in Afghanistan and regional leader of the group]". *BBC Persian.* 19 Oct. 2015. 12 Dec. 2015 <http://www.bbc.com/persian/afghanistan/2015/10/151019_fm_>.

Black, Ian. "Saudi clerics declare ISIS terrorism a 'heinous crime' under sharia law". *The Guardian.* 17 Sept. 2014. 1 Dec. 2015 <http://www.theguardian.com/world/2014/sep/17/saudi-clerics-fatwa-declares-terrorism-heinous-crime-sharia-la>.

—. "Second Saudi Arabia suicide bombing fuels ISIS campaign fears". *The Guardian.* 29 May 2015. 15 Nov. 2015

<http://www.theguardian.com/world/2015/may/29/saudi-arabia-suicide-bomb-attack-kills-four-in-damman>.

'Boko Haram leader: "We will sell the girls on the market"' [video]. *The Guardian*. 6 May 2014. 11 Sept. 2014 <http://www.theguardian.com/world/boko-haram?page=8>.

Botelho, Greg, Yousuf Basil, and Sugam Pokharel. "ISIS says it's behind deadly Shiite mosque attack in Bangladesh". *CNN*. 27 Nov. 2015. 1 Dec. 2015 <http://edition.cnn.com/2015/11/27/asia/bangladesh-isis-attack-claim>.

Burke, Jason. "Abu Yahya al-Libi obituary". *The Guardian*. 6 June 2012. 12 Apr. 2016 <http://www.theguardian.com/world/2012/jun/06/abu-yahya-al-libi>.

—. *The 9/11 Wars*. London: Penguin Book, 2011. 10-11

Caris, Charles, and Samuel Reynolds. *ISIS Governance in Syria*. Report 22. Washington, DC: The Institute for the Study of War, 2014. 12 Oct. 2014 <www.understandingwar.org/report/isis-governance-syria>.

Charles River Editors. *The Islamic State of Iraq and Syria*. Marson Gate, 2014.

Cholvo, Martin. "Explosion in Syria kills senior leadership of Ahrar al-Sham". *The Guardian*. 10 Sept. 2014. 16 Nov. 2014 <http://www.theguardian.com/world/2014/sep/10/explosion-syria-kills-leadership-ahrar-al-sham>.

Cockburn, Patrick. *The Rise of Islamic State: ISIS and the New Sunni Revolution*. London: Verso, 2014.

Cole, Juan. "'Too Extreme for al-Qaeda': Al-Zawahiri Disowns ISIL". *Mideast Posts*. 5 Feb. 2014. 22 Sept. 2014 <http://mideastposts.com/middle-east-politics-analysis/extreme-al-qaeda-al-zawahiri-disowns-isil>.

"European jihadists: 'It ain't half hot here, mum'—why and how Westerners go to fight in Syria and Iraq". *The Economist*. 30 Aug. 2014. 9 Sept. 2014 <http://www.economist.com/news/middle-east-and-africa/21614226-why-and-

how-westerners-go-fight-syria-and-iraq-it-aint-half-hot-here-mum>.

Gambill, Gary. "Abu Musab al-Zarqawi: A biographical sketch". The Jamestown Foundation, 2004. 15 Dec. 2014 <http://www.jamestown.org/single/?tx_ttnews%5D=27304#.Vw1Nl4-cHIU>.

Gerges, Fawaz "Islamic State: Can its savagery be explained?" *BBC World Service* 9 Sept. 2014. 5 Dec. 2015 <http://www.bbc.co.uk/news/world-middle-east-29123528>.

—. *The Far Enemy: Why Jihad Went Global*. Cambridge: Cambridge UP, 2005.

Hall, John. "The ISIS map of the world: Militants outline chilling five-year plan for global domination as they declare formation of caliphate - and change their name to the Islamic State". *The Daily Mail*. 1 July 2014. 15 Sept. 2014 <http://www.dailymail.co.uk/news/article-2674736/ISIS-militants-declare-formation-caliphate-Syria-Iraq-demand-Muslims-world-swear-allegiance.html#ixzz3DNq610qN>.

Hoodbhoy, Pervez. "What's next after Karachi's carnage?" *3 Quarks Daily*. 14 May 2007 <http://3quarksdaily.blogs.com/3quarksdaily/2007/05/what_next_after.html>.

Jeffries, Stuart. "ISIS's destruction of Palmyra: 'The heart has been ripped out of the city'". *The Guardian*. 2 Sept. 2015. 28 Nov. 2015. <http://www.theguardian.com/world/2015/sep/02/isis-destruction-of-palmyra-syria-heart-been-ripped-out-of-the-city>.

Joscelyn, Thomas. "Jailed jihadi ideologue says that ISIS is a deviant organisation". *Long War Journal*. 28 May 2014. 18 Sept. 2015 <http://www.longwarjournal.org/archives/2014/05/jailed_jihadist_ideo.php>.

Kirdar, M. J. "Al-Qaeda in Iraq". Center for Strategic and International Studies, June 2011. 1-15.

Lacroix, Stephane. "Between Revolution and Apoliticism: Nasir al-Din al-Albani and his Impact on the Shaping of Contemporary Salafism". Meijer, Roel, ed. *Global Salafism: Islam's New Religious Movement*. London: Hurst, 2009. 58-80.

"Lessons of Lal Masjid". Editorial. *Daily Times*. 11 July 2007. 14 Feb. 2016 [editorial summarizes daily reports accessed 4 Dec. 2010] <http://archives. dailytimes.com.pk/editorial/11-Jul-2007/editorial-lessons-of-lal-masjid>.

Lia, Brynjar. "'Destructive Doctrinarians': Abu Mus'ab al-Suri's Critique of the Salafis in the Jihadi Current". Meijer, Roel, ed. *Global Salafism: Islam's New Religious Movement*. London: Hurst, 2009. 281-300.

Maley, William. "Interpreting the Taliban". Introduction. *Fundamentalism Reborn? Afghanistan and the Taliban*. Ed. Maley. London: Hurst, 2001. 1-28.

Malik, Shiva, Ali Younes, Spencer Ackerman, and Mustafa Khalili. "How ISIS crippled al-Qaida". *The Guardian*. 10 June 2015. 1 Dec. 2015 <http://www.theguardian.com/world/2015/jun/10/how-isis-crippled-al-qaida>.

Meijer, Roel, ed. "Commanding Right and Forbidding Wrong as a Principle of Social Action: The Case of the Egyptian al-Jama'a al-Islamiyya". Meijer, Roel, ed. *Global Salafism: Islam's New Religious Movement*. London: Hurst, 2009. 189-220.

Melvin, Don, and Ray Sanchez. "Russian plane crashes in Sinai, killing all 224 people on board". *CNN*. 1 Nov. 2015. 28 Nov. 2015 <http://edition.cnn.com/2015/10/31/ middleeast/egypt-plane-crash>.

Metcalf, Barbara, ed. *Islamic Contestations: Essays on Muslims in India and Pakistan*. New Delhi: Oxford UP, 2004.

—. *Islamic Revival in British India: Deoband, 1860-1900*. New Delhi: Oxford UP, 1982.

Moghadam, Assaf, and Brian Fishman, eds. *Fault lines in global jihad: Organizational, strategic, and ideological fissures* (London: Routledge, 2011).

Muhammad Sa'ad Ababakar, et al. "Open Letter to Dr. Ibrahim Awwad al-Badri, Alias 'Abu Bakr al-Baghdadi', and to the Fighters and Followers of the Self-Declared 'Islamic State'". 24th Dhul-Qi'da 1435 AH. 19 Sep. 2014. 18 Sep. 2015. <http://www.lettertobaghdadi.com/ar>.

Najafizadah, Haroon. "Ruyarui-ye Taliban wa Da-esh [Confrontation between the Taliban and ISIS]". Report. *BBC Persian*. 25 June 2015. 29 June 2015 <http://www.bbc.com/ persian/afghanistan/2015/06/150625_mar_isis_harun_analysis>.

Naji, Abu Bakr. *The Management of Savagery*. Trans. William McCants. John M. Olin Institute for Strategic Studies (Harvard University, 2006).

"Niroohaye Jaish al-islam viduie az koshtan-e 18 uzu-e Daesh montasher Kardand [Jaish-al Islam Forces show, in a video, that they have killed 18 members of ISIS]". *BBC Persian*. 1 July 2015. 20 Aug. 2015 <http://www.bbc.com/ persian/world/2015/07/ 150701_an_syria>.

Noraiee, Hoshang. Rev. of *My Life With the Taliban* by Abdul Salam Zaeef. *Academia.edu*. 2014. 10 Nov. 2014 <http:// www.academia.edu/8740651/A_review_of_Zaeefs_ Autobiography_My_Life_With_Taliban>.

"Pakistan Taliban sack spokesman Shahidullah Shahid for IS vow". *The Guardian*. 21 Oct. 2014. 24 Oct. 2014 <http:// www.bbc.co.uk/news/world-asia-29640242>.

"Paris attacks: The latest news and opinion on the attacks across Paris". *The Guardian*. 13 Nov. 2015. 28 Nov. 2015 <http://www.theguardian.com/world/paris-attacks>.

Paz, Reuven. "Debates Within the Family: Jihadi-Salafi Debates on Strategy, Takfir, Extremism, Suicide Bombings, and the Sense of the Apocalypse". Meijer, Roel, ed. *Global Salafism: Islam's New Religious Movement*. London: Hurst, 2009. 267-280.

Quran. Surah 9, at-Tawbah, 107-110.

Ra'ees, Wahabuddin. "Building Polity within [a] Secular Framework of Political Activities in Egypt, Tunisia and Turkey in Reference to Ibn Khaldun's Theory of State". *Al-Shajarah* 18.1 (2013): 59-84.

"Rahbare Taliban be havadaranash: naw javanân ra estekhdam nakonid (The leader of Taliban to his supporters: Don't recruit children)". *BBC Persian*. 27 May 2015. 28 Oct. 2015 <http://www.bbc.com/persian/afghanistan/2015/10/151027_k02-taliban-leader-message>.

Rashid, Ahmed. *Taliban: The Power of Militant Islam in Afghanistan and Beyond*, 2nd ed., I. B. Tauris, 2010.

Riedel, Bruce. "Baghdadi vs. Zawahri: Battle for global jihad". *Al-Monitor*. 24 Nov. 2014. 10 June 2015 <http://www.al-monitor.com/pulse/originals/2014/11/battle-global-jihad-bin-laden-legacy.html>.

Roy, Olivier. "Has Islamism a Future in Afghanistan?" *Fundamentalism Reborn? Afghanistan and the Taliban*. Ed. William Maley. London, Hurst , 2001.

Shaheen, Kareem. "ISIS claims responsibility as suicide bombers kill dozens in Beirut". *The Guardian*. 12 Nov. 2015. 1 Dec. 2015 <http://www.theguardian.com/world/2015/nov/12/beirut-bombings-kill-at-least-20-lebanon>.

Simon, Allison. *The Islamic State: Why Africa should be worried*. Policy brief. Institute for Security Studies, 2014. 12 Sep. 2014. 19 Nov. 2014 <https://www.issafrica.org/the-islamic-state-why-africa-should-be-worried>.

Smith, David. "Boko Haram continues its ascent as the world looks away: With Abuja focusing on the Ebola outbreak and Washington on ISIS, Islamic militants continue to rampage in northern Nigeria". *The Guardian.* 11 Sept. 2014. 11 Sept. 2014 <http:// www.theguardian.com/world/2014/sep/11/world-attention-boko-haram-continues-ascent>.

Smith, Lewis. "Five dead in Saudi Arabia mosque shooting - ISIS claims responsibility". *The Independent.* 17 Oct. 2015. 1 Dec. 2015 <http://www.independent.co.uk/news/world/middle-east/five-dead-in-saudi-arabia-mosque-shooting-isis-claims-responsibility-a6697596.html>.

Starr, Barbara, Joshua Berlinger, and Raja Razek. "U.S. military carries out airstrikes; aid drops to Iraqi town surrounded by ISIS". *CNN.* 30 Aug. 2014. 11 Sept. 2014 <http://edition.cnn.com/2014/08/30/world/meast/isis-iraq-syria>.

Steinberg, Guido. "Jihadi-Salafism and the Shi'is: Remarks about the Intellectual Roots of Anti-Shiism". Meijer, Roel, ed. *Global Salafism: Islam's New Religious Movement.* London: Hurst, 2009. 107-125.

Stern, Jessica, and Berger, J. M. *ISIS: The State of Terror.* London: William Collins, 2015.

"The militant schoolgirls who terrorised a Pakistan community." Video. Journeyman Pictures. 26 June 2007. 12 Apr. 2016 <http://www.youtube.com/watch?v=n4f89Jg-TnY&feature= fvw>.

"The trouble with madrassas in Pakistan". *The Express Tribune.* 25 Jan. 2012. 18 Sept. 2014 <http://tribune.com.pk/story/326941/the-trouble-with-madrassas-in-pakistan>.

Urquart, Conal. "Iraq crisis: ISIS militants plan to 'marry' captured Yazidi women". *The Independent.* 17 Aug. 2014. 11 Sept. 2014 <http://www.independent.co.uk/news/world/ middle-east/iraq-crisis-isis-militants-plan-to-marry-captured-yazidi-women-9674922.html>.

Variyar, Mugdha. "ISIS threatens Ramadan attack in Bahrain; minister calls for common mosques for Shias and Sunnis after Kuwait bombing". *International Business News.* 29 June 2015. 1 Dec. 2015 <http://www.ibtimes.co.in/isis-warns-ramadan-attack-bahrain-minister-calls-common-mosque-shias-sunnis-637431>.

Wagemakers, Joas. "The Transformation of a Radical Concept: *al-wala' wa-l-bara'* in the Ideology of Abu Muhammad al-Maqadisi". Meijer, Roel, ed. *Global Salafism: Islam's New Religious Movement.* London: Hurst, 2009. 81-106.

Walker, Andrew. *'Eat the Heart of the Infidel'—The Harrowing of Nigeria and the Rise of Boko Haram.* London: Hurst, 2016.

Weaver, Matthew. "Militant group releases UN peacekeepers held hostage in Syria: Jabhat al-Nusra releases all 45 Fijian UN peacekeepers after holding them hostage for two weeks". *The Guardian.* 11 Sept. 2014. 17 Sept. 2014 <http://www.theguardian.com/ world/2014/sep/11/ jabhat-al-nusra-releases-hostages-fijian-syria>.

Weiss, Michael and Hassan Hassan. *ISIS: Inside the Army of Terror.* New York: Regan Arts, 2015.

Welsford, Katie. *When borders are meaningless: The Islamic State in Iraq and al-Sham.* London: Institute for Islamic Strategic Affairs. July 2014. 15 Nov. 2014 <http://iisa.org.uk/wp-content/uploads/2014/07/When-borders-are-meaningless-ISIS.pdf>.

"Yemen crisis: Islamic State claims Sanaa mosque attacks". *BBC World Service.* 21 Mar. 2015. 1 Dec. 2015 <http://www.bbc.co.uk/news/world-middle-east-31989844>.

Zaeef, Abdul Salam. *My Life With the Taliban.* Ed. Alex Strick van Linschoten and Felix Kuchen. London: Hurst, 2010.

Endnotes

1 M. J. Kirdar, "Al-Qaeda in Iraq" (Center for Strategic and International Studies June 2w011) 1-15.

2 See Patrick. Cockburn, *The Rise of Islamic State: ISIS and the New Sunni Revolution* (London: Verso, 2014).

3 See Jessica Stern and J. M. Berger, *ISIS: The State of Terror* (London: William Collins, 2015).

4 Hannah Arendt, *The Origins of Totalitarianism* (London: HBJ, 1975).

5 See Michael Weiss and Hassan Hassan, *ISIS: Inside the Army of Terror* (New York: Regan Arts, 2015) 29.

6 See Jason Burke, *The 9/11 Wars* (London: Penguin Books, 2011) 10-11.

7 Ahmed Rashid, *Taliban: The Power of Militant Islam in Afghanistan and Beyond*, 2nd ed. (I. B. Tauris, 2010).

8 See Charles Caris and Samuel Reynolds, *ISIS Governance in Syria*, Report 22 (Washington, DC: The Institute for the Study of War, 2014), 12 Oct. 2014 <www.understandingwar.org>.

9 Boko Haram in Nigeria, led by Abubakar Shekau, kidnapped more than 279 school girls in April 2014.Then, Abubakar Shekau claimed that he would sell them on the market. See "Boko Haram leader: 'We will sell the girls on the market'" [video], *The Guardian* 6 May 2014 11 Sept. 2014 <http://www.theguardian.com/world/boko-haram?page=8>.
See also David Smith, "Boko Haram continues its ascent as the world looks away: With Abuja focusing on the Ebola outbreak and Washington on ISIS, Islamic militants continue to rampage in northern Nigeria", *The Guardian* 11 Sept. 2014 <http://www.theguardian.com/world/2014/sep/11/world-attention-boko-haram-continues-ascent>.
For an historical perspective, see Andrew Walker, *'Eat the Heart of the Infidel'—The Harrowing of Nigeria and the Rise of Boko Haram* (London: Hurst, 2016).
See also Allison Simon, *The Islamic State: Why Africa Should Be Worried*, policy brief (Institute for Security Studies, 2014), 19 Nov. 2014.

10 Conal Urquart, "Iraq crisis: ISIS militants plan to 'marry' captured Yazidi women", *The Independent* 17 Aug. 2014, 11 Sept. 2014 <http://www.independent.co.uk/news/world/ middle-east/iraq-crisis-isis-militants-plan-to-marry-captured-yazidi-women-9674922.html>, accessed 11 Sept. 2014.
See also Barbara Starr, Joshua Berlinger, and Raja Razek, "U.S. military carries out airstrikes, aid drops to Iraqi town surrounded by IS", CNN 31 Aug. 2014, 11 Sept. 2014 <http://edition.cnn.com/2014/08/30/world/

meast/isis-iraq-syria>.

11 Stuart Jeffries, "ISIS's destruction of Palmyra: 'The heart has been ripped out of the city'", *The Guardian* 2 Sept. 2015, 28 Nov. 2015 <http://www.theguardian.com/world/2015/ sep/02/isis-destruction-of-palmyra-syria-eart-been-ripped-out-of-the-city>.

12 See *Qur'an*, Surh 9, at-Tawbah. 107-110.

13 See Caris and Reynolds (2014).

14 See Abdul Salam Zaeef, *My Life with the Taliban*, ed. Alex Strick van Linschoten and Felix Kuchen (London: Hurst, 2010) 84.

15 Olivier Roy, "Has Islamism a Future in Afghanistan?" ed. William Maley, *Fundamentalism Reborn? Afghanistan and the Taliban* (London: Hurst, 2001) 211, p. 211. See also Rashid (2010) and Zaeef (2010).

16 However, al-Zarqawi, as an inspirational strategist and founding father of this leftist brand of al-Qaeda in Iraq, which later developed into ISIS, was a lay person with poor education and a petty criminal record in his early age. See Burke (2011).
See also Gary Gambill, "Abu Musab al-Zarqawi: A biographical sketch" The Jamestown Foundation, 2004, 15 Dec. 2014 <http://www.jamestown.org/single/?tx_ttnews %5D= 27304>.

17 "European Jihadists: 'It ain't half hot here, mum'—why and how Westerners go to fight in Syria and Iraq", *The Economist* 30 Aug. 2014, 9 Sept. 2014 <http://www.economist.com/news/middle-east-and-africa/21614226-why-and-how-westerners-go-fight-syria-and-iraq-it-aint-half-hot-here-mum>.

18 However, the Taliban – particularly the Pakistani Taliban – have, to some extent, changed their attitudes towards women. For example, women may be used for organising and performing certain aspects of jihad including suicide attacks. Active participation of women in the Red Mosque event, in which over 100 female seminary students were killed in clashes with security forces, is a notable example of this. This event happened in early July 2007. Some interesting materials can be seen in YouTube videos and pictures illustrating the militant activities in which the female students were involved.
See "The militant schoolgirls who terrorised a Pakistan community," video, Journeyman Pictures, 26 June 2007 <http://www.youtube.com/watch?v=n4f89Jg-TnY&feature=fvw>.
Additionally, see the photos in Pervez Hoodbhoy, "What's next after Karachi's carnage?" *3 Quarks Daily* 14 May 2007 <http://3quarksdaily.blogs.com/3quarksdaily/2007/ 05/what_next_after.html>.
See also a summary of brief day-by-day reports on the insurgency (published by a Pakistani periodical): "Lessons of Lal Masjid", editorial, *Daily Times*, 11 July 2007, 14 Feb. 2016 [editorial summarizes daily reports

accessed 4 Dec. 2010] <http:// archives.dailytimes.com.pk/editorial/11-Jul-2007/editorial-lessons-of-lal-masjid>.

19 See "European jihadists: 'It ain't half hot here, mum'—why and how Westerners go to fight in Syria and Iraq" (2014).

20 Burhanuddin Rabbani, Ahmad Shah Massoud, and Gulbuddin Hekmatyar were Islamists who split in the 1970s. Rabbani was a pro-Muslim Brotherhood founder of Jamiat-e Islami [the Islamic Society] who became president of Afghanistan; while the pro-Pakistani Hekmatyar, an early member (as was Massoud) of Jamiat-e Islami, became the founder of Hezb-e Islami [the Islamic Party] and prime minister of Afghanistan.

21 See Barbara Metcalf, *Islamic Revival in British India: Deoband, 1860-1900* (New Delhi: Oxford UP, 1982). See also Rashid (2010). Additionally, see Hoshang Noraiee, rev. of *My Life with the Taliban*, by Abdul Salam Zaeef, *Academia.edu* 2014, 10 Nov. 2014 <http://www.academia.edu/8740651/A_review_of_Zaeefs_Autobiography_My_Life_With_Taliban>.

22 See Metcalf (1982).

23 "The trouble with madrassas in Pakistan", *The Express Tribune* 25 Jan. 2012, 18 Sept. 2014 <http://tribune.com.pk/story/326941/the-trouble-with-madrassas-in-pakistan>.

24 See William Maley (2001), "Interpreting the Taliban", introduction, William Maley (ed.), *Fundamentalism Reborn? Afghanistan and the Taliban* (London, Hurst, 2001) 1-28. See also Rashid (2010) and Burke (2011).

25 See Zaeef (2010).

26 See Barbara Metcalf (2004) *Islamic Contestations: Essays on Muslims in India and Pakistan* (New Delhi: Oxford University Press, 2004). See also Rashid (2010).

27 See Roel Meijer (ed.), *Global Salafism: Islam's New Religious Movement* (London: Hurst, 2009). See also Metcalf (1982) regarding Ahle Hadith. Ahle Hadith is the subcontinent version of the Salafist school/movement at present time. Now, there is a huge network of madrassas associated with this school in Pakistan; but it not as popular as Deobandi. The radical jihadi organisation ideologically associated with Ahle Hadith in Pakistan is Lashkar-e Tayybah, for which the Kashmir issue is its primary interest.

28 Quraish was an aristocratic tribe to which Mohammad belonged. Descendants of Mohammad are usually called *syed*.

29 See Stephane Lacroix, "Between Revolution and Apoliticism: Nasir al-Din al-Albani and his Impact on the Shaping of Contemporary Salafism", *Global Salafism: Islam's New Religious Movement*, ed. Roel Meijer (London, Hurst, 2009) 73-74.

30 See Raji (2004). See also Brynjar Lia, "'Destructive Doctrinairians':

Abu Mus'ab al-Suri's Critique of the Salafists in the jihadi Current", *Global Salafism: Islam's New Religious Movement*, ed. Roel Meijer (London: Hurst, 2009) 281-300.

31 See Lia 286.

32 However, it should be noticed that al-Maqdisi, similar to al-Zawaheri, criticised Zarqawi for using extreme tactics in Iraq. See Stern and Berger (2015) 278.

33 See Reuven Paz, "Debates within the Family: Jihadi-Salafist debates on Strategy, Takfir, Extremism, Suicide Bombing, and the Sense of the Apocalypse", *Global Salafism: Islam's New Religious Movement*, ed. Roel Meijer (London: Hurst, 2009) 269.

34 See Joas Wagemakers, "The Transformation of a Radical Concept: *al-wala' wa-l-bara'* in the Ideology of Abu Muhammad al-Maqadisi", *Global Salafism: Islam's New Religious Movement*, ed. Roel Meijer (London: Hurst 2009) 95.

35 See Rashid (2010) and Roy (2001).

36 See Zaeef (2010) and Noraiee (2014).

37 See Abu Bakr Naji, *The Management of Savagery: The Most Critical Stage Through Which the Umma Will Pass*, trans. William McCants, John M. Olin Institute for Strategic Studies (Cambridge: Harvard University, 2006). For discussion of form and content with regards to building polity, see Wahabuddin Ra'ees, "Building Polity within [a] Secular Framework of Political Activities in Egypt, Tunisia and Turkey in Reference to Ibn Khaldun's Theory of State", *Al-Shajarah* 18.1 (2013): 59-84.

38 Caris and Reynolds (2014).

39 Stern and Berger 117.

40 Abdallah Suleiman Ali, "ISIS announces Islamic caliphate, changes name", ed./trans. Pascale El-Khoury, *Al-Monitor* 30 June 2014 <http://www.al-monitor.com/ pulse/ar/security/2014/06/iraq-syria-isis-announcement-islamic-caliphate-name-change.html>.

41 John Hall, "The ISIS map of the world: Militants outline chilling five-year plan for global domination as they declare formation of caliphate – and change their name to the Islamic State", *The Daily Mail* 1 July 2014, 15 Sept. 2014 <http://www. dailymail.co.uk/news/article-2674736/ISIS-militants-declare-formation-caliphate-Syria-Iraq-demand-Muslims-world-swear-allegiance.html#ixzz3DNq610qN>.

42 Ahmad Rashid's (2010) book is still one of the most reliable books available on the Taliban. (Be aware, however, that some parts of it are now out of date.)

43 For explaining these strategies, see Fawaz Gerges, *The Far Enemy: Why Jihad Went Global* (Camridge: Cambridge UP, 2005).

44 See Fawaz Gerges, "Islamic State: Can its savagery be explained?" *BBC*

World Service 9 Sept. 2014, 5 Dec. 2015 <http://www.bbc.co.uk/news/world-middle-east-29123528>.

45 Al-Libi was killed in Pakistan in 2012. See Jason Burke, Abu Yahya al-Libi, Obituary, *The Guardian* 6 June 2012.

46 Paz 276.

47 Quoted in Paz 277.

48 Paz 277.

49 Quoted in Roel Meijer, "Commanding Right and Forbidding Wrong as a Principle of Social Action: The Case of the Egyptian al-Jama'a al-Islamiyya", *Global Salafism: Islam's New Religious Movement*, ed. Roel Meijer (London: Hurst, 2009) 204.

50 Naji (2006).

51 See Lia (2009).

52 Stern and Berger (2015).

53 See Charles River Editors, *The Islamic State of Iraq and Syria: The History of ISIS/ISIL* (CreateSpace: Marson Gate, 2014).

54 Quoted in Lia 287. For a comparative view of different approaches between Salafists and Muslim Brotherhood religious nationalists, see Peter Picucci, *Terrorism's Operational Code: An Examination of the Belief Systems of Al-Qaeda and Hamas*, Diss. Lawrence: U. of Kansas, 2008 (Ann Arbor: UMI, 2008. ATT 3307710) 263.

55 Lia 296. See also Assaf Moghadam and Brian Fishman, eds., *Fault lines in global jihad: Organizational, strategic, and ideological fissures* (London: Routledge, 2011).

56 Lia 294-298.

57 Quoted in Lia 295.

58 See Weiss and Hassan 179-180.

59 Gambill (2004).

60 Naji (2006).

61 Guido Steinberg, "Jihadi-Salafism and the Shi'is: Remarks about the Intellectual Roots of anti-Shi'ism", *Global Salafism: Islam's New Religious Movement*, ed. Roel Meijer (London: Hurst, 2009) 122-123.

62 See Caris and Reynolds (2014).

63 Juan Cole, "'Too Extreme for al-Qaeda': Al-Zawahiri Disowns ISIL", *Mideast Posts* 5 Feb. 2014, 22 Sept. 2014 <http://mideastposts.com/middle-east-politics-analysis/extreme-al-qaeda-al-zawahiri-disowns-isil>.

64 Martin Cholvo, "Explosion in Syria kills senior leadership of Ahrar al-Sham", *The Guardian* 10 Sept. 2014, 16 Nov. 2014 <http://www.theguardian.com/world/2014/sep/10/ explosion-syria-kills-leadership-ahrar-al-sham>.

65 "Niroohaye Jaish al-islam viduie az koshtan-e 18 uzu-e daesh montasher Kardand [Jaish-al Islam Forces show, in a video, that they have

killed 18 members of ISIS]", *BBC Persian* 1 July 2015, 20 Aug. 2015 <http://www.bbc.com/persian/world/2015/07/150701_ an_syria>.

66 Charles River Editors (2014).

67 Ali (2014).

68 Thomas Joscelyn, "Jailed jihadist ideologue says the ISIS is a deviant organisation", *Long War Journal* 28 May 2014, 18 Sept. 2015 <http://www. longwarjournal.org/archives/2014/05/jailed_jihadist_ideo.php>.

69 Mohamed al-Daameh, "Abu Qatada, Maqdisi can unify Islamist ranks against ISIS: experts", *Aawsat* 27 Sept. 2014, 23 Oct. 2014 <http://www. aawsat.net/2014/09/article 55336996>.

70 Shiva Malik, Ali Younes, Spencer Ackerman, and Mustafa Khalili, "How ISIS crippled al-Qaida", *The Guardian* 10 June 2015, 1 Dec. 2015 <http://www. theguardian.com/ world/2015/jun/10/how-isis-crippled-al-qaida>.

71 Malik et al. (2015).

72 Stern and Berger 186.

73 Muhammad Sa'ad Ababakar, et al., "Open Letter to Dr. Ibrahim Awwad al-Badri, Alias 'Abu Bakr al-Baghdadi', and to the Fighters and Followers of the Self-Declared 'Islamic State'", 24th Dhul-Qi'da 1435 AH, 19 Sep. 2014, 18 Sep. 2015 <http://www. lettertobaghdadi.com/pdf/Booklet-Arabic.pdf>. 3 Mar. 2016 <http://www. lettertobaghdadi.com/14/english-v14.pdf>. (For a list of the latest signatories, see <http://www. lettertobaghdadi.com/new-signatories>.)

See also "Over 1000 Indian Islamic scholars issue world's biggest fatwa against ISIS", *India* 9 Sept. 2015, 3 Mar. 2016 <http://www.india.com/news/india/ over-1000-indian-islamic-scholars-issue-worlds-biggest-fatwa-against-isis-541080/>.

74 Shaykh Muhammad al-Yaqoubi, *Refuting ISIS: A Rebuttal of Its Religious and Ideological Foundations* (USA: Sacred Knowledge, 2015). (As of 2016, a new edition of *Refuting ISIS* is now available in Arabic.)

Min. 19: "hatred is a source of...self-destruction"—Sheikh Muhammad al-Yaqoubi, interview with Shelagh Fogarty. *Heart and Soul*, BBC 31 Mar. 2014, 3 Mar. 2016 <https://www.youtube.com/watch?v=K4pP4nXdTv8>. Formerly available at <http://www.bbc.co.uk/programmes/p01w4v2r>.

75 Al-Yaqoubi (2015).

76 Ian Black, "Saudi clerics declare ISIS terrorism a 'heinous crime' under sharia law", *The Guardian* 17 Sept. 2014, 1 Dec. 2015 <http://www. theguardian.com/world/2014/sep/17/saudi-clerics-fatwa-declares-terrorism-heinous-crime-sharia-law>.

77 Following hostage taking, the al-Nosrah Front asked the UN to lift their name from the terrorist blacklist, release the prisoners, and facil-

itate aid to the areas they control (but which are being besieged by the Syrian Government). However, they withdrew these demands later and released the hostages. The terms they put forward were quite unusual for a hard-line jihadist group. On the one hand, it could be interpreted as a new strategy towards recognition of UN authority. But on the other, they were likely to show their power and desire to strengthen relations with other Syrian anti-Assad organisations—rather than recognition of UN legitimacy.

See Matthew Weaver, "Militant group releases UN peacekeepers held hostage in Syria: Jabhat al-Nusra releases all 45 Fijian UN peacekeepers after holding them hostage for two weeks", The Guardian 11 Sept. 2014, 17 Sept. 2014 <http://www. theguardian.com/world/2014/sep/11/ jabhat-al-nusra-releases-hostages-fijian-syria>.

78 Naji (2006).

79 "Paris attacks: The latest news and opinion on the attacks across Paris", *The Guardian* 13 Nov. 2015, 28 Nov. 2015 <http://www.theguardian.com/ world/paris-attacks>.

80 Don Melvin and Ray Sanchez, "Russian plane crashes in Sinai, killing all 224 people on board", *CNN*, 1 Nov. 2015, 28 Nov. 2015 <http://edition. cnn.com/ 2015/10/31/middleeast/egypt-plane-crash/>.

81 Stern and Berger 96.

82 See Bruce Riedel, "Baghdadi vs. Zawahri: Battle for global jihad", *Al-Monitor* 24 Nov. 2014, 10 June 2015 <http://www.al-monitor.com/ pulse/originals/2014/11/battle-global-jihad-bin-laden-legacy.html>.See also Simon (2014).

"Ansar al Sharia Libya's tight relationship with AQIM is no secret inside Libya. The Islamic State's 'province' in Libya, which is opposed to al Qaeda and its front groups, has even complained about the "closeness" of the two organizations' leaders"—Thomas Joscelyn, "Al Qaeda in the Islamic Maghreb honors Ansar al Sharia's slain military commander", *Long War Journal* 29 Oct. 2015, 7 Mar. 2016 <http://www.longwarjournal.org/ar- chives/ 2015/10/al-qaeda-in-the-islamic-maghreb-honors-ansar-al-shari- as-slain-military-commander.php>.

83 Stern and Berger 177-198 (chap. 8).

84 Simon (2014). See also "Pakistan Taliban sack spokesman Shahidul- lah Shahid for IS vow", *BBC World Service* 21 Oct. 2014, 24 Oct. 2014 <http://www.bbc.co. uk/news/world-asia-29640242>.

85 See Stern and Berger 177-198 (chap. 8).

86 Kareem Shaheen, "ISIS claims responsibility as suicide bombers kill dozens in Beirut", *The Guardian* 12 Nov. 2015, 1 Dec. 2015 <http://www.theguardian. com/ world/2015/nov/12/beirut-bombings-kill-at-least-20-lebanon>.

87 Mugdha Variyar, "ISIS threatens Ramadan attack in Bahrain; minister calls for common mosques for Shias and Sunnis after Kuwait bombing", *International Business News* 29 June 2015, 1 Dec. 2015 <http://www.ibtimes.co.in/isis-warns-ramadan-attack-bahrain-minister-calls-common-mosque-shias-sunnis-637431>.

88 "27 killed in ISIS attack on Kuwait mosque", *Al-Arabiya* [English] 26 June 2015, 1 Dec. 2015 <http://english.alarabiya.net/en/News/middle-east/2015/06/26/Explosion-hits-mosque-in-Kuwait-during-Friday-prayers-.html>.

89 Ian Black, "Second Saudi Arabia suicide bombing fuels ISIS campaign fears", *The Guardian* 29 May 2015, 3 Mar. 2016 <http://www.theguardian.com/world/2015/may/29/saudi-arabia-suicide-bomb-attack-kills-four-in-damman>. See also Lewis Smith, "'Five dead in Saudi Arabia mosque shooting - ISIS claims responsibility", *The Independent* 17 Oct. 2015, 1 Dec. 2015 <http://www.independent.co.uk/news/world/middle-east/five-dead-in-saudi-arabia-mosque-shooting-isis-claims-responsibility-a6697596.html>.

90 "Yemen crisis: Islamic State claims Sanaa mosque attacks", *BBC World Service* 21 Mar. 2015, 1 Dec. 2015 <http://www.bbc.co.uk/news/world-middle-east-31989844>.

91 Greg Botelho, Yousuf Basil, and Sugam Pokharel, "ISIS says it's behind deadly Shiite mosque attack in Bangladesh", *CNN* 27 Nov. 2015, 1 Dec. 2015 <http://edition.cnn. com/2015/11/27/asia/bangladesh-isis-attack-claim>.

92 Haroon Najafizadah, "Ruyarui-ye Taliban wa Da-esh [Confrontation Between the Taliban and ISIS]", report, *BBC Persian* 25 June 2015, 29 June 2015 <http://www.bbc.com/ persian/afghanistan/2015/06/150625_mar_isis_harun_analysis>.

93 Najafizadah (2015).

94 See "Rahbare Taliban be havadaranash: naw javanân ra estekhdam nakonid [The leader of the Taliban to his supporters: Don't recruit children]", *BBC Persian* 28 Oct. 2015 <http://www.bbc.com/persian/afghanistan/2015/10/151027_k02-taliban-leader-message>.

95 "Beruz-e ekhtelaf mian-e farmandeh-e Daesh dar Afghanistan ba rahbare mantaqeh-ei in gruh [Eruption of differences between ISIS commander in Afghanistan and the regional leader of the group]", *BBC Persian* 19 Oct. 2015, 12 Dec. 2015 <http://www.bbc.com/ persian/afghanistan/2015/10/151019_fm_isil_afghanistan_ withdrew_support_khorasan_ chief>.

كان حزب الله هم الغالبون

المقاومة الإسلامية في سوريا

لبَّيكَ يا زَينبُ

SECTION 3

ISIS, ISLAMIC REPUBLIC OF IRAN AND HEZBOLLAH

Abstract

ISIS's aggressive and violent activities in Syria and Iraq have created a serious threat to currently well-established international borders, particularly in the Middle East. ISIS has openly and deliberately violated many basic, universally-accepted values. The nature and dimensions of this threat to Iran, as a more sensible case, can be understood if ISIS's extremist anti-Shia ideology is taken into account. However, the Islamic Republic of Iran, in certain political and ideological aspects, shares common ground with ISIS. In this article, some aspects of sectarian elements, both in terms of ideology and politics of the jihadists/Islamists, will be explained. It will be explained why the threat of ISIS is so real for Iran. To gain further insight regarding Iranian concerns, the nature of the relationships between the Islamic Republic of Iran and the Sunni communities inside the country will be examined.

Key words: ISIS, Iran, Salafists, Baluchistan, Kurdistan, Sunnis, Shias, Saudi Arabia, al-Zarqawi.

3.1: Introduction

The Islamic Republic of Iran (IRI), established in 1979, was the first Islamic state which emerged in the modern era. It was an Islamist state in which the political field merged with judicial, religious, and cultural aspects of life, to enforce a unified totalitarian Islamic system. It was different, for instance, even from Saudi Arabia, where political leadership had not dissolved their sphere of power into a total religious system. Iranian Islamists led, by Ayatollah Khomeini, in the Shia tradition, initiated a new system of power in which the boundaries between public and private spheres were removed. This encouraged many new Islamic groups, both among Sunnis and Shias, to redefine their political strategies to conquer political power as a starting point for Islamisation.

Either as a reaction to IRI, or as influence of it, new radical Sunni jihadists, particularly among Salafists and Deobandis, emerged. These political groups were of a breed different from the Muslim Brotherhood or Jamaat-e-Islami. Although they had had clear political strategies even before Khomeini, the Brotherhood and Jamaat-e-Islami were seen as rather softer and political-minded, compared with the new jihadists. Khomeini had a clear political strategy; but before the revolution, he was not willing (at least openly) to be involved in organising any armed militant Islamist force. But during his rule as *Vali-ye Faqih* (supreme leader), he adopted a hard-line, militant policy against non-Muslims and secular rulers. Militant Salafists emerged as hard-line anti-Shias. Yet in many respects, they shared with Khomeinism certain ideological and political values, such as giving priority to the establishment of an Islamic state, to the full implementation of the Islamic rules; and to the "revival" of Islam to its "glorious" time of "superiority". So it is not very surprising to identify many common values between Salafist jihadis (like ISIS and al-Qaeda) on the one hand and Khomeinism on the other. But at the same time, and in many respects, they have adopted competing interpretations of Islamic traditions.

▓ 'Them' and 'us' in the language of Khomeini and Sunni Salafist jihadists

It is not necessary to have a theocratic political system to use religion as an instrument against rivals. Since the Iranian revolution and the emergence of a theocratic regime in Iran, this has become more normal, particularly in Middle Eastern countries. There, the norm has been to use Islam as a political instrument to control Islamism and the Islamisation of society from above. But it is not exactly the same for the Islamists and jihadists. Their intent has been to capture political power from below and to implement Islamic values as a comprehensive political, social, and ideological project.

Giving superiority to their own projects, and putting strong emphasis on their puritanical nature, are some common ideological features. Absolute rejection of 'others' as the devil is not uncommon. Strong belief in the polarisation of people between 'us' (as believers) and 'them' (as non-believers) – and acting accordingly – makes the radical jihadists distinctive from ordinary, moderate Muslims. Both Sunni jihadists and Shia radicals share similar ideas. Khomeinist political ideology can be seen as a combination of ideas both from Islamists and from puritanical Sunni jihadists (including Salafists). However, a large section of Salafi jihadists reject Shias as non-believers.

The strategy of exporting the Islamic revolution and spreading the Khomeinist version of an "Islamic awakening" was based on the idea of a Shia interpretation of *al-wala'* (loyalty), and *wal-bara'*—disavowal of the apostates and polytheists. This rejectionist and exclusionary idea even targeted those Muslims whom Khomeini derogatorily called "American Muslims".

Khomeini rejected his opponents' interpretations of Islam, and brutally suppressed them. This thesis enforced highly autocratic and sectarian policies. To hate and exclude 'others' on the basis of their being viewed as heretics, non-Muslims, or just not 'real' Muslims, became policy. This was a political and ideological objective: to establish a 'totalitarian' Islamic state, through purification of the Islamic ideas, on the basis of a specific Shia interpretation.

Khomeini said that announcing disavowal (*wal-bara'*) of polytheists is a pillar of monotheism and is the political obligation of the religious duty of pilgrimage. He ordered Mehdi Karroubi[1], his representative in Hajj affairs, to organise Iranian pilgrims to take part in demonstrations and suggested that the Hajj should "resound" with "the noise of" thunderous "shouts of disavowal" denouncing "the polytheists and heretics of the world superpowers", "particularly the criminal America... [You] should not neglect from expressing your anger and hatred regarding the enemies of the God and people". [2] He said that this is the Prophet's tradition—a tradition which should not be limited to the time of pilgrimage ceremony. He also said that Muslims should make "the whole world full of love and loyalty to the God [,] and hatred for and anger at the enemies of God".[3]

To pursuit, his ideas of *wal-bara'* and of the purification of Islam, exporting the Islamic revolution was a necessity. For this reason, Khomeini persistently ignored Saudi rules of Mecca pilgrimage, and insisted on spreading his ideas, through demonstrations and political chanting, even within Mecca itself—where the large majority of the pilgrims were Sunnis. The majority of pilgrims had little desire to politicise the sacred pilgrimage ceremony or to breach the rules established by Saudi Arabia. But the IRI had a different, revolutionary agenda.[4]

The strategy of expansionism, a removal of national boundaries, and the establishment of an Islamic empire were some political 'talking points' which Khomeini had openly announced.[5] Exporting the Islamic revolution by Khomeini was a double-edged strategy. On the one hand, it boosted the confidence of many Islamist movements from different approaches, encouraging them to pursue a clear political agenda. On the other hand, many secular governments and Sunni religious authorities in the Middle East considered this to be an aggressive policy and a real threat. Such concerns were not discouraged by Khomeini's announcement that

With God's will, we will break the hands of invaders, and end the oppression of all oppressors in the Islamic countries. And with the exportation of our revolution, which in reality, is the exportation of the true Islam and instructions of the Prophet, we will bring to an end the dominance of oppression of the superpowers. And with the help of God, we will level the path for the emergence of the saviour and the reformer of all, *Imam Zaman* [Messiah], as the absolute legitimate Imamat.[6]

This is clearly an idea which excludes others, particularly the Sunnis; because in this context, 'true Islam' is a highly selective and subjective issue. Obviously, it is a Shia-related interpretation of political Islam, which Ayatollah Khomeini represented in Iran. It is an idea which is based on the principle of *imamat* (leadership), in particular, the absence and then reappearance and rule of the *Imam Zaman*. In Sunni traditions, these ideas – particularly the legitimacy of *imamat* – are not accepted because these contradict their own principles and the legitimacy of their belief in four *Rashidun*) caliphs.[7]

However, it may not be very strange that Ayatollah Khomeini, in Shia tradition, used language similar to that of Sayyid Qutb; or that he also possessed ideas similar to those of radical Salafists al-Maqdisi and al-Libi (see Chapter 1). Al-Maqdisi is a senior anti-Shia Salafist ideologue. He was the mentor of al-Zarqawi, whose strategies has been followed by ISIS. Similar to Khomeini, al-Maqdisi had strong ideas regarding supporting the principle of 'loyalty and disavowal'—*Al-wala' wa-l-bara'* (loyalty to God and Muslims alone) and disavowal of other religions and non-Muslims). From both points of view, the 'real' Islam is limited to their own versions. As stated earlier in Section 1, Al-Maqdisi believed:

It is compulsory for you (*fa-l-wajib 'alayka*) – if you want Paradise – to disbelieve in him (the modern-day *taghut)*, disavow him and his servants and his friends (*awlialya'ihi*) and to hate them (*tubghidulhun*) and to make them detestable (*tubaghghidulum*) for your children and your family, to work and wage jihad (*tujahidu*) all of your life for his destruction and his annulment (*min ajl hadmihi wa-ibtalhi*) and that you do not give up [that you will not] be satisfied or happy unless [there is] the rule of God the Most High and his legislation alone. Otherwise there is hell. Hell![8]

For Khomeini, as for other jihadists and Islamists such as Qutb, secular states/government are considered corrupt, oppressive, usurpative, tyrannical (*taghut*), and rebellious against God's rules.[9] The nature of governments could be explained in terms of the level of their loyalty to Islam and their rejection of secularism. Khomeini had said that 'Oppressive governments, their judges, their executives and their other professions are "rebellious", because they have disobeyed and rebelled against God's orders and have established laws based on their own will and performed judgement and execution of laws accordingly'.[10]

Come, oh Muslims, to your honour—to your victory. By Allah, if you disbelieve in democracy, secularism, nationalism, as well as all the other garbage and ideas from the West, and rush to your religion and creed, then by Allah, you will own the earth[—]and the East and West will submit to you. This is the promise of Allah to you. This is the promise of Allah to you.[11]

Similar language was used by Khomeini to attack these. He believed that Islamic laws want to remove all boundaries and implement the universal law of *sharia* and that Western nationalism, democracy, freedom, monarchism, and republicanism are anti-Islamic ideas. Khomeini rejected the nationalist concepts of pan-Iranianism and pan-Turkism, and pointed out that "nationalism is a big plot" by colonialists in order to 'divide and conquer' Muslims and ruin Islam by secularizing political and civic life.[12]

This was a basis for attacking the secular leaders of the Islamic countries as being either apostate or *taghut*, or as supporters of American Islam. In this regard, Khomeini also used language similar to that of Sunni jihadists such as al-Libi. As stated earlier in Section 1, Abu Yahya al-Libi, in contrast with more moderate Wahhabis and Salafists, believed that "We should fight all the infidels, whether apostates or crusaders, nationals or foreigners, Arabs or non-Arabs, whether their names are 'Abd al-'Aziz Boutaeflika, 'Abdallah ibn 'Abdal-Aziz, 'Abdallh ibn Husayn, Mu'mmar Qadhafi or George Bush, Tony Blair, Sarkozy or Olmert", even he believed that the enemies from inside are more dangerous than foreign crusaders.[13]

Rivalries between Saudi Arabia and the Islamic Republic of Iran

Politicising Shia-Sunni conflicts was an important consequence of this process, which erupted into further rivalries between Saudi Arabia and the Islamic Republic of Iran (IRI). This rivalry developed into a sort of Cold War between two camps represented by Shia Iran on the one hand, and Sunni Saudi Arabia on the other. But this did not lead to further order. Instead, it created more sectarian conflicts in many Islamic countries, particularly within Pakistan in the 1980s. These conflicts also influenced many jihadists associated with war in Afghanistan. Saudi Arabia used its abundant financial resources and cultural and religious resources to influence a majority of the Sunni population in most Islamic countries.[14] So Saudi Arabia flooded Sunni countries as well as Sunni populations in Shia countries, not only with financial support, but also with cultural, institutional and ideological resources.[15] It did so, whether officially or through its Wahhabi-associated religious institutions and businessmen. This was a process of exporting and internalising strict anti-Shia Wahhabi ideas.

This was a counter-policy Saudi Arabia used to confront or undermine Shia influence, whether potentially or immediately. Theocratically and ideologically among the Sunni Schools, Hanbali-Wahhabism spread by Saudi Arabia, is and has been the most radical anti-Shia approach. This also supported Salafism as a version of the Sunni interpretation of Islam closest to Wahhabism, more so than any other Sunni school, and equipped with crucial resources. Most radical jihadists, in many respects, and through either measured or non-deliberate policies, have roots in the political and ideological contexts created through rivalry between two camps, the first led by Saudi Arabia on the one hand and the second led by the Islamic Republic of Iran on the other. However, it is no longer easy for these countries, particularly Saudi Arabia, to escape from the threats the radical jihadists have imposed on their regime. Therefore, the anti-Shia, approach of al-Qaeda, ISIS, and all other radical Sunni Salafists and Deobandis cannot be fully understood in isolation from these political rivalries.[16].

In spite of supporting the US-led coalition against ISIS by Saudi Arabia, and in spite of threats against Saudi Arabia by Salafist groups such as al-Qaeda and ISIS, the private donors from Saudi Arabia have continued to support radical jihadists abroad so as to confront Shiism/Iran.[17] This, too, has not led to a reduction of the rivalry between Iran and Saudi Arabia. Neither has it led them to abandon sectarian political provocations against each other.

3.2: Is ISIS a threat to Iran?

Now ISIS is a real threat, not only to the Middle Eastern countries (including Saudi Arabia), but also to many other parts of the world. Since it openly and brutally challenges some of the most respected ethical and social values established in modern life, it neither accepts nor leaves much space for negotiation and compromise. Beyond, this, ISIS has openly rejected the current established national boundaries (particularly boundaries based on the Sykes-Picot agreement). And it has not hidden its intention and political ambition to use force to remove the existing national borders and political systems. It is their agenda to establish a vast Islamic caliphate (empire) ruled by the newly-appointed caliph, Abu Bakr al-Baghdadi. Western powers (led by the US) – the national "apostate" powers – are considered as enemies and barriers to their ambitions. But Shias, mainly led by IRI, are seen as the "worst" enemies from within.

ISIS's anti-Shia approach is clearly a continuation of the same ideology and strategy which was established and implemented by al-Zarqawi in Iraq in 2004.[18] Following many important Salafist-Wahhabi *fatwas*[19], al-Zarqawi, with a strong sense of hatred and anger, believed that the Shia were unbelievers and that killing them could be lawful. He had said that the Shia are "the most evil of mankind... the lurking snake, the crafty and malicious scorpion, the spying enemy, and the penetrating venom".[20] Al-Zarqawi and his successors, including Abu Omar al-Baghdadi, were defeated by the US, and their local allies. However, as whole, the US lost the war. Iran, without overtly fighting, emerged as the main winner in the post-Saddam era. Since then, they have been successful in strengthening their area of influence through a secular but Shia-dominated regime in Iraq.

ISIS against the alliance of Iran, Syria, and Iraq

The influence of the Iranian Islamic regime in Syria has a longer history of supporting the minority-based Alawite Shia. But the secular regime of the Assad 'dynasty' can hardly be explained purely on the basis of the Iranian ideological interests. This close relationship was cemented during the Iran-Iraq war when the Ba'athist Assad regime was the only regime which supported Iran against the Iraqi Ba'athists. In spite of his Islamist mission, Khomeini even rejected the request for help of the Syrian Muslim Brotherhood, who had (through their ideologue Sa'id Hawwa) turned to Khomeini for help in the early 1980s. Hafez al-Assad was supported by Iran, in spite of his killing of about 5,000-25,000 Muslim Brotherhood insurgents in the late 1970s and early 1980s.[21] This was an important reason for the Syrian Muslim Brotherhood's taking of an anti-Shia position since then.[22] This was also a politically-oriented decision by the Muslim Brotherhood of Syria, because mainstream branches in Egypt and other countries had not had an anti-Shia approach and had even supported the Iranian Islamic regime.

The Iranian regime's support of Bashar al-Assad, done to suppress initially-peaceful protests in 2011, in reality renewed and exacerbated the earlier hostilities between IRI and the Syrian Islamists. It even damaged IRI relationship with other branches of the Muslim Brotherhood in Palestine and Egypt. Iran has been seen by the Syrian Islamists, and even most Sunnis in other countries, as representative of Shias who are seen to have been encouraging the al-Assad regime to restrain itself from taking genuine steps to reform the system and widen the scope of political participation.

Even beyond that, IRI has sent special military/security forces and advisors to Syria to help Bashar al-Assad. From the beginning of the protests, the Islamic Republic of Iran supported the Assad regime and with same voice called the protesters "terrorists", "*takfirists*", and so on. General Hossein Hamadani, who was killed in Syria, had explained their decisive role in the formation of *basijs* (volunteer militias) both in Syria and in Iraq.[23] *Modafeon*, the official website of the militias organised under the name Modafean Haram (Defenders of the Shrine), was established in 2014. However, many of the participant groups existed and had played a similar role from 2011 on.[24] It was formed by many factions including by 7 main groups of Shias in different countries on the basis of these criterion: "Faith In Islam, resisting against *takfirist* terrorists, and accepting the leadership of *Vali-ye Faqih* (Ayatollah Khamenei).[25] It has also been announced that they have cleared *takfirists* from a space surrounding the Zainab Shrine and that they have also fought against them in Syria and Iraq and liberated Shia areas. It has emphasised the fundamental role that Iran had played in founding Modafean Haram and in providing military training and supporting it in all respects.[26]

According to a BBC report, it is estimated that there are 4,000 volunteers from throughout Iran. They have been chosen from Provincial Units of Saberin and sent by the Revolutionary Guard to Syria. The Iranian Sepah-e Qods (Quds Force) has recruited, organised, and trained Iraqi militias, Afgan Hazaras, and Pakistani Shias in a systematic way. It was reported that Afghani Shia Hazaras, who were recruited into and organised in the *Liwa Fatemiyoun* (Fatemiyoun Brigade), were from communities of poor Hazara refugees settled in the suburbs of the large cities such as Mashahed and Qom. The

Shia Pakistani were from Parachinar in Pakistan and were organised in the *Liwa Zainebiyoun* (Zainebiyoun Brigade). Iraqi militias under the authority of Harakat Hezbollah al-Nujaba were organised by Sepah al-Badr.[27] There have been reports that Pakistani militias [28] and Afghanis[29] from the brigades mentioned have been killed in battle in Syria.

A similar policy (though in a different context) has been pursued by Iran to support the Shia regime of Maliki, who moved towards marginalisation of the Sunni communities in the Iraqi social and political life. The high level of corruption and the use of extreme measures to marginalise Sunnis in Iraq, affected the Sunnis' attitudes towards the conflicts.[30] In reality, the situation in Iraq was a continuation of the Arab Spring, which had already started in other Arab countries but had already started to move in a different direction in Syria. The Arab Spring, which was seen by Khamenei as an Islamic awakening, had already started to show its darkest, most radical, sectarian side. This was the wave of the Arab Spring which reached Iraq and developed into ISIS-led uprisings.

In the context of suppressive and discriminatory policies both in Syria and Iraq, some large sections of the Sunnis became indifferent or became an easy source of recruitment for the radical jihadists such as ISIS. It is estimated that many Sunni tribal militias, who were once member of the "awakening movement" and who had played a crucial role in defeating Iraqi al-Qaeda, were initially excluded from the system and then joined ISIS in desperation.[31] Sectarian divisions and further polarisation of communities along Sunni-Shia religious lines have been exacerbated further by conflicts in Bahrain, and then made even worse in Yemen, where Houthis insurgencies started.

Iran has also been accused of sending ammunition and logistical facilities to both Houthis in Yemen and Shias in Bahrain. But Saudi Arabia sent forces directly to both Bahrain and Yemen to supress insurgents and rebuke Iran by sending the message not to interfere with affairs in Arabic countries. The Allied forces led by Saudi Arabia bombarded Houthi areas, in Yemen. This was a very clear sign of further rivalries between Iran and Saudi Arabia.

Fear of ISIS inside Iranian borders

The Iranian media, for a long period, have paid close attention to the ISIS phenomenon and have discussed the issue in much detail. However, the Iranian media outlets, which are dominantly controlled by the regime, to a large extent considered it to be a foreign issue and have either overlooked or underestimated the direct threat to Iran. They have always tried to look at ISIS as a small and insignificant force. But Iran's great concern has been reflected in the volume of discussion they have given to the issue. Iranian officials have implicitly, and to some extent explicitly, shown how dangerous ISIS activities have been along to the Iranian borders and how worried they have been about these developments.

Yahya Rahim Safavi, the military advisor to Ayatollah Khamenei; Mahmood Alavi, the intelligence minister; Abdolreza Rahmani Fazli, the interior minister; General Hossein Dehghan, the chief of staff; and Ahmad Reza Pourdastan, commander of the army, have taken on the issue of ISIS either to highlight its threat to Iran's borders or to ridicule ISIS and to question its ability and strength. However, Safavi has said "why [should we] support Iraq and Syria? I reply [:] if we don't fight with criminal and irreligious ISIS across the borders and do not secure our country in these areas, then we should fight with these terrorist[s] near our borders".[32]

Alavi has reported that the members of secret ISIS cells within Iran had been arrested. He also announced that the enormous efforts made by ISIS to spread insecurity inside Iran, particularly along the borders, have failed.[33] The dimensions of the threat had even been reflected in statements made by Khamenei. Once, he had told Haider al-Abadi, the Iraqi prime minster, that they would consider the security of Iraq as their own security.[34] In a speech in a military university, Khamenei said he knew that the enemy supported by some 'stupid' leaders in the Persian Gulf area had intentions to create proxy wars close to Iranian borders. He also said that in the case of any devilish measure, the reaction of the Islamic Republic would be very strong.[35]

Now that ISIS has aggressively moved close to western Iranian borders, the IRI regime has become more nervous. There have been claims that ISIS militants have clashed with Iranian security forces inside the north-western Iranian borders.[36] Even if it is not true, as IRI officials have stated, the reports reflect the tactics that ISIS adopts to create fear inside Iran, by encouraging the Iranian Sunnis to rise and challenge the Iranian Shia regime.

Iranian officials have also announced that they have recently arrested many so-called "Salafists" or "*takfirists*", including ISIS supporters in Iran.[37] In some other cases, they have reported that they have destroyed or arrested many ISIS cells inside Iranian borders, particularly along western borders (Kermanshah/Kurdistan)[38] or in the south-east (Sistan and Baluchistan Province).[39] At the same time, in contradictory statements, Iranian security officials have announced that they would not allow ISIS in Iraq to enter an exterior buffer zone extending 40 km from the Iranian border.

Atrocities have not been limited to the Iraqi Government and Iraqi Shias, or Syrian Alawite Shias and Assad. ISIS has already threatened Shias in Lebanon and addressed Hezbollah as a "party of Satan", said that ISIS's martyrs "love the blood of Rafida"[40]. On a few occasions, ISIS has even attacked Shias in Saudi Arabia[41], Yemen, Kuwait, Egypt, and other countries farther afield like Bangladesh (see Chapter 1). ISIS has built their *velayats* (provinces) in Khorasan and many other places. Creating these organisations and attacking Shia shrines and mosques are not only deliberate and well-calculated actions designed to create fear and harassment among Shias and challenge the Iranian regime. But they are also designed to create further polarisation in the Sunni Muslim countries, particularly Arab countries. They also undermine the power of regimes considered by both ISIS and al-Qaeda to be "apostate". They hope that by creating an atmosphere of fear, uncertainty, and insecurity, they can recruit more jihadists and find space to establish their *velayats* as a new step forward in the process of waging offensive jihad.[42]

It seems that ISIS has already started to besiege Iran from different directions and to 'find footsteps' along the Iranian borders. Iranian Security forces, possibly for the same reasons, very openly tried to become closer to their old enemy, the Taliban. For example, security forces openly invited the Taliban's officials (led by Tayyab Agha) to Tehran.[43] Previously, however, there were reports that Iranian security forces had a relationship with the Taliban in order to confront US forces. Even Iran had allowed the Taliban to open an office in Zahedan.[44]

From the evidence provided, it is not very difficult to understand the IRI's concerns and the very difficult position they are in. Iran has little choice but to act seriously against ISIS. But at the same time, it is also clear that open and direct involvement of Iran in Syria and Iraq have easily boosted ISIS's position. ISIS may take advantage of the new situation by looking at the conflict as a 'total war' between Shias and

Sunnis. In that case, ISIS may find more opportunities to gain more sympathy among the conservative and even quietist Sunni authorities in Sunni countries. Involvement of the IRI in their conflicts in Syria and Iraq has already created much tension between Iran and Saudi Arabia. This can generate further tension between the Iranian regime and its Sunni population inside Iran. Not only does ISIS wish this, but such tension also makes Saudi Arabia and its allies desire to act.

Any invasion of ISIS into Iranian borders is a matter of life and death for IRI as well as the Shia majority population, in spite of their different political approaches including secular and reformist ones. They are aware that ISIS's sectarian approach does not allow ISIS to distinguish religious Shia from secular ones. This is enough for all Iranian Shias, to be highly motived for fighting against ISIS. Even the Iranian reformists are aware of this problem. Saeed Hajjarian, for instance, has recently come to the belief that, given the similar conditions during the war between Iran and Iraq, the invasion of ISIS into Iranian borders can create a strong consensus, to the benefit of national interests.[45] This may be true of the Shia communities, but it is very doubtful that Sunni communities in many parts of Iran actively support the regime against ISIS, as they were hardly willing to join the war against Iraq in the 1980s.

In any critical condition, the current divisions can be used as a basis for the placement of further suspicion and pressure on Sunni communities. In case of an ISIS invasion, whatever the consequence may be, it certainly increases ethnic, religious, and sectarian tensions to the level of religious and ethnic cleansing. In that circumstance, Sunnis may be considered by radical Shias to be a unified community and a fifth column of the enemy. Now, there are some radical clerics such as Grand Ayatollah Naser Makarem Shirazi, and Shia websites which consider Iranian Sunnis as a whole to be Wahhabis and warn about their rapid population increase within Iran and their plan to migrate to and buy properties in cities like Mashhad.[46]

It is nearly impossible for ISIS to gain much success in the Iranian mainland. But, it can create serious problems in marginalised areas where Sunnis population are concentrated, particularly in Sistan and Baluchistan in the east (and, to lesser extent, in Kurdish areas along the western borders), where many Sunnis feel alienated and discriminated against by the Shia regime of Iran.

Being aware of this discontent among the Sunnis in Iran, an advisor to the Iranian Foreign Ministry, Mohammad Sadr, has recently denied that ISIS is a threat inside Iranian borders. But he has seen power sharing with Iranian Sunnis as a solution to reduce the risk of the ISIS threat inside Iran's borders.[47] This shows that some authorities among the reformists have a desire to tackle some of the internal problems between Shias and Sunnis. But what are these problems? This is a question which will be examined in more detail in following section.

3.3: Shia Islamism in Iran and discrimination against Sunnis

There is no precise figure available specifying the population percentage of Sunnis in Iran. The national census considers them as part of the Muslim faith in general. But Shiism is considered by the constitution to be the official religion.[48] It is estimated that Sunnis constitute about 10%-15% of the whole population of 75-80 million people in Iran.[49] The Kurdish Sunnis are mainly settled along the western and north-western borders, in Kurdistan, Kermanshah, and Western Azerbaijan. The Baluch Sunnis are located along the south-eastern

borders in Sistan and Baluchistan. And the Turkmen Sunnis
are located in Turkmen Sahra (now Golestan Province) in the
north. Geographically, there is a lesser concentration of Sunnis among Arabs in Khuzestan. There are also many Sunnis in
other provinces such as Kerman, Fars, and Hormozgan. There
are Persian-speaking Sunnis in many parts of Khorasan, and
there are also some smaller communities of Sunnis in Gilan
Province. Apart from these, there are a considerable number
of Sunnis in larger cities within Shia-dominant areas, particularly in Tehran and Mashhad.

The areas with majority Sunni populations, which are
likely to be linguistically distinctive from other Shia-dominant
areas, tend to be the less-developed areas of the country.[50] The
Sunnis in Iran strongly believe that since the 1979 emergence
of the Islamic Republic of Iran, they have been deliberately
and structurally discriminated against by the hard-line Shia
government on the basis of their ethnicity and religion.

Iranian Sunnis, for example, argue that according to the
Iranian constitution, a Sunni can't be president and (even
more obviously) can't attain the purely Shia-based position of
Vali-ye Faqih (supreme leader).[51] The Sunnis also argue that
they have been excluded from key positions such as ministerial, diplomatic, high-ranking military, and security positions,
and even from key provincial posts such as governorships.
Furthermore, they argue that they have not been allowed to
build their own mosques in Tehran while simultaneously the
Shias have been supported by the government in building
many mosques and *hussainyehs* in many small towns and vil-
lages in Sunni-dominant areas—even if there are just a few
Shias or not even any Shias settled there at all.

The Sunnis also argue that Shia religious groups are supported by the government. They say high-ranking Shia clerics
frequently arrange tours all over the Sunni areas for mission-

ary purposes and freely hold their own ceremonies and are trying to convert Sunnis to the Shia faith, but that the Sunnis are not given similar opportunities in Shia-dominated areas. If they do take any similar step, they face much pressure and are accused of being Wahhabis. They also argue that the whole Sunni population is branded as Wahhabi (particularly by hardliner Shias), and is placed under surveillance accordingly.

The Sunnis are also denied equal access to economic resources or to business and employment opportunities. Even by devising an official list of names to choose from, a large number of ethnic names have been excluded. With few exceptions, nearly all streets, schools, and other public spaces are named for contemporary Iranian Shia religious figures, or to a lesser extent, Iranian classical figures. Cultural and linguistic activities by these ethnic-religious groups are not easily allowed, or are easily banned and suppressed by security forces. Amnesty International[52] and Ahmed Shaheed[53] have also documented many forms of pressures placed on Sunnis in Iran.

The Shia regime has used a deliberate and systematic policy of excluding Sunnis, on the basis of suspicion of their being an 'outsider' or enemy 'fifth column'. This has been a matter of concern for some high-ranking reformist officials. For example, take Ali Yunesi – the previous minister of intelligence in Khatami's government, and now the special assistant of President Rouhani in religious and ethnic minority affairs. He criticised those people who consider some minorities to be "outsiders and [who] say that sensitive, confidential and secretive positions cannot be offered to these outsiders...this is not a fair perspective to consider some sections of Iranian people as outsiders".[54]

To gain more insight on Sunnis, the Sunni community in the Kurdish areas will be examined in the next part.

Kurdish Sunnis along the Western borders

Iranian Kurds are spread within a few provinces, particularly among Kurdistan, Kermanshah, and West Azerbaijan. Altogether, these 3 provinces constitute about 5.6% of the total area of the country. Their populations are quite diverse and include Sunnis, Shias, and Ahle Haq. It is very difficult to identify a precise figure for the number of Kurdish Sunnis. But it is very likely to be the biggest section of the Sunni population in Iran. It may be estimated to be about 3-4 million, out of a total population of 6.5 million in 3 provinces.[55] Kurdish Sunnis are dominantly Shafi'i—and among them, Sufi orders have quite a strong influence. Secular politics with a reasonably pluralistic view, rather than a narrowly ethnic approach, has quite deep roots in Iranian Kurdistan. They have a reasonably long history of political and military activities against the Iranian regimes (both Pahlavi and then the IRI).

The Kurdish nationalists have always rejected separatism and demanded a greater share in Iranian national power and more autonomy for ethno-linguistic "nationalities" including Kurdish ones. Possibly, the Democrat Party and Komelah may still be the most influential political organisation among Iranian Kurds. More recently, however, and with a more violent approach, Pezhvak, which is considered to be an affiliation of the PKK, has also become active. These secular organisations take quite a firm stand against ISIS, which is already at war with their close fellow Kurd both in Iraq and in Syria.

It is difficult to estimate the influence of religious groups, but they have also been actively involved in Kurdish politics. After the 1979 Revolution, Ahmad Moftizadeh was an influential religious nationalist figure who founded Shams (the Central Council of the Sunni Community). Molavi Abdul Aziz Mollazadeh, a moderate Sunni figure in Sistan and Baluchistan, also became a prominent member of Shams. Moftizadeh protested against the constitutional articles which considered Shiism to be the official religion and which required for the president to be elected from the official religion. Moftizadeh was demanding autonomy for Kurdistan and was known for establishing "Maktab-e Quran" (Quran School).[56]

The Shams group is still involved in low-level internet activities, but it is not easy to understand its influence in Kurdish areas. It supports reformists in Iran and asks for improvement of social and political conditions in Sunni areas and acceptance of their equal rights within Iran.[57] Now, there are some other Kurdish religious organisations, some of which are mainly influenced by moderate Islamists, particularly Muslim Brotherhood organizations such as Jamaat-e Dawat va Islah-e Iran (The Society of Mission and Reform in Iran).[58] Apart from these groups, another Kurdish group called Harkat-e Islami Ahle Sunnat wa Jamaat-e-Iran, led by Sheikh Abdolqader Tawihidi, has held to a more radical position and is very critical of the Iranian regime, based on the principle of *Velayat-e Faqih* ('government of the jurist'). In an announcement regarding the "Week of Solidarity", which is held by the Iranian regime to emphasise solidarity between Shias and Sunnis, they stated their belief that such a commemoration is hypocritical when the Iranian regime violates the "rights of Sunnis", and that 'unity' is a meaningless claim. However they go beyond that and believe that Shiism has been a misleading and divisive sect which has been creating disunity among Muslims throughout history.[59]

Ansar al-Islam is a quite well-known Salafist jihadist organisation with Kurdish connections. Recruiting from Kurdish regions in Western Iran and Iraq, it has developed a close relationship with al-Qaeda. They are also known for sheltering Zarqawi after he had escaped from Afghanistan. Al-Zarqawi had entered Iran (according to Weiss and Hassan). And with the support of Gulbuddin Hekmatyar, he was sent from Zahedan to Tehran, where he was trained by an IRGC camp in Mehran prior to going to Kurdistan. These writers also mention that General Qasem Soleimani, head of the Quds Corps, had boasted that Ansar al-Islam and al-Zarqawi could move freely in Iran.[60] It is believed that Ansar al-Islam now has a very close cooperation with ISIS. The presence of sporadic elements of ISIS in Kurdistan has been confirmed by the announcements of secular Kurdish organisations such as the Democrat Party.[61] But it is difficult to know how much influence they have among the Kurds.

ISIS's recent invasions of Kurdish areas of Iraq and against Kobani in Syria have created a strong, united backlash from the Kurdish communities all over the world, as well as from within Iran.[62] Iran is more likely to regard Iqlim Kurdistan (the autonomous Kurdish government in Iraq) as a buffer zone to stop ISIS's further advancement towards the Iranian borders.

But Kurdish suspicion of Iranian activities was soon to become apparent. In confronting ISIS, the IRGC – particularly Sepah-e Qods – actively organised and armed Shia mobilisation groups in Iraq. This further undermined and discredited the ability of the Iraqi government, police, and army in Iraq while strengthening Iran's role in Iraq. Hard-line mobilisation forces were seen as a new threat against both Sunni and Kurdish secular forces. For the same reason, Masrour Barzani, head of Kurdistan's security forces, warned about the danger of Shia militias organised and supported by Iran as being even worse than ISIS in Iraq.[63]

In spite of hostility and a long history of brutal suppression by the IRI of the secular Iranian Kurdish political organisations, the intelligence minister, Mahmood Alavi, has announced that they have negotiated with the Iranian Kurdish political organisations such as Komelah and the Democratic

Party of Kurdistan.[64] In Iran, independent demonstrations are not tolerated by the security forces. And yet, there were many demonstrations in Iran against ISIS attacks on Kobani. It seems that the Iranian government had allowed and even facilitated these demonstrations. One main reason for this may relate to the direct threat posed by ISIS. But also, Iran may intend to use the Kurdish issue against their rivals such as Turkey and Saudi Arabia, and to strengthen Bashar al-Assad's position in Syria.

As was mentioned earlier, the security forces have claimed they had arrested some ISIS-related cells located in the Kurdish region.[65] However, this claim should be considered with a great deal of caution and scepticism because the Iranian government, for the purpose of publicity, may arrest some religious or even non-religious activists who have nothing to do with ISIS—falsely accusing them of being ISIS members.

Because of shared experiences, cross-border solidarity, and quite strong secular traditions among the Iranian Kurdish people, ISIS may find it more difficult to influence them. But it is a quite different situation among Sunnis in Sistan and Baluchistan.

Sistan and Baluchistan—south-eastern borders

Possibly after the Kurdish community, the Baluch are the largest Sunni community in Iran. The Sunnis in this area, apart from small groups in neighbouring provinces, are settled in Sistan and Baluchistan, and mainly in Baluchistan. The Sunni population in this province is, again, subject to estimation, but it could be as high as 1.5 to 2 million people.[66] Spanning about 182,000 square kilometres, over 11% of the whole country, it is the second-largest province in Iran—very slightly smaller than Kerman Province. In contrast to the Kurdish Sunnis, they are Hanafi-Deobandis. Through the widespread reach of shared religious institutions such as madrasahs and Tablighi Jamaat, they have close connections with religious institutions in Pakistan and also have influence in and are influenced by political developments in both Afghanistan and Pakistan.

Along the Eastern borders, in Sistan and Baluchistan, secular ethnic traditions are much weaker than in Kurdistan. The whole province, particularly Baluchistan, is suffering from insecurity, robberies, drug trafficking, and numerous skirmishes organised by militant groups. Sunni-dominant populations in the province are, by and large, very suspicious of all security measures the Iranian regime have taken in the area.

It is not very strange among the Baluch that when they talk about their problems, they talk about Shias, the government, discrimination, corruption, poverty, unemployment, insecurity, and lack of attention to the province. Possibly the majority of Sunnis in the area widely and strongly believe that Iranian security forces are involved in all sorts of corruption, robberies, and insecurities. One such issue is the spread of corruption among security forces, whose officers are mainly non-Sunni appointments sent from other parts of Iran. They are using low-ranking *basijis* (officially-sanctioned volunteer militia) from the area. The local Sunnis spread stories that security officers, shortly into their mission, become millionaires by controlling checkpoints and receiving millions in bribes from both petty and wealthy smugglers. Supposedly, such posts are supposed to cut down on crime. In reality, though, these posts are bought and sold by high-ranking officers as a lucrative investment to make themselves 'filthy rich' in a short period. Then they 'take the money and run'—leaving the area as soon as possible (for good reason). They say that security officers have no intention of fighting corruption or robbery, and that they don't have anywhere near high enough morale for actually entering into any serious fighting against criminals. For example, Jaish al-Adl, an insurgent Sunni militant group, had arrested five security forces, particularly low-ranking guards, in 2013. How? They were all sleeping at their post. When four of them were released in 2014, Mohammad Esmail Kausari, an MP from Tehran who has served on the National Security and Foreign Policy Committee, insisted that these security forces should be put on trial because they were sleeping during their military duty.[67]

To strengthen their own stereotypical outlook and biased judgments, the Sunnis also blame local Shias – particularly, Sistanis – as the main source of pressure and discrimination. For instance, they spread rumours claiming that Sistani Shias are responsible for killing their patients in hospitals. For example a quite liberal-minded, secular person sent a WhatsApp message to me about a man who had had an accident and who had then been taken north to Zahedan but who died:

> Here there is neither good treatment nor [are there] good doctors; most nurses are Zabolis who dedicate themselves to other Zabolis. [...] Governor Dahmardeh [(the previous governor)] and Shahriari (an MP) have spread bad publicity against the Baluch. If a patient is a Baluch, they don't treat him properly so in this way he/she dies.[68]

Hard-line Baluch nationalists or militant Sunnis with a strong sense of hatred accuse Zaboli nurses and doctors of deliberately and systematically killing not only Baluch male patients, but also women and even babies.

These narratives by Sunnis, in many respects may be completely biased, or to some extent overstated or even without any true foundation. But they do reflect the deep suspicion of the Sunnis, in the area, regarding the Shias. The spread of insecurity in the area, has led to heavy attendance of Revolutionary Guards in the province, to command directly the operation in certain areas along the border but the problems have increased even further and even led to more clashes.[69] The special forces like Mersad (Ambush) with a 'shoot to kill' policy, target any suspicious people without any responsibility. Mersad and other security forces, in 2015, according to a local report, had shot and killed at least 52 Baluch on the roads, claiming that they had refused to stop while they were carrying smuggled goods, mainly (flammable) fuel.[70]

As a result, this long-term and systematic exclusionary policy by the Iranian regime has generated some damaging effects on a large section of the Sunni population in Iran. A large section of the Sunnis, particularly in Baluchistan in Iran, consider the Iranian regime to be even worse than Maliki's regime in Iraq. So it is not unexpected when they show some sympathy or become indifferent towards ISIS in Iraq and Syria. Possibly for the same reason, many Sunnis believe that the current news coverage of ISIS's violent actions is propaganda made by Iran or by Western sources to give a bad name to real Muslims. Some others argue that, in many respects, they do not see much difference between the Iranian regime and ISIS because in Iran, they have experienced plenty of executions, public hangings, floggings, and amputation of hands, amputation of other organs, stoning, and attacks on women because of *hijab* laws. Hezbollah groups had also sprayed acid on the faces of men and women for the crime of wearing T-shirts. So because of this, some of them argue that at least ISIS is a Sunni group which might not put pressure on them on the same scale.

An educated person, speaking under condition of anonymity, said that within private circles, possibly 50% of the young people support ISIS. Another educated person said:

> Don't say 'Daesh' [a pejorative term for ISIS], say 'Iraqi Sunni community' here, ordinary people

support Daesh. The Shia Government's position is clear! Shias are against Sunnis, it means [they are called by Shias] Daesh. Previously we were called [by the Shia government in Iran] Wahhabis, then Salafists; now [we are called] Daeshi. So many people are killed by Iran, Israel and the USA but nobody says anything about them. Now that a Sunni Government enforces the God's law and the prophet's tradition, the whole world, including Jews, Christians, and Shias, join together to destroy the Sunnis.[71]

Someone in the UK but originally from the same area, speaking as an educated secular person, echoed the same arguments and told me that "all are [(everyone is)] against Sunnis"[72].

While the Sunni religious websites in Iran find it difficult to express their genuine ideas, many of them have tried to condemn ISIS as much as they condemn other forms of violence by other forces. Molavi Abdul Hamid has condemned using any form of violence, and blamed the big powers, particularly Russia for adopting violent policies rather than finding a peaceful solution based on negotiation and consensus. Molavi Abdul Hamid is an outspoken critic of hardliners in Iran and is a well-known and influential Sunni authority and the religious leader of Sunnis in Sistan and Baluchistan. He has distanced himself from any form of extremism but has not taken a very clear anti-ISIS position.[73] However, Molavi has not made it clear how such conciliation can be achieved, given that ISIS can't tolerate Ahrar al-Sham, the Taliban, or even al-Qaeda.

Deep dissatisfaction with the Iranian Shia regime became more apparent when Iranian security forces recruited Sunni Baluch from Sistan and Baluchistan and dispatched them to Syria to defend Assad forces. The Sunnis' participation was widely publicised, by Iranian officials, as a sign of unity between Sunnis and Shias in supporting IRI's policy against opponents in Syria and against ISIS.

In the context of high unemployment and poverty in this province, paying the volunteers more than US $700 (2.5 million tumans) per month is very tempting.[74] After two Sunni Baluch, Khojasteh and Mollazahi, along with five or so Shia Baluch, were killed in Syria, they (both Sunni and Shia) were regarded as martyrs who together had heroically supported pure Mohammedan Islam against a terrorist group "associated with [the] US and Israel".[75] According to Zahedan Express, a conservative hard-line Shia site, in this way Sunnis in Iran had given opportunity to "Sunni intellectuals and real Muslims" to 'lift up' or "raise their heads" in honour and pride.[76] Following this, some top officials, including the health minister, visited the Sunni victims' families to formally express gratitude and appreciation for their sons' actions in Syria.[77]

Figure 3-1 Training militia from Sistan and Baluchistan Province (Zahedan press Web site)

Ironically, however, what was intended by the Shia authorities to be a unifying action has become a step towards even further division, because it has caused more polarisation between Shias and Sunnis in the province. Regarding recruitment of the local Sunnis, many Sunni clerics issued religious edicts (*fatwas*) that those who attend Syria to support al-Assad to kill Sunnis are heretics and should not be considered Muslims. Therefore, according to one of these *fatwas*, holding religious ceremonies for the people killed are forbidden, their wives are automatically divorced, and they are not considered martyrs. However, there have not been any edicts by these clerics regarding the Baluch Sunnis who have joined ISIS.[78] Even so, some believed that those who make jihad in God's Path and join 'real' Muslims are right.[79]

In the context of insecurity, dissatisfaction, and high levels of unemployment, the militant ethnic-religious organisations have not hidden their sympathies for the progress of ISIS in Iraq. For example, Jaish al-Adl has seen ISIS's activities as the "Popular Revolution" in Iraq.[80] Other militant jihadist organisations such as Jama't Ansar al-Furqan (Harakat al-Ansar and Al-Furqan merged in 2013) and Jaish al-Nasr-e Iran (a split from Jaish al-Adl) are more likely to show even stronger sympathy with ISIS.[81] Sepah-e Sahab-e Iran, recently (in 2015) offered their allegiance to Salahuddin Farooqi the leader of Jaish al-Adl.[82] Now, it seems, these are two competing alliances which already have an uneasy relationship between themselves.[83]

These militant organisations have not openly associated themselves with Salafist jihadists such as al-Qaeda or ISIS—but they never condemn their activities either. Their own Islamic aims, language, and appeals are quite similar to those of the radical jihadists but are mixed with some ethnic issues. Jondollah, in their operations, acted similar to al-Zarqawi. They are actively using social media in Arabic to communicate with communities outside Iran. There have been some

reports that some individuals or members of the current organisations have been active in ISIS. For example, in a report
published by the Guardian, Nasser Balochi is mentioned as an
IT/social media strategist.[84]

The secular Baluch nationalists are very weak and highly fragmented. Simultaneously, they have ambiguously vague
and even, in some cases, supportive positions regarding the
local Sunni jihadists. An educated nationalist is more likely
to be excited about any attack on the Iranian regime—and for
such a nationalist, the precise ideological nature and political
strategies of the attackers does not seem to matter. For example, someone expressed the belief that the Sunni and the Baluch are oppressed and killed – and no one supports them—so
let the "criminal regime" be punished by ISIS. When I asked
another activist about his position on religious jihadists in
Baluchistan, he said that as far as they help to make Baluchistan independent (separate), they are fine. Someone else with
a more moderate approach said they do not admire them but
that they would not openly reject them merely to make the
Islamic Republic of Iran happy. Some also argue that they are
not in the position to criticise local jihadists, especially those
who can threaten and harm their families inside Iran. Notice
should be taken of the fact that Baathist nationalist officers in
Iraq played a key role in supporting ISIS's capture of important cities such as the seizure of Mosul in June 2014. In Iranian Baluchistan, in a similar way, there is some possibility that
some nationalist groups may join them.

For finding footholds in south-eastern Iran, ISIS could
easily exploit the cross-border facilities in both Pakistan and
Afghanistan and even in the Gulf countries. ISIS have already
mobilised forces inside Pakistan and Afghanistan. And according to a secret report from the Baluchistan chief minister to the
central government, in Pakistan, ISIS had been actively build-

ing alliances and recruiting radicals from within groups such as Lashkar-e Jhangvi and Tehrik-e Taliban Pakistan (TTP) in Pakistani Baluchistan.[85] Radical Sunnis in groups such as Sepah-e Sahabeh Pakistan and Lashkar-e Jangvi, along with some Taliban, already have a strong presence in the Pakistani part of Baluchistan. They have already been involved in many sectarian killings of Shias in this area very close to Iranian borders. Lashkar-e Jhangvi and Taliban-e Pakistan, along with some other smaller groups, are believed to have a close relationship with ISIS as well.[86] For instance, a training camp has been established in the name of Abdul Rasheed Ghazi (who died at Lal Masjid) in an area controlled by Ansar al-Islam in Iraq.[87]

There are some other developments which are worth mentioning here. It seems that after the cut-off of diplomatic relations between Saudi Arabia and IRI, Sunnis in Iranian Baluchistan – as far as what was reflected in social media, particularly Whatsapp – widely supported Saudi Arabia. It also seems that recently among Saudi Arabia and her allies in the Gulf countries, there have been further efforts to bring together Sunni opponents, both jihadists and nationalists, in Iranian Baluchistan, to play a stronger role against the IRI. At the same time, this measure may also be an active step by Gulf countries to undermine any strong ISIS influence among the Sunnis in the area. Both moderate ethnic nationalists such as Baluchistan People's Party (BPP), and ethno-jihadists such as Jaish al-Adl, have shown interest in gaining support from Gulf countries led by Saudi Arabia."[88]

Whether BPP, as a secular group, and JAD, as a religious one, are willing to creating an alliance, is still a matter of speculation. It it seems that two groups have already developed quite close relationships, but according to Rahim Bandui, a member of the Central Council and Executive Bureau of the BPP: "for BPP to be the political wing of a religious armed struggle[Jaish-e Adl] is out of question".[89]

In spite of some efforts made by Rouhani's government which had been intended to improve the relationship between Shias and Sunnis, particularly by the appointment of a more moderate and reformist Shia governor in Baluchistan along with the appointment of more Sunni Baluch in some middle-ranking management positions, hard-line conservatives have been a big barrier against making further and more visible progress.

Locally, these tensions, intensified further by polarizing the populace into Shias and Sunnis, have led to some destructive measures. For example, a hard-line conservative MP, Hossein-Ali Shahriari, a Shia MP from Zahedan in Sistan and Baluchistan, believes that the area may serve as a corridor for entrance of the enemy and emergence of another Mosul-like catastrophe in Iran.[90] Considering the power and pressure of the conservative hard-line elements, it is understandable why, so far, there has not been significant improvement in the relationship between Shias and Sunnis in this province. Even this relationship has been deteriorated after the Iranian regime took an active role in Syria and Iraq.

In time of greater crisis, such conflicts could intensify even further, because it is very likely that the radical groups from both sides widely target ordinary people on the grounds of their ethnicity and religion. Sectarian divisions and the propaganda of hatred have already generated a level of polarisation between Shias and Sunnis. This has weakened the boundaries between rational and irrational thinking. If ISIS succeeds in operating within this province, it is very likely that the resulting conditions could rapidly lead to ethnic and religious cleansing. This, in turn, could develop into a new wave of refugees (whether genuine or jihadist) seeking entry into neighbouring Gulf States. Such a scenario could create further insecurity.

3.4: Conclusion

There are many reasons to believe that the Iranian regime is strongly worried about the current progress of ISIS in the neighbouring countries very close to the Iranian border. Iran's main concerns are based on different factors.

ISIS is, both ideologically and theologically, an extremist anti-Shia force, one which considers Shias to be non-believers, polytheists, enemy fifth columns, heretics, etc. For them, this is a basis for religious legitimisation of massacres, seizure of properties and the ruining of Shia shrines, lands, and houses.

ISIS has been in a direct war with Shia and Alawite governments in Iraq and Syria. There, Iran has actively influenced political life and developed a close relationship with the Assad regime in Syria, as it has done with successive governments in Iraq. Beyond that, the evidence shows that Iran has militarily supported the Assad regime and has even, for this purpose, mobilised Shia militias from other countries such as Pakistan, Afghanistan, Lebanon, and Iraq. Lebanese Hezbollah, with a great deal of support from Iran, has been an active supporter of the Syrian government and has openly participated in the war against Sunni jihadists and against opposition groups in Syria.

Therefore, for all Sunni opponents of Shiism – particularly, for ISIS and other Salafist jihadis in Syria – the IRI is considered to be their main enemy, and "Shia" are suspect of being conspirators. ISIS has already imposed challenges to the Iranian leadership and to the Iranian Islamic system by attacking Shia-related communities, mosques, shrines, and other forms of identity. They have done so, not only in Syria and Iraq, but also in many other countries in the Middle East. The danger of invasion into Iranian territory from the western border and, with even greater possibility, from the eastern borders adjacent to Afghanistan and Pakistan, still exist. Along both the eastern and western borders, there have already been reports by Iranian security forces who claim that they have arrested members of cells affiliated with ISIS. Furthermore, ISIS has actively recruited forces and organised squads of jihadists in many countries surrounding Iran. This seems to be an attempt to besiege Iran.

The conflicts in Iraq and Syria have also affected a great number of Sunnis in Iran. The dimensions of the problem can be better understood by paying more attention to the concerns of the majority of Iranian Sunnis who are deeply discontented with IRI's Shia-based policies. Moreover, the majority of Iranian Sunnis are ethnically identified as Kurds, Baluch, Turkmen, and Arabs. The majority of them are also concentrated in highly strategic areas. For example, they are located adjacent to Iraq, Pakistan, and Afghanistan as well as the Persian Gulf and the Oman Sea.

In Iran, there are many fundamental barriers, including constitutional ones, against implementing genuine reforms in relation to the Sunnis and other minorities. This is even truer in relation to non-Muslim religions. But still, there do exist some civic spaces in which to improve social conditions— both by providing Sunnis with more opportunities, and by inclusively promoting a sense of mutual belonging rather than considering them to be "outsiders".

Creating a more effective foundation and shared common ground for resolving the Shia-Sunni tensions in the area is nearly impossible without genuine political cooperation between Middle Eastern countries in tackling sectarian religious approaches in their policies. Friendly relationships among these countries, particularly between Saudi Arabia and Iran, can create a better foundation for addressing the problems of indiscrimination against Shias or Sunnis and other ethnic and religious groups in the whole area. This can help them undertake reasonable reforms in their socio-political and educational systems. The goal would be to minimise opportunities for the radical jihadists, including ISIS and al-Qaeda, to exploit the issue for political purposes.

To address these problems, it is necessary for the global players such as the UN, the US, the European Union, and even Russia and China to initiate fundamental programmes and take appropriate measures to actively persuade the countries involved in these conflicts to build constructive, consensual relationships between Sunnis and Shias and to build regional institutions to tackle not only jihadist issues but the wider problems of security including social, economic, and political issues.

If competition between Saudi Arabia and Iran continues, it will cause even more problems in the whole area in which ISIS's position to recruit forces will be strengthened. If polarisation of people along Shia and Sunni religious lines intensifies, and sectarian conflicts continue in the neighbouring countries, it is likely that ISIS will succeed in creating serious problems along the south-eastern borders of Iran and other Sunni communities. This can lead to disastrous conditions which will risk causing ethnic cleansing and further waves of refugees within a newly expanded geographical area.

References

"400 die as Iranian marchers battle Saudi police in Mecca; Embassies smashed in Teheran". *New York Times.* 2 Aug. 1987. 22 Mar. 2016 <http://www.nytimes.com/1987/08/02/world/400-die-iranian-marchers-battle-saudi-police-mecca-embassies-smashed-teheran.html>.

"Afradi az Daesh dar gharb-e Iran dastgir shodehand [Some of Daesh's people have been arrested in West Iran]". *Deutsche Welle* [Persian ed.]. 17 Nov. 2015. 10 Dec. 2015 <http://www.dw.com/fa-ir/a-18856643>.

Ahady, Anwar-ul-haq. "Saudi Arabia, Iran and the Conflicts in Afghanistan". Ed. William Malley. *Fundamentalism Reborn? Afghanistan and the Taliban.* London: Hurst, 2001. 117-135.

Ahmadi, Hamid. "Bakhsh-e sheshom: zamineha wa che-goonagi-e shoru'-e jang [Section 6: The background and conditions of the breakthrough of the war]". *Negahi ejmali be Jang-e 6 saleh A'raq a'lih-e Iran wa Iran a'lih-e A'raq* [An outline of the 6-year war of Iraq against Iran and Iran against Iraq]. *Negaresh.* 7 Mehr 1389 *hs* [29 Sept. 2010]. 22 Mar. 2016 <http://negaresh.de/didgah/ahmadi_jang_1. htm>.

"Ahzab-e Kurd az hozur-e Daesh dar Kurdistan-e Iran khabar midahand [Kurdish parties reports about attendance of ISIS in Kurdistan]". *Al-Arabiya.* 15 Aug. 2014. 15 Dec. 2015 <http://farsi.alarabiya.net/fa/iran/2014/08/15>.

Alavi, Mahmood. "Niruhay-e Daesh be arzuhayeshan baray-e na amni-ye Iran narasidand [ISIS forces' dreams of making Iran insecure were not realised]". *BBC Persian.* 13 June 2015. 10 Sept. 2015 <http://www.bbc.com/persian/iran/2015/06/150613_l12_ iran_isis_alavi>.

Alhntoshi, Mishari. "مستمر إيرانى واضطهاد لقمع نتعرض :البلوشية لمقاومة ولن نتنازل عن حقنا فى تقرير المصير [Baloch resistance: we are continually exposed to Iranian repression and persecution, but we will not give up our right to self-determination]". *Sabq.* 3 Mar. 2016. 22 Mar. 2016 <https://sabq.org/kTYcSp>.

"Amir-e Daesh dar Iran dastgir shod/shekast sangin Daesh dar Sistan wa Baluchistan/ natayej pezuhesh yek nehad amnyyati dar bareh tamayol-e ahl-e sunnat-e Iran [Daesh Emir arrested in Iran/ Heavy defeat of Daesh in Sistan and Baluchistan/ The results of research by security forces regarding [the] tendency of the Iranian Sunnis to favour Daesh]". *Zahedan Press.* 25 Shahrivar 1393 *hs* [16 Sept. 2014]. 22 Mar. 2016 <http://zahedanpress. com/22404>.

Amnesty International. *Iran 2013.* Annual report. *Amnesty*

International. 23 May 2013.24 Mar. 2016 <http://www.amnestyusa.org/research/reports/annual-report-iran-2013>.

—. *Iran 2015-2016.* Annual report. *Amnesty International.* 12 Sept. 2015. 22 Mar. 2016 <https://www.amnesty.org/en/countries/middle-east-and-north-africa/iran/report-iran>.

—. *Iran: Human Rights Abuses against the Baluchi Minority.* MDE 13/104/2007. *Amnesty International.* 17 Sept. 2007. 16 Mar. 2016 <https://www.amnesty.org/en/documents/MDE13/104/2007/en>.

—. *Iran: Human rights abuses against the Kurdish minority.* MDE 13/088/2008. *Amnesty International.* 30 July 2008. 17 Mar. 2016 <https://www.amnesty.org/en/documents/MDE13/088/2008/en>.

Anon. Correspondence with author. *WhatsApp.* 13 Jan. 2016.

Anon (HD). Correspondence with author. 13 Dec. 2015.

Anon. Correspondence with author. 10 Apr. 2015.

Anon. Correspondence with author. 18 Sept. 2014.

"Aya marzbanan ezafeh khdmat mikhorand [Are the border corps extra-relaxed in their service?]". *Esfahan Shargh.* 18 Farvardin 1393 *hs* [7 Apr. 2014]. 15 Mar. 2016 <http://esfahanshargh.ir/16362>.

"Ayatollah Khamenei: Iran amnyyat-e A'raq ra amnyyat khod midand [Ayatollah Khamenei: Iran considers the security of Iraq to be its own security]". *BBC Persian.* 21 Oct. 2014. 6 Nov. 2014 <http://www.bbc.co.uk/persian/iran/2014/10/141021_l12_iran_ iraq_ibadi_pm_visit_tehran>.

Batatu, Hanna. "Syria's Muslim Brethren". Ed. Fred Halliday and Hamza Alavi. *State and Ideology in the Middle East and Pakistan.* New York: Monthly Review Press, 1988. 112-133.

"Beyanyeh Shoray-e Markazi Sunnat (shams) dar khosus matelbat wa khasthay-e ahle sunnat [An announcement of the Sunni Central Council (Shams) regarding demands of Iranian Sunnis]". *Sunni News.* 3 Esfand 1388 *hs* [22 Feb. 2010]. 2 Nov. 2012 <http://sunninews.org/FA/articles. aspx?selected_article_no=4807>.

Charles River Editors. *The Islamic State of Iraq and Syria: The History of ISIS/ISIL.* CreateSpace: Marson Gate, 2014.

Cockburn, Patrick. *The Rise of Islamic State: ISIS and the New Sunni Revolution.* London: Verso, 2014.

"Dastgiry-e 53 Haami-e Daesh dar Iran/tajrobeh 69000 hamleh-e siberi be Iran [Arrest of 53 supporters of Daesh in Iran/ 69000 cyber attack on Iran]". *Zahedan Press.* 16 Azar 1394 *hs* [7 Dec. 2015]. 22 Mar. 2016 <http://zahedanpress.com/27576>.

Ebrahimi, Hamzah. "Jang-e dakheli dar Suryyeh; Iran dar jonub-e Halab cheh mikonad? [Civil War in Syria; What does Iran do in South Aleppo?]". *BBC Persian.* 19 Dec. 2015. 20 Dec. 2015 <http://www.bbc.com/persian/ world/2015/12/151217_l10_sepah_syria_aleppo>.

"Edea'ay dargiri Dae'sh ba nirohay-e nezami-y-e Iran [ISIS's claim of clashes with Iranian security forces]". *BBC Persian.* 29 Aug. 2014. 26 Oct. 2014 <http://www.bbc. com/persian/world/2014/08/140829_u07_isis_iran_west_ tweet>.

"Enfejar-e bombe souti dar Iranshahr shishehay-e Bimarestan-e ra shekast [The sound bom exploision in Iranshahrbroke the glass of an Iranian hospital]". *Zahedan Press.* 25 Mehr 1394 [17 Oct. 2015]. 10 Dec. 2015 <http:// zahedanpress.com/26502>.

Eslahe. [Website] *Eslahe.* 23 Mar. 2016 <http://eslahe.com>.

"Ettelaeih ettehad-e mujahedin-e hezb-e al-Forqan wa harkat al-Ansar [Announcement of an alliance between Hizb al-Forqan mujahidin and Harkat al-Ansar]". *Blogspot*. 11 Daey 1392 *hs* [1 Jan. 2014]. 12 Dec. 2015 <http://hezbulfurqan.blogspot.co.uk/2014/01/ blog-post.html>.

Forqan, Ansar. *Twitter* [account suspended]. <https://twitter.com/a_alfurqan_3>.

Gambill, Gary. "Abu Musab al-Zarqawi: A Biographical Sketch". Washington: Jamestown Foundation, 2004. 15 Dec. 2014 <http://www.jamestown.org/single/?tx_ttnews%5D= 27304>.

"Goshayesh-e daftar-e nomayandagi-ye Taliban dar Zahedan [The opening of a Taliban representative's office in Zahedan]". *Deutsche Welle* [Persian ed.]. 2 Aug. 2012. 14 Dec. 2015 <http://www.dw.com/fa-ir/a-16139351>.

"Hafteh vahdat dar beynayeh Harkat-e Islami Sunnat wa Jamaat [Week of Solidarity addressed in an announcement of Harkat-e Islami Ahle Sunnat wa Jamaat-e-Iran]". *Sunni News*. 4 Mar. 2010. 2 Sept. 2011 <http://sunninews.org/FA/articles.aspx?selected_article_ no=4946>.

Hajjarian, Saeed. "Reformists must remain viable and teach the spiritual ... The government must correct its shortcomings and [...] recover [...] the cabinet [...]". *Tir Press*. 15 Aug. 2015. 18 Mar. 2016 <http://www.tirpress.ir/265266/ر-بکوشند-باید-طلبان-اصلاح-حجاریان-سعید.>.

"Haya't-e siasi-ye Taliban dar Tehran [The Taliban's political representative in Tehran]". *Hamshahri Online*. 29 Ordibehesht 1394 *hs* [19 May 2015]. 14 Dec. 2015 <http://www.hamshahrionline.ir/details/295616/Iran/foreignpolicy>.

"Hoshdar-e Ayatollah Makarem-e Shirazi dar bareh khatare bozrg baray-e Mashhad [Ayatollah Makarem Shirazi's warning on great danger for Mashhad]". *Afsaran*. 24 Mordad 1393 *hs* [15 Aug. 2014]. 15 Mar. 2016 <http://www.afsaran.ir/link/674780>.

Iran Human Rights Documentation Center. "On the Margins:

Arrest, Imprisonment and Execution of Kurdish Activists in Iran Today". *Iran HRDC*. 11 Apr. 2012. 23 Mar. 2016 <http://www.iranhrdc.org/english/publications/reports/1000000089-on-the-margins-arrest-imprisonment-and-execution-of-kurdish-activists-in-iran-today.html>.

Islamic Republic of Iran. Constitution. Approved 24 Oct. 1979. Enforced from 3 Dec. 1979. Amended 28 July 1989. *Iran Online*. Accessed 10 Oct. 2015 <http://www.iranonline.com/iran/iran-info/government/constitution-9-1.html>.

Jaish al-Adl [Army of Justice]. "Sazeman-e Jiashe al-Adl sazemani dafaei dar rastay-e dafaa' az haysyyat wa hoquq-e Baluch wa ahle sunnat [The Jaish al-Adl defence organization in the defence of the rights of the Baloch nation...]". *Blogspot*. 22 Mar. 2016 <http://jashuladl3.blogspot.co.uk>.

"Jozeyat-e kashf wa khonsasazi-ye bomb 21 kiloi dar shahrestan-e sarbaz/awamel-e bobgozari shonasaie shodand [Details of the discovery and detonation of a 21-kilogram bomb in the district of Sarbaz/ The people involved with the bomb were identified]". *Zahedan Press*. 25 Azar 1394 *hs* [16 Dec. 2015]. 17 Mar. 2016 <http://zahedanpress.com/27516>.

Kampain-e Faa'lin-e Baloch [The Baloch Activists Campaign]. "Vakonesh-e mojadad-e olamay-e ahl-e sumnat nesbat be ea'zam-e rustayian-e manateq mahroom be surryeh [Another reaction by Sunni clerics regarding the dispatching of people in the poor countryside areas to Syria]". *Balochcampaign.com*. 14 Azar 1394 *hs* [5 Dec. 2015]. 11 Dec. 2014 <http://balochcampaign.com/index.php/news/balochestan-news/item/ 3068-2015-12-05-08-57-59>.

Kampain Fa'alin-e Baloch [The Baloch Activists Campaign].

"Sepah jawanan ra dar tangna qrar midaha ke be suryeh berawand [The Revolutionary Guard put pressure on the young people to go to Syria]". *Balochcampaign.com*. 12 Aban 1394 *hs* [3 Nov. 2015]. 16 Dec. 2015 <http://baloch-campaign.com/index.php/all-category/gozaresh/item/3001-2015-11-03-12-15-38>.

Khomeini, Ruhollah. "Pyam-e tarikhi Imam be hojjaj-e Baytullah- al-Haram [Historic Message of the Imam, for Pilgrims to Mecca]". *Manshur-e Jomhury-e Islami* [Charter of the Islamic Republic]. Tehran: Sazeman-e Tablighta-e Islami, 1988. 15-58.

Khuhro, Zarrar. "Militant camp in Iraq named after Lal Masjid's Abdul Rasheed Ghazi". *Dawn*. 7 Mar. 2014. 10 Dec. 2015 <http://www.dawn.com/news/1091567>.

Kirdar, M. J. "Al-Qaeda in Iraq". Center for Strategic and International Studies, June 2011. 1-15.

"Modafea'an-e Haram-e Sunni mazhab, olguy-e vaqaei eslam-e nab-e Mohammadi [Sunni defenders of the shrine: the example of real, pure Muhammadan religion]". *Zahedan Press*. 19 Azar 1394 *hs* [10 Dec. 2015]. 10 Dec. 2015 <http://zahedanpress.com/ 27613>.

Modafean Haram. "Gozaresh-e tasviri/tashyeea' haft Shahid-e Modafea' Heram dar Qom [A pictoral report/ memorial ceremony of 7 Martyrs of the Defenders of the Shrine in Qom]". *Modafeon*. 7 Azar 1394 *hs* [28 Nov. 2015]. 10 Jan. 2016 <http://modafeon.blog.ir/ post/958>.

—. "Sepah-e Bain al-Malali-e Modafean-e Haram [The International Army of the Defenders of the Shrine]". *Modafeon*. 8 Shahrivar 1393 *hs* [30 Aug. 2014]. 10 Jan. 2016 <http://modafeon.blog.ir/post/79>.

—. "Tashyeea' Paykare Do Shahi-e Afghan of Defenders of Shrine farad dar karaj [memorial ceremony for the bodies of 2 Afghan Martyrs of the Defenders of the Shrine will be held in Karaj tomorrow]". *Modafeon.* 28 Mordad 1394 *hs* [19 Aug. 2015]. 10 Jan. 2016 <http://modafeon.blog.ir/post/455>.

"Mokhalefate olamaye sunni-ye Iran ba hamalat-e hawaei-ye rusiyeh dar suryeh [Rejection, by Sunni clerics in Iran, of Russian attacks in Syria]". *Deutsche Welle* [Persian ed.]. 12 Oct. 2015. 15 Mar. 2016 <http://www.dw.com/fair/a-18777200>.

"Moqam-e Kurdistan-e Iraq dar mored hamkary-e shebeh-e nezamian-e Shia-e ba artesh hoshdar dad [Warning of a senior official in Iraqi Kurdistan regarding cooperation of Shia militia with the army]". *BBC Persian.* 17 Mar. 2015. 12 Dec. 2015 <http://www.bbc.com/persian/world/2015/03/150317_l03_iraq_is_iran>.

Nazesh, Kiran. "The Islamic State Is Spreading Into Pakistan". *New Republic.* 23 Sept. 2014. 13 Dec. 2015 <https://newrepublic.com/article/119535/isis-pakistan-islamic-state-distributing-flags-and-flyers>.

Naji, Abu Bakar. *The Management of Savagery: The Most Critical Stage Through Which the Umma Will Pass.* Trans. William McCants. John M. Olin Institute for Strategic Studies (Cambridge: Harvard University, 2006). <https://www.google.co.uk/url?sa=t&rct=j&q=&esrc=s&source=web&cd=4&cad=rja&uact=8&ved=0ahUKEwjeiKCYuaHLAhWJwxQKHXpXBtcQFggtMAM&url=https%3A%2F%2Fazelin.files>.

Noraiee, Hoshang. "Globalization and Islam: Modernity, Diversity and Identities". Ed. Farhang Morady and Ismail Siriner. *Globalisation, Religion and Development. . International Journal of Politics and Economics.* 15 Apr. 2011. 39-62.

—. "Jadal-e ben-ejaishe-adl wajaish-e nasr:jihad baray-e khoda, jihad baraye mellat, jihad baraye qodrat? [Conflicts between Jaish al-Adl and Jaish al-Nasr: Jihad for God, Jihad for the Nation, Jihad for Power?]". *Taptan.* 16 Aug. 2014. 20 Sept. 2014 <http://www.taptan.com/?p=129>.

—. "Khawarmianeh wa kashmakesh bain-e Iran wa Arabistan Saudi [The Middle East and conflicts between Iran and Saudi Arabia]". *Taptan.* April 2011. 17 Nov. 2014 <www.taptan.com/?page_id=84>.

—. "Sunni Militants in Iran: Activities, Ideological Sources and Political Strategies". *International Research Journal of Social Science.* 2015 Vol. 4(3), 79-87. 22 Mar. 2016 <http://www.isca.in/IJSS/Archive/v4/i3/14.ISCA-IR-JSS-2014-331.pdf>.

"Jamia't va khanavar-e shahrestanhay-e keshvar be tartib-e ostan [The country's population, households, and city, according to the provinces]". 2011 Population Census. *Amar.* 30 July 2012. 16 Mar. 2016 <http://www.amar.org.ir/Portals/2/pdf/jamiat_shahrestan_keshvar.pdf>.

Pars News Agency. "Goft o guy montasher nashodeh ba sardar-e Shahid Husain-e Hamadani [Unpublished interview with Martyr Husain Hamadani, general]". *Pars News Agency.* 19 Mehr 1394 *hs* [11 Oct. 2015]. 10 Jan. 2016 <http://www.farsnews.com/ 13940719000626>.

Paz, Reuven. "Debates Within the Family: Jihadi-Salafi Debates on Strategy, Takfir, Extremism, Suicide Bombings, and the Sense of the Apocalypse". Ed. Roel Meijer. *Global Salafism: Islam's New Religious Movement.* London: Hurst, 2009. 267-280.

Qutb, Sayyid. *Milestones.* New Delhi: Islamic Book Services, 2002.

"Rahim Safavi: Be Daesh pyam dadim ke agar nazdik-e a'tabat beshawad mostaqim wared mishavim [Rahim Safavi: We sent a message to ISIS: if they approach the shrines, we would straightly enter the war]". *BBC Persian.* 29

June 2015. 29 June 2015 <http://www.bbc.com/persian/
iran/2015/06/150629_l12_iran_safavi_iraq_is>.

Riedel, Bruce. "Islamic State cell strikes Shiites in Saudi Arabia". *Al-Monitor*. 28 Nov. 2014. 1 Dec. 2014 <http://www.
al-monitor.com/pulse/originals/2014/11/saudi-shiite-is-
lamic-state-terrorism.html>.

Sadr, Mohammad. "Hamkary-e Iran wa Amerika alih-e
Daesh momken ast [Cooperation between Iran and the
US on ISIS is possible]". *BBC Persian*. 20 Mordad 1393
hs [11 Aug. 2014]. 13 Aug. 2014 <http://www.bbc.co.uk/
persian/iran/2014/08/140811_l12_ iran_isis_iran_us_co-
operation_iraq.shtml>.

"Sal-e 2015 dast-e kam 53 nafar az shahrwandan Baluch dar
tirandazi-ye mamuran koshteh wa zakhmi shodehand
[In 2015, at least 52 Baluch citizens have been shot dead
or have been injured by security forces]". *Balochcam-
paign.com*. 5 Bahman 1394 *hs* [25 Jan. 2016]. 25 Jan. 2016
<http://www.balochcampaign.com/index.php/news/
balochestan-news/item/3179-2015-52>.

Sangachin, P.Farzam, Esmail Salehi and Mortaza Dinarwandi. "Sanjesh-e sath-e tawse' yaftagi ostanhay-e keshvar-e
Iran be roikard-e tahlil-e ameli [Measuring the extent of
development of Iran's provinces with the method of factor analysis]". amayesh sar zamin [Measuring the coun-
try], Winter 1391hs [2012-2013], 4:2 (5-26). <https://jtcp.
ut.ac.ir/article_30343_0.html>.

Sepah-e Sahabeh Iran. "Ettehad wa hambastagy-e Sepah-e
Sahbeh Iran with Sazeman-e Jaish al-Adl [Alliance and
Solidarity of Sepah-e Sahabeh Iran with the Jaish al-Adl
organisation]". *Blogspot*. 25 Farvardin 1394 *hs* [14 Apr.
2015]. 19 Dec. 2015 <http://www.ss-iran.blogspot.co.uk>.

"Shahadat-e awalin razmandagan-e Baluch-e ostan dar
nabard ba niroohaye takfiri-ye Daesh dar Manateqh-e

suryyeh + asami wa tasvir-e shohada [The First Baluch Martyrs from fighting with Takfirist Daesh Forces in the region of Syria + names and pictures of the Martyrs]". *Zahedan Press*. 6 Azar 1394 *hs* [27 Nov. 2015]. 9 Dec. 2015 <http://zahedanpress.com/27327>.

Shaheed, Ahmed. "March 2016 report of the Special Rapporteur on the situation of human rights in the Islamic Republic of Iran". United Nations: Human Rights Council. 10 Mar. 2016. 24 Mar. 2016 <http://shaheedoniran.org/english/dr-shaheeds-work/march-2016-report-of-the-special-rapporteur-on-the-situation-of-human-rights-in-the-islamic-republic-of-iran>.

Shaheed, Ahmed. "October 2011 report of the Special Rapporteur on the situation of human rights in the Islamic Republic of Iran". United Nations: General Assembly. 23 Sept. 2011. 24 Mar. 2016 <http://shaheedoniran.org/english/dr-shaheeds-work/latest-reports/report-of-the-special-rapporteur-to-the-un-general-assembly-dr-ahmed-shaheed-2011>.

Shahriari, Husain-Ali. "Negranam zamani berasad ke Sistan wa balochistan be mousel tabdil shawad" [I am worried that one day, Sistan and Balochistan will become a Mosul]". *Baloch Press*. 20 Aban 1393 *hs* [11 Nov. 2014]. 13 Nov. 2014 <http://balochpress.net>.

Shams Iran. [web site] *Shams Iran*. 23 Mar. 2016 <http://www.shams-iran.org>.

"Sistan wa Baluchistan: tasavire vazir behdasht dar didar ba jawantarin shahid moqadas [Sistan and Baluchistan: pictures of the minister of health visiting the home of the youngest martyr of Moqadas]". *Hamshahri Online*. 4 Dey 1394 *hs* [25 Dec. 2015]. 15 Mar. 2016 <http://www.hamshahrionline.ir/details/319278/Defence/imposedwar>.

"Sokhanan-e Moulvi Fazlol Rahman Kuhi dar tahrim-e

ea'zam-e jawanan be suryyeh [Moulvi Fazlol Rahman's
words regarding sanction of dispatching the youth to Syr-
ia]". *Sunni News.* 7 Nov. 2015, 11 Dec. 2015 <http://ww-
w.sunni-news.com/fa/ articles.aspx?article_no=35351>.

Steinberg, Guido. "Jihadi-Salafism and the Shi'is: Remarks
about the Intellectual Roots of Anti-Shiism". Ed. Roel
Meijer. *Global Salafism: Islam's New Religious Movement.*
London: Hurst, 2009. 107-125.

Stern, Jessica, and J. M. Berger. *ISIS: The State of Terror.* London: William Collins, 2015.

"Tazahorat dar Kurdistan-e Iran wa dar hemayat–az kobani + aks" [Demonstrations in Iranian Kurdistan against
ISIS–and in support of Kobani + pictures]". *Eslamabad Khabar.* 19 Mehr 1393 *hs* [11 Oct. 2014]. 10 Nov.
2014 <http://eslamabadkhabar.ir/shownews. php?id-
news=255346>.

"Tim-e terroristi barnameh Kharabkari dar ejtemaa't-e shia
wa Sunni ye Sistan wa Bluchistan dasht+ new detail
[A terrorist cell had a plan to sabotage the relationship
between Shia and Sunni communities in Sistan and
Baluchistan + new detail]". *Zahedan Press.* 1 Azar 1394
hs [22 Nov. 2015]. 22 Mar. 2016 <http://zahedanpress.
com/27114>.

Townsend, Mark, and Toby Helm. "Jihad in a social media
age: how can the West win an online war?" *The Guardian.*
23 Aug. 2014. 13 Dec. 2015 <http://www.theguardian.
com/world/2014/aug/23/jihad-social-media-age-west-
win-online-war>.

"Vazir-e Ettellaa't: 130 aamel takfiri dar Iran bazdasht
shodand [Intelligence minister: 130 takfirist Agents
were arrested in Iran]". *Mashregh* [Mashriq] *News.* 15
Mehr 1393 *hs* [7 Oct. 2014]. 22 Mar. 2016 <http://www.
mashreghnews.ir/fa/news/352065/130>.

"Vazir-e Ettellaa't: Ba Komeleh ham mazakereh mikonim" (Minister of intelligence: we even negotiate with Komeleh". *Radio Zamaneh*. 15 Mehr 1393 *hs* [7 Oct. 2014]. 16 Oct. 2014 <http://www.radiozamaneh. com/180409>.

Wagemakers, Joas. "The Transformation of a Radical Concept: *al-wala' wa-l-bara'* in the Ideology of Abu Muhammad al-Maqdisi". Ed. Roel Meijer. *Global Salafism: Islam's New Religious Movement*. London: Hurst, 2009. 81-106.

Weiss, Michael and Hassan Hassan. *ISIS: Inside the Army of Terror*. New York: Regan Arts, 2015.

Welsford, Katie. "When borders are meaningless: The Islamic State in Iraq and al-Sham". London: Institute for Islamic Strategic Affairs. *IISA Blog*. 18 July 2014. 11 Nov. 2014 <http://iisablog.org/2014/07/18/18-july-2014-when-borders-are-meaningless-the-islamic-state-in-iraq-sham>.

Younesi, Ali "Doulat Natawanest be aqqalyathay-e qawmi wa mazhabi ostandari wa vazarat bedahad [The government failed to offer ministerial and provincial governorships to the religious and ethnic minorities]". *BBC Persian*. 13 Azar 1392 *hs* [4 Dec. 2013]. 13 Aug. 2014 <http://www. bbc.co.uk/persian/iran/2013/12/131204_ l39_younesi_minorities_appointments.shtml>.

Zaidi, Mubashir. "IS is recruiting thousands in Pakistan, govt. warned in 'secret' report". *Dawn*. 8 Nov. 2014. 13 Dec. 2015 <http://www.dawn.com/news/1143133>.

Endnotes

1 Mehdi Karroubi also became Speaker of the Assembly, a two-time presidential candidate, and a leader of the reformist movement. Since 2009, he has been kept under house arrest by Iranian Islamic authorities.

2 See p. 18 of Ruhollah Khomeini, "Pyam-e tarikhi Imam be hojjaj-e Baytullah- al-Haram [Historic Message of the Imam, for Pilgrims to Mecca]", *Manshur-e Jomhury-e Islami* [Charter of the Islamic Republic] (Tehran:

Sazeman-e Tablighta-e Islami, 1988) 15-58.

3 Khomeini 19.

4 After the revolution, in spite of the dissatisfaction of Saudi Arabia, Iranian pilgrims were organising political demonstrations every year. In 31 July 1987, the protests led to bloody clashes between Iranian pilgrims and Saudi Arabia's security forces, in which about 400 pilgrims, mostly from Iran, were killed. See "400 die as Iranian marchers battle Saudi police in Mecca; Embassies smashed in Teheran", *New York Times* 2 Aug. 1987, 22 Mar. 2016 <http://www.nytimes.com/1987/08/02/world/400-die-iranian-marchers-battle-saudi-police-mecca-embassies-smashed-teheran.html>.

5 Hamid Ahmadi, "Bakhsh-e sheshom: zamineha wa chegoonagi-e shoru'-e jang [Section 6: The background and conditions of the breakthrough of the war]", *Negahi ejmali be Jang-e 6 saleh A'raq a'lih-e Iran wa Iran a'lih-e A'raq* [An outline of the 6-year war of Iraq against Iran and Iran against Iraq], Negaresh 7 Mehr 1389 *hs* [29 Sept. 2010], 22 Mar. 2016 <http://negaresh.de/didgah/ahmadi_jang_1.htm>.

For conversion from Persian *(hs)* to English dates, see <https://www.vercalendario.info/en/calendars/persian-calendar/compare-1395.html>.

6 Khomeini 56. See also Hoshang Noraiee, "Khawarmianeh wa kashmakesh bain-e Iran wa Arabistan Saudi [The Middle East and conflicts between Iran and Saudi Arabia]", *Taptan* Sep. 2013, 17 Nov. 2014 <www.taptan.com/?page_id=84>.

7 In the Sunni tradition, the 'Imamat' is not accepted as a legitimate principle. And they believe that 4 caliphs – Abubakr, Omar, Osman, and Ali – were the legitimate senior deputies of the Prophet Mohammad. But in Shia tradition, the caliphate of Abu Bakr, Omar ibn al-Khattab, and Uthman (Osman) ibn Affan were illegitimate and only Ali and his 11 descendants were the only legitimate Imams. Shia Muslims believe that the 12th Imam – the Mahdi or Imam Zaman – disappeared, and he will reappear to rule and bring real justice.

8 See p. 95 of Joas Wagemakers, "The Transformation of a Radical Concept: al-wala' wa-l-bara' in the Ideology of Abu Muhammad al-Maqdisi", ed. Roel Meijer, *Global Salafism: Islam's New Religious Movement* (London: Hurst, 2009) 81-106.

9 See p. 58 of Sayyid Qutb, *Milestones* (New Delhi: Islamic Book Services, 2002).

10 See p. 46 of "Globalization and Islam: Modernity, Diversity and Identities", ed. Farhang Morady and Ismail Siriner, *Globalisation, Religion and Development*, ISBN 978-0956825605, *International Journal of Politics and Economics*, 15 Apr. 2011, 39-62.

11 See p. 117 of Jessica Stern and J. M. Berger, *ISIS: The State of Terror*

(London: William Collins, 2015).

12 Noraiee 47.

13 See p. 277 of Reuven Paz, "Debates Within the Family: Jihadi-Salafi Debates on Strategy, Takfir, Extremism, Suicide Bombings, and the Sense of the Apocalypse", ed. Roel Meijer, *Global Salafism: Islam's New Religious Movement* (London: Hurst, 2009) 267-280.

14 Cockburn quoted the European Parliamentary Department of Foreign Affairs's statement that Saudi Arabia, since the 1980s, had spent $10 billion to spread Wahhabism See p. 100 of Patrick Cockburn, *The Rise of Islamic State: ISIS and the New Sunni Revolution* (London: Verso, 2014).

15 Anwar-ul-haq Ahady, "Saudi Arabia, Iran and the Conflicts in Afghanistan", ed. William Malley, *Fundamentalism Reborn? Afghanistan and the Taliban* (London: Hurst, 2001) 117-135.
See also p. 116 of Guido Steinberg, "Jihadi-Salafism and the Shi'is: Remarks about the Intellectual Roots of Anti-Shiism", ed. Roel Meijer. *Global Salafism: Islam's New Religious Movement* (London: Hurst, 2009) 107-125.

16 The term 'radical Deobandis' refers to the jihadist political groups such as the Afghani Taliban, Pakistani Taliban, Lashkar-e Janguhi, and Sepah-e Sahbah Pakistan, mainly in Pakistan and Afghanistan.

17 Patrick Cockburn quotes an ex-director of MI-6 that Saudi Arabia has a contradictory policy of fighting the jihadists from inside, yet supporting them abroad to confront Iran (Cockburn 36).

18 Gary Gambill, "Abu Musab al-Zarqawi: A Biographical Sketch" (Washington: Jamestown Foundation, 2004) 15 Dec. 2014 <http://www.jamestown.org/single/?tx_ttnews%5D=27304>.
See also Charles River Editors, *The Islamic State of Iraq and Syria: The History of ISIS/ISIL* (CreateSpace: Marson Gate, 2014).

19 For example, an important religious figure in Saudi Arabia, Abdullah Ibn Jibrin, who issued a *fatwa* in 1991, considered Shias as polytheists whose killing can be lawful by Muslims. See Steinberg 115, 122-123.

20 Quoted from Robert S. Leiken (CBS News, 18 May 2004) in Charles River Editors (2014).

21 See p. 129 of Hanna Batatu, "Syria's Muslim Brethren", ed. Fred Halliday and Hamza Alavi, *State and Ideology in the Middle East and Pakistan* (New York: Monthly Review Press, 1988) 112-133.

22 See Steinberg 119 and Batatu 113.

23 Pars News Agency, "Goft o guy montasher nashodeh ba sardar-e Shahid Husain-e Hamadani [Unpublished interview with Martyr Husain Hamadani, general]", *Pars News Agency* 19 Mehr 1394 *hs* [11 Oct. 2015], 10 Jan. 2016 <http://www.farsnews.com/13940719000626>.

24 Modafean Haram, "Sepah-e Bain al-Malali-e Modafean-e Heram

[The International Army of the Defenders of the Shrine]", *Modafeon* 8 Shahrivar 1393 *hs* [30 Aug. 2014], 10 Jan. 2016 < http://modafeon.blog.ir/post/79>.

25 The 7 main Shia groups are:
Hezbollah Lebanon led by Seyyed Hossein Nasr,
Liwa Abu al-Fadhal al-Abbas formerly led by Maher Ajib Jazza (Abu Ajib);
Liwa Zulfiqar led by Abu Shahad al-Juburi;
Saraya al-Salam (previously Jaish al-Mahdi), led by Muqtada al-Sadr,
Sepah badr Iraq led by Hadi al-Amiri,
Asa'ib Ahl al-Haq (Khazali Network) led by Shekyh Qais al-Khaza'li;
Kata'ib Hezbollah Iraq led by Sheikh Abbas al-Mahdavi
There are also Harakat al-Nujaba, Kataeb Sayed al-Shuhada, and Saraya al-Khorasani, among others.

26 Modafean Haram (30 Aug. 2014).

27 Hamzah Ebrahimi, "Jang-e dakheli dar Suryyeh; Iran dar jonub-e Halab cheh mikonad? [Civil War in Syria; What does Iran do in South Aleppo?]", *BBC Persian* 19 Dec. 2015, 20 Dec. 2015 <http://www.bbc.com/persian/world/2015/12/151217_l10_sepah_syria_aleppo>.

28 Modafean Haram, "Gozaresh-e tasviri/tashyeea' haft Shahid-e Modafea' Heram dar Qom [A pictoral report/ memorial ceremony of 7 Martyrs of the Defenders of the Shrine in Qom]", *Modafeon* 7 Azar 1394 *hs* [28 Nov. 2015], 10 Jan. 2016 <http://modafeon.blog.ir/post/958>.

29 Modafean Haram, "Tasheia'Paykare Do Shahi-e Afghan of Defenders of Shrine farad dar karaj [memorial ceremony for the bodies of 2 Afghan Martyrs of the Defenders of the Shrine will be held in Karaj tomorrow]", *Modafeon* 28 Mordad 1394 *hs* [19 Aug. 2015], 10 Jan. 2016 <http://modafeon.blog.ir/post/455>.

30 Cockburn 66.

31 Charles River Editors (2014).

32 "Rahim Safavi: Be Daesh pyam dadim ke agar nazdik-e a'tabat beshawad mostaqim wared mishavim [Rahim Safavi: We sent a message to ISIS: if they approach the shrines, we would straightly enter the war]", *BBC Persian* 29 June 2015, 29 June 2015 <http://www.bbc.com/persian/iran/2015/06/150629_l12_iran_safavi_is>.

33 Ibid. See also Mahmood Alavi, "Niruhay-e Daesh be arzuhayeshan baray-e na amni-ye Iran narasidand [ISIS forces' dreams of making Iran insecure were not realised]", *BBC Persian* 13 June 2015, 10 Sept. 2015 <http://www.bbc.com/persian/iran/2015/06/ 150613_l12_iran_isis_alavi>.

34 See "Ayatollah Khamenei: Iran amnyyat-e A'raq ra amnyyat khod midand [Ayatollah Khamenei: Iran considers the security of Iraq to be its

own security]", *BBC Persian* 21 Oct. 2014, 6 Nov. 2014 <http://www.bbc. co.uk/persian/iran/2014/10/141021_ l12_iran_iraq_ibadi_pm_visit_tehran>.

35 "Rahim Safavi: be daesh pyam dadim ke agar nazdik-e a'tabat beshawad mostaqim wared mishavim" (29 June 2015).

36 "Edea'ay dargiri Dae'sh ba nirohay-e nezami-y-e Iran [ISIS's claim of clashes with Iranian security forces]", *BBC Persian* 29 Aug. 2014, 26 Oct. 2014 <http://www.bbc.com/ persian/world/2014/08/140829_u07_isis_ iran_west_tweet>.

37 "Vazir-e Ettellaa't: Ba Komeleh ham mazakereh mikonim" (Minister of intelligence: we even negotiate with Komeleh", *Radio Zamaneh* 15 Mehr 1393 *hs* [7 Oct. 2014], 16 Oct. 2014 <http://www.radiozamaneh. com/180409>.

"Vazir-e Ettellaa't: 130 aamel takfiri dar Iran bazdasht shodand [Intelligence minister: 130 takfirist Agents were arrested in Iran]", *Mashregh* [Mashriq] *News* 15 Mehr 1393 *hs* [7 Oct. 2014], 22 Mar. 2016 <http:// www.mashreghnews.ir/fa/news/352065/130>.

38 "Afradi az Daesh dar gharb-e Iran dastgir shodehand [Some of Daesh's people have been arrested in West Iran]", *Deutsche Welle* [Persian ed.] 17 Nov. 2015, 10 Dec. 2015 <http://www.dw.com/fa-ir/a-18856643>.

39 "Dastgiry-e 53 Haami-e Daesh dar Iran/tajrobeh 69000 hamleh-e siberi be Iran [Arrest of 53 supporters of Daesh in Iran/ 69000 cyber attack on Iran]", *Zahedan Press* 16 Azar 1394 *hs* [7 Dec. 2015], 22 Mar. 2016 <http://zahedanpress.com/27576>.

See also "Amir-e Daesh dar Iran dastgir shod/shekast sangin Daesh dar Sistan wa Baluchistan/ natayej pezuhesh yek nehad amnyyati dar bareh tamayol-e ahl-e sunnat-e Iran [Daesh Emir arrested in Iran/ Heavy defeat of Daesh in Sistan and Baluchistan/ The results of research by security forces regarding [the] tendency of the Iranian Sunnis to favour Daesh]", *Zahedan Press* 25 Shahrivar 1393 *hs* [16 Sept. 2014], 22 Mar. 2016 <http://zahedanpress. com/22404>.

40 Katie Welsford, "When borders are meaningless: The Islamic State in Iraq and al-Sham", London: Institute for Islamic Strategic Affairs, *IISA Blog* 18 July 2014, 11 Nov. 2014 <http://iisablog.org/2014/07/18/18-july-2014-when-borders-are-meaningless-the-islamic-state-in-iraq-sham>.

41 Bruce Riedel, "Islamic State cell strikes Shiites in Saudi Arabia", *Al-Monitor* 28 Nov. 2014, 1 Dec. 2014 <http://www.al-monitor.com/ pulse/originals/ 2014/11/saudi-shiite-islamic-state-terrorism.html>.

42 Abu Bakar Naji, *The Management of Savagery: The Most Critical Stage Through Which the Umma Will Pass*, trans. William McCants, John M. Olin Institute for Strategic Studies (Cambridge: Harvard University, 2006). <https://www.google.co.uk/url?sa=t&rct=j&q=&esrc=s&-

source=web&cd=4&cad=rja&uact=8&ved=0ahUKEwjeiKCYuaHLAh-
WJwxQKHXpXBtcQFggtMAM&url=https%3A%2F%2Fazelin.files.>.

43 "Haya't-e siasi-ye Taliban dar Tehran [The Taliban's political representative in Tehran]", *Hamshahri Online* 29 Ordibehesht 1394 *hs* [19 May 2015]., 14 Dec. 2015 <http://www.hamshahrionline.ir/details/295616/Iran/ foreignpolicy>.

44 "Goshayesh-e daftar-e nomayandagi-ye Taliban dar Zahedan [The opening of a Taliban representative's office in Zahedan]", *Deutsche Welle* [Persian ed.] 2 Aug. 2012, 14 Dec. 2015 <http://www.dw.com/fair/a-16139351>.

45 Saeed Hajjarian," Reformists must remain viable and teach the spiritual ... The government must correct its shortcomings and [...] recover [...] the cabinet [...]", *Tir Press* 15 Aug. 2015, 18 Mar. 2016 <http://www.tirpress.ir/265266/سعید-حجاریان-اصلاح-طلبان-باید-بکوشند-ر->.

46 "Hoshdar-e Ayatollah Makarem-e Shirazi dar bareh khatare bozrg baray-e Mashhad [Ayatollah Makarem Shirazi's warning on great danger for Mashhad]", *Afsaran* 24 Mordad 1393 *hs* [15 Aug. 2014], 15 Mar. 2016 <http://www.afsaran.ir/link/674780>.

47 Mohammad Sadr, "Hamkary-e Iran wa Amerika alih-e Daesh momken ast [Cooperation between Iran and the US on ISIS is possible]", *BBC Persian* 20 Mordad 1393 *hs* [11 Aug. 2014], 13 Aug. 2014 <http://www.bbc.co.uk/persian/iran/ 2014/08/140811_l12_iran_isis_iran_us_cooperation_iraq.shtml>.

48 Islamic Republic of Iran, Constitution, approved 24 Oct. 1979 (enforced from 3 Dec. 1979), amended 28 July 1989, *Iran Online*, accessed 10 Oct. 2015 <http://www.iranonline.com/iran/iran-info/government/constitution-9-1.html>.

49 For the population of different provinces, see "Jamia't va khanavar-e shahrestanhay-e keshvar be tartib-e ostan [The country's population, households, and city, according to the provinces]". 2011 Population Census. *Amar.* 30 July 2012. 16 Mar. 2016 <http://www.amar.org.ir/Portals/2/pdf/jamiat_shahrestan_keshvar.pdf>.

50 Farzan, P. Sangachin, Salehi, Esmail, and Mortaza Dinarwandi. "Sanjesh-e sath-e tawse' yaftagi ostanhay-e keshvar-e Iran be roikard-e tahlil-e ameli [Measuring the extent of development of Iran's provinces with the method of factor analysis]". amayesh sar zamin [Measuring the country], Winter 1391hs [2012-2013], 4:2 (5-26). <https://jtcp.ut.ac.ir/article_30343_0.html>.

51 Islamic Republic of Iran (1979).

52 Amnesty International, *Iran 2013*, annual report, *Amnesty International* 23 May 2013, 24 Mar. 2016 <http://www.amnestyusa.org/research/

reports/annual-report-iran-2013>.
See also Amnesty International, *Iran 2015-2016*, annual report, *Amnesty International* 12 Sept. 2015, 22 Mar. 2016 <https://www.amnesty.org/en/countries/middle-east-and-north-africa/iran/report-iran>.
Additionally, see Amnesty International, *Iran: Human Rights Abuses against the Baluchi Minority*, MDE 13/104/2007, *Amnesty International* 17 Sept. 2007, 16 Mar. 2016 <https://www.amnesty.org/en/documents/MDE13/104/2007/en>.
Regarding the Kurds, see Amnesty International, *Iran: Human rights abuses against the Kurdish minority*, MDE 13/088/2008, *Amnesty International* 30 July 2008, 17 Mar. 2016 <https://www.amnesty.org/en/documents/MDE13/088/2008/en>.
See also Iran Human Rights Documentation Center, "On the Margins: Arrest, Imprisonment and Execution of Kurdish Activists in Iran Today", *Iran HRDC* 11 Apr. 2012, 23 Mar. 2016 <http://www.iranhrdc.org/english/publications/reports/1000000089-on-the-margins-arrest-imprisonment-and-execution-of-kurdish-activists-in-iran-today.html>.
53 Ahmed Shaheed, "October 2011 report of the Special Rapporteur on the situation of human rights in the Islamic Republic of Iran", United Nations: General Assembly, 23 Sept. 2011, 24 Mar. 2016 <http://shaheedoniran.org/english/dr-shaheeds-work/latest-reports/report-of-the-special-rapporteur-to-the-un-general-assembly-dr-ahmed-shaheed-2011>.
See also Ahmed Shaheed, "March 2016 report of the Special Rapporteur on the situation of human rights in the Islamic Republic of Iran", United Nations: Human Rights Council, 10 Mar. 2016, 24 Mar. 2016 <http://shaheedoniran.org/english/dr-shaheeds-work/march-2016-report-of-the-special-rapporteur-on-the-situation-of-human-rights-in-the-islamic-republic-of-iran>.
54 Ali Younesi: "Doulat Natawanest be aqqalyathay-e qawmi wa mazhabi ostandari wa vazarat bedahad [The government failed to offer ministerial and provincial governorships to the religious and ethnic minorities]", *BBC Persian* 13 Azar 1392 *hs* [4 Dec. 2013], 13 Aug. 2014 <http://www.bbc.co.uk/persian/iran/2013/12/131204_l39_younesi_ minorities_appointments.shtml>.
55 See "[Of the country's population and households, province and city, respectively]" (30 July 2012).
56 Shams Iran, [web site], *Shams Iran* 23 Mar. 2016 <http://www. shams-iran.org>.
57 "Beyanyeh Shoray-e Markazi Sunnat (shams) dar khosus matelbat wa khasthay-e ahle sunnat [An announcement of the Sunni Central Council (Shams) regarding demands of Iranian Sunnis]", *Sunni News* 3 Esfand

1388 *hs* [22 Feb. 2010], 2 Nov. 2012 <http://sunninews.org/FA/articles. aspx?selected_article_no=4807>.
58 Eslahe, [web site], *Eslahe* 23 Mar. 2016 <http://eslahe.com>.
59 "Hafteh vahdat dar beynyeh Harkat-e Islami Sunnat wa Jamaat [Week of Solidarity addressed in an announcement of Harkat-e Islami Ahle Sunnat wa Jamaat-e-Iran]", *Sunni News* 4 Mar. 2010, 2 Sept. 2011 <http:// sunninews.org/FA/articles.aspx?selected_article_no= 4946>.
60 See p. 54 of Michael Weiss and Hassan Hassan, *ISIS: Inside the Army of Terror* (New York: Regan Arts, 2015).
61 "Ahzab-e Kurd az hozur-e Daesh dar Kurdistan-e Iran khabar midahand [Kurdish parties reports about attendance of ISIS in Kurdistan]", *Al-Arabiya* 15 Aug. 2014, 15 Dec. 2015 <http://farsi.alarabiya.net/fa/ iran/2014/08/15>.
62 "Tazahorat dar Kurdistan-e Iran wa dar hemayat–az kobani + aks" [Demonstrations in Iranian Kurdistan against ISIS–and in support of Kobani + pictures]", *Eslamabad Khabar* 19 Mehr 1393 *hs* [11 Oct. 2014], 10 Nov. 2014 <http://eslamabadkhabar.ir/shownews.php?idnews=255346>.
63 "Moqam-e Kurdistan-e Iraq dar mored hamkary-e shebeh-e nezamian-e Shia-e ba artesh hoshdar dad [Warning of a senior official in Iraqi Kurdistan regarding cooperation of Shia militia with the army]", *BBC Persian* 17 Mar. 2015, 12 Dec. 2015 <http://www.bbc.com/persian/ world/2015/03/150317_l03_iraq_is_iran>.
64 See "Vazir-e Ettellaa't: Baa Komeleh ham mazakereh mikonim" (7 Oct. 2014) and "Vazir-e Ettellaa't: 130 aamel takfiri dar Iran bazdasht shodand" (7 Oct. 2014).
65 "Afradi az Daesh dar gharb-e Iran dastgir shodehand" (17 Nov. 2015).
66 According to a 2011 population census, the population of Sistan and Baluchistan Province was over 2.5 million people. It should be noticed that the majority of Sistan's population, and possibly about 50% of Zahedan's population, are Shia. The same holds true for the capital. Other larger cities such as Iranshahr, Chahbahar, Saravan, and Khash also have a considerable number of Shias. See "[Of the country's population and households, province and city, respectively]" (30 July 2012).
67 "Aya marzbanan ezafeh khdmat mikhorand [Are the border corps extra-relaxed in their service?]", *Esfahan Shargh* 18 Farvardin 1393 *hs* [7 Apr. 2014], 15 Mar. 2016 <http://esfahanshargh.ir/16362>. See additionally: http://www.tehrantimes.com/index_View.asp?code=173131
68 Anon., correspondence with author, *WhatsApp*, 13 Jan. 2016.
69 "Enfejar-e bombe souti dar Iranshahr shishehay-e Bimarestan-e ra shekast [The sound bom exploision in Iranshahrbroke the glass of an Iranian hospital]", *Zahedan Press* 25 Mehr 1394 [17 Oct. 2015], 10 Dec. 2015

<http://zahedanpress.com/26502>.
Additionally, see "Jozeyat-e kashf wa khonsasazi-ye bomb 21 kiloi dar shahrestan-e sarbaz/awamel-e bobgozari shonasaie shodand [Details of the discovery and detonation of a 21-kilogram bomb in the district of Sarbaz/ The people involved with the bomb were identified]", *Zahedan Press* 25 Azar 1394 *hs* [16 Dec. 2015], 17 Mar. 2016 <http://zahedanpress. com/27516>.
See also "Tim-e terroristi barnameh Kharabkari dar ejtemaa't-e shia wa Sunni ye Sistan wa Bluchistan dasht+ new detail [A terrorist cell had a plan to sabotage the relationship between Shia and Sunni communities in Sistan and Baluchistan + new detail]", *Zahedan Press* 1 Azar 1394 *hs* [22 Nov. 2015], 22 Mar. 2016 <http://zahedanpress.com/27114>.
70 "Sal-e 2015 dast-e kam 53 nafar az shahrwandan Baluch dar tirandazi-ye mamuran koshteh wa zakhmi shodehand [In 2015, at least 52 Baluch citizens have been shot dead or have been injured by security forces]", *Balochcampaign.com* 5 Bahman 1394 *hs* [25 Jan. 2016], 25 Jan. 2016 <http://www.balochcampaign.com/ index.php/news/balochestan-news/ item/3179-2015-52>.
71 Anon. Correspondence with author. 18 Sept. 2014.
72 Anon. Correspondence with author. 10 Apr. 2015.
73 "Mokhalefate olamaye sunni-ye Iran ba hamalat-e hawaei-ye rusiyeh dar Suryeh [Rejection, by Sunni clerics in Iran, of Russian attacks in Syria]", *Deutsche Welle* [Persian ed.] 12 Oct. 2015, 15 Mar. 2016 <http:// www.dw.com/fa-ir/a-18777200>.
74 Kampain Fa'alin-e Baloch [The Baloch Activists Campaign], "Sepah jawanan ra dar tangna qrar midaha ke be suryeh berawand [The Revolutionary Guard put pressure on the young people to go to Syria]", *Balochcampaign.com* 12 Aban 1394 *hs* [3 Nov. 2015], 16 Dec. 2015 <http:// balochcampaign.com/index.php/all-category/gozaresh/item/3001-2015-11-03-12-15-38>.
75 The majority of them were from Bazman, an area in the East of Iranshahr District, where there is a small population of native Baluchi-speaking Shias.
76 "Modafea'an-e Haram-e Sunni mazhab, olguy-e vaqaei eslam-e nab-e Mohammadi [Sunni defenders of the shrine: the example of real, pure Muhammadan religion]", *Zahedan Press* 19 Azar 1394 *hs* [10 Dec. 2015], 10 Dec. 2015 <http://zahedanpress.com/27613>.
See also "Shahadat-e awalin razmandagan-e Baluch-e ostan dar nabard ba niroohaye takfiri-ye Daesh dar manateqh-e Suryyeh + asami wa tasvir-e shohada [The First Baluch Martyrs from fighting with Takfirist Daesh Forces in the region of Syria + names and pictures of the Martyrs]", *Zahedan Press* 6 Azar 1394 *hs* [27 Nov. 2015], 9 Dec. 2015 <http://zahedanpress.com/27327>.

77 "Sistan wa Baluchistan: tasavire vazir behdasht dar didar ba jawan-tarin shahid moqadas [Sistan and Baluchistan: pictures of the minister of health visiting the home of the youngest martyr of Moqadas]", *Hamshahri Online* 4 Dey 1394 *hs* [25 Dec. 2015], 15 Mar. 2016 <http://www.hamshahrionline.ir/details/319278/Defence/imposedwar>.

78 "Sokhanan-e Moulvi Fazlol Rahman Kuhi dar tahrim-e ea'zam-e jawanan be suryyeh [Moulvi Fazlol Rahman's words regarding sanction of dispatching the youth to Syria]", *Sunni News* 7 Nov. 2015, 11 Dec. 2015 <http://www.Sunni-news.com/fa/articles. aspx?article_no=35351>. See also Kampain-e Faa'lin-e Baloch [The Baloch Activists Campaign], "Vakonesh-e mojadad-e olamay-e ahl-e sumnat nesbat be ea'zam-e rustayian-e manateq mahroom be surryeh [Another reaction by Sunni clerics regarding the dispatching of people in the poor countryside areas to Syria]", *Balochcampaign.com* 14 Azar 1394 *hs* [5 Dec. 2015], 11 Dec. 2014 <http://balochcampaign.com/index.php/news/balochestan-news/item/3068-2015-12-05-08-57-59>.

79 Anon (HD). Correspondence with author. 13 Dec. 2015.

80 See Hoshang Noraiee, "Jadal-e ben-ejaishe-adl wajaish-e nasr:jihad baray-e khoda, jihad baraye mellat, jihad baraye qodrat? [Conflicts between Jaish al-Adl and Jaish al-Nasr: Jihad for God, Jihad for the Nation, Jihad for Power?]", *Taptan* 16 Aug. 2014, 20 Sept. 2014 <http://www.taptan.com/?p=129>.

81 "Ettelaeih ettehad-e mujahedin-e hezb-e al-Forqan wa harkat al-Ansar [Announcement of an alliance between Hizb al-Forqan mujahidin and Harkat al-Ansar]", *Blogspot* 11 Daey 1392 *hs* [1 Jan. 2014], 12 Dec. 2015 <http://hezbulfurqan.blogspot.co.uk/ 2014/01/blog-post.html>.

82 Sepah-e Sahabeh Iran, "Ettehad wa hambastagy-e Sepah-e Sahbeh Iran with Sazeman-e Jaish al-Adl [Alliance and Solidarity of Sepah-e Sahabeh Iran with the Jaish al-Adl organisation]", *Blogspot* 25 Farvardin 1394 *hs* [14 Apr. 2015], 19 Dec. 2015 <http://www.ss-iran.blogspot.co.uk>.

83 Hoshang Noraiee, "Sunni Militants in Iran: Activities, Ideological Sources and Political Strategies", *International Research Journal of Social Science*, 2015 Vol. 4(3), 79-87, 22 Mar. 2016 <http://www.isca.in/IJSS/Archive/v4/i3/14.ISCA-IRJSS-2014-331.pdf>. See also Sepah-e Sahabeh Iran (14 Apr. 2015). Ansar Forqan, Twitter [account suspended], <https://twitter.com/a_alfurqan_3>. Jaish al-Adl [Army of Justice"Sazeman-e Jiashe al-Adl sazemani dafaei dar rastay-e dafaa' az haysyyat wa hoquq-e Baluch wa ahle sunnat [The Jaish al-Adl defence organization in the defence of the rights of the Baloch nation...]", *Blogspot* 22 Mar. 2016 <http://jashuladl3.blogspot.co. uk>.

84 Mark Townsend and Toby Helm, "Jihad in a social media age: how can the West win an online war?" *The Guardian* 23 Aug. 2014, 13 Dec. 2015

<http://www. theguardian.com/world/2014/aug/23/jihad-social-media-age-west-win-online-war>.

85 Mubashir Zaidi, "IS is recruiting thousands in Pakistan, govt. warned in 'secret' report", *Dawn* 8 Nov. 2014, 13 Dec. 2015 <http://www.dawn.com/news/ 1143133>.

86 Kiran Nazesh, "The Islamic State Is Spreading Into Pakistan", *New Republic* 23 Sept. 2014, 13 Dec. 2015 <https://newrepublic.com/article/119535/isis-pakistan-islamic-state-distributing-flags-and-flyers>.

87 Zarrar Khuhro, "Militant camp in Iraq named after Lal Masjid's Abdul Rasheed Ghazi", *Dawn* 7 Mar. 2014, 10 Dec. 2015 <http://www.dawn.com/news/1091567>.

88 For a statement by Nasser Boladei, leader of the Baluchistan People's party, see Mishari Alhntoshi, " مقاومة البلوشية: نتعرض لقمع واضطهاد إيرانى مستمر ولن نتنازل عن حقنا فى تقرير المصير [Baloch resistance: we are continually exposed to Iranian repression and persecution, but we will not give up our right to self-determination]", *Sabq* 3 Mar. 2016, 22 Mar. 2016 <https://sabq.org/kTYcSp>.

89 Rahim Bandui. Email to Author on 22 March 2016. Bandui also confirmed this point in a face to face conversation with author on 31 March 2016.

90 Husain-Ali Shahriari, "Negranam zamani berasad ke Sistan wa balochistan be mousel tabdil shawad" [I am worried that one day, Sistan and Balochistan will become a Mosul], *Baloch Press* 20 Aban 1393 *hs* [11 Nov. 2014], 13 Nov. 2014 <http://balochpress.net>.

Jaish Adl – Adalat News

SUNNI MILITANTS IN SOUTH-EASTERN IRAN

Abstract

In this section, the ideological and strategic approaches of militant Sunni groups in south-eastern Iran will be explored. The ability of these militants to survive, and their capacity for popularity and action, are not just associated with the strong sense of alienation and discrimination among the local Sunnis in the area, but also with their ethnic and religious networks which exist across borders. In this way, they have strengthened their positions in the wake of turbulent conditions in adjacent countries, particularly in Pakistan and Afghanistan. The militant groups in the area are not homogeneous, but vary from quietists and ethnic-religious nationalists to sectarians and global-oriented jihadists.

In this section, Jondollah has been chosen as the main case study. Jondollah, as the predecessor of most existing groups, emerged in the wake of turbulent circumstances following the invasion of Afghanistan by the US and her allies. In this context, Jondollah overemphasised differences with 'the other'. By so doing, Jondollah tried to replace or mix what they called the '"truth"' of ethnicity with the '"truth"' of religiously-defined '"ethnic"' politics. While Jondollah preached hatred and intolerance towards Shias as being 'the other', ethnic-religious cleansing was being praised and encouraged.

Nearly all of these militants in the marginalised corner of south-eastern Iran have adopted a strong anti-Shia approach influenced, both politically and ideologically, by radical Deobandis as well as by Wahhabis and Salafists. With serious threats imposed by ISIS along her western borders, the Shia regime in Iran has become more aware of the dimensions of the problem, particularly in the area of Sistan and Baluchistan.

This research is based on secondary data partly published in Balochi and mainly published in Farsi.

Key words: Abdolmalek Rigi, al-Qaeda, al-Zawahiri, Ansar al-Forqan, Baloch, Baluchistan, Deobandi, Harkat-e Ansar-e Iran, Hezb-e al-Forqan (Sazman-e Hezb-e Ahl-e Sonnat-e Iran), Iran, Jaish al-Adl, Jaish al-Nasr, jihadist, Jondollah, Lashkar-e Jhangvi, Lashkar-e Rasool Ullah, Monem Group, Moulvi Abdolhamid Esmailzah, Pakistan, Ramzi Yousef, Sepah-e Sahaba-Iran, Sheikh Khaled Mohammad, Sistan, Sistanis, Sunni, Shia, Taliban, Wafaq Al Madris Al Arabia.

4.1 Introduction[1]

The Sunnis constitute about 15% of Iran's population. They are settled in different areas, but mainly they reside in Kurdistan along the country's western and north-western borders adjacent to Iraq and Turkey, as well as in Sistan and Baluchistan (Balochistan) along the south-eastern boundaries next to Pakistan and Afghanistan. There is a strong belief among the Sunnis in Iran that they are being discriminated against by the Shia theocratic regime in matters such as freedom of religious practice, the sharing of political power, and access to resources, particularly access to business and employment opportunities.

Recently, even Ali Younesi[1] – the former Minister of Intelligence and currently President Rouhani's special assistant in religious and ethnic minority affairs – criticised top Iranian authorities who considered Sunni minorities to be outsiders. This long-term policy of systematic alienation by the Iranian Shia regime has developed into a damaging process which has given rise to resentment among most Sunnis in Iran. So it

---

1 In this section, parts 3.1 and 3.2 were published in 2015 but they were further edited and prepared for this book. See Noraiee, Hoshang. "Sunni Militants in Iran: Activities, Ideological Sources and Political Strategies." *International Research Journal of Social Science Vol* 4.3 (2015): 79-87. <http://www.isca.in/IJSS/Archive/v4/i3/14.ISCA-IRJSS-2014-331.pdf>.

has not been unexpected that many Sunnis would show some kind of sympathy towards radical jihadists in Iraq, Syria, and Afghanistan (see Section 2).

Human Rights Watch, the United Nations Human Rights Council, and Amnesty International have regularly reported violations of human rights in Iran (as was mentioned in Section 2). The violation of the rights of ethnic and religious minorities, including the issues facing Sunnis in areas such as Sistan and Baluchistan, has been well documented in their reports.

Sistan and Baluchistan, along the south-eastern border, has 1,210 km. of land-based territorial boundaries consisting of 288.5 km. with Afghanistan and 921.7 km. with Pakistan. This province also has 370 km. of coastal border along the Arabian Sea and the Gulf of Oman, not far from Persian Gulf. The figures show that Sistan and Baluchistan province constitutes about 17% of the total Iranian boundary.

This province occupies a large area, about 187,500 km^2 (comprised of Baluchistan's 172,000 km^2 and Sistan's 16,000 km^2)—about 11.5% of Iran's territory. It has a population slightly higher than 2.5 million people, with a population density of lower than 13 people per square km.^{2} The Sunni population are mainly dispersed in the Baluchistan area and are estimated to be around 1.5 to 2 million people, who are also considered as being ethnically Baluch (Baloch).

The local political history of Sistan and Baluchistan is different from that of Kurdistan. In Sistan and Baluchistan, secular ethnic traditions are weak, and Sunni political and religious networks have been strongly influenced by the troublesome conditions in neighbouring Pakistan and Afghanistan. Considering the political circumstances in the region and widespread discontent of the Sunni population in this province, it is not so strange to see that most influential radical jihadists in

Iran have emerged from this part of the country. These groups have been diverse in terms of their religious ideologies, political strategies, and methods of operation. In terms of typology, as defined by Hegghammer, the ethnic-religious or nationalist-oriented approaches have been growing in usage among them; but there are also those who hold to non-political quietist, sectarian, and global-oriented approaches as well.[3]

As was explained in Section 2, the development and spread of the new threats posed by the extremist anti-Shia ISIS jihadists in Iraq and Syria has further highlighted Iran's level of sensitivity tothe serious problems (whether current or potential) brewing in the region. To tackle these problems, President Rouhani has tried to adopt a more moderate policy to improve the Sunnis' conditions and strengthen the position of quietists and moderate Sunnis to weaken radical groups in south-eastern Iran.[4]

Methodology

This research is based on secondary data which has been culled from various online publications, particularly websites and weblogs associated with militant groups in Sistan and Baluchistan. The sources include many speeches, interviews, and announcements which had been made available in published form during the last 10 years of their activities. Many of these websites or weblogs may no longer be available anymore because of filtering systems used by the Iranian security forces.

The source materials have been mainly published in Farsi. The lack of precise dates for many documents, and the highly rhetorical language by which they were originally presented, makes it difficult to create an appropriate assessment of the political context at the time the announcements were made and also makes it difficult to assess their validity and reliability for understanding the real intentions behind their ideas.

Methodologically, the main concerns are not just about the reliability and accuracy of the data but also about assessments of the claims and counterclaims made by different parties involved in the struggle for protecting or gaining power. In this context, however, the parties – Jondollah, on the one hand, and the Iranian government on the other – are unequal powers. There is still a 'fog of war' which cloaks and obscures the conflicts; and both sides are fully aware of the power of spectacular events and know that "if it bleeds, it leads" (as noticed by Cockburn).[5] Cockburn, as an experienced war journalist, held that "Everyone in a war has a more-than-usual strong motive for misrepresenting their achievements and failures, and usually it's difficult to disprove their claims".[6]

IRI controls the reporting of media outlets and resources inside Iran; while Jondollah and other Sunni groups, as opponents, are from minority groups which have limited resources to the extent that they sometimes only rely on using the power of rumour and the internet, such as Facebook and YouTube. Many official data sources presented by the Iranian government are very unreliable—for example, some are based on TV propaganda and prisoners' confessions which have been extracted under severe pressure and even physical torture. However, in different ways, this is also the case with opponent Sunni groups.

The following parts of this section are organised in two chapters. First, the process of development of the radical Sunni groups, in south-eastern Iran, along with the sources of their ideological and political strategies, will be explained. Second, to have a more profound understanding of dimensions of the development of the current conflicts and to gain some more insights about the directions that the incidents may take in this area, the case of Jondollah will be examined in more detail.

A local enemy or a global one?

Jihadists' strategies have been widely discussed in terms of dichotomous approaches to either the 'far enemy' or the 'near enemy'.[7] Broadly speaking, the Sunni radical groups which operate in south-eastern Iran, particularly in the provinces of Sistan and Baluchistan as in Khorasan, have apparently followed two different strategies. The first such strategy is one in which priority is given to transnational or cross-border enemies. The second such strategy is one in which priority is given to local or domestic enemies. Similar strategies are used by many Sunni militant groups in Pakistan.[8]

Forces which have followed an externally-oriented strategy have directed their "jihad" towards enemies beyond their own borders. In this case, some radical Sunni forces in south-eastern Iran consider the Taliban as their main ally, and some regard American-NATO's forces as well as the government of Afghanistan as their main enemies. In this case, al-Forqan would be a good example.[9] Those who have an internally-oriented strategy consider the Shias and the IRI as their main enemy, so their jihad is mainly directed against the IRI and against Shias. In reality, there is no such thing as an impenetrable border between these two strategies, for the militants share the same goal of achieving an Islamic state or, in its broader meaning, a caliphate run by the Sunni militant forces on the basis of sharia law.

Some militant groups have shifted over time from one strategy to another or have even considered a hybrid strategy. Working in wider networks with strong cross-border linkages has given them more flexibility in movement, security, and survival, and even a higher level of strategic choice. At the same time, strategic or tactical ties with cross-border powers (particularly the Pakistani government or security forces) may push these groups to cross their ideological 'red lines' and even enter into sectarian conflicts among themselves.

Sources of ideas

There is no single source of inspiration for the mobilization of radical Sunni forces in south-eastern Iran. In one way or another, their ideas are based on radical developments in Deobandism, Salafism/Ahl-e Hadithi, and Wahhabism. While there are some 'Islamists' (to use Roy's term), particularly among the more urban-educated people, who are inspired by the Muslim Brotherhood and Jamat-e Islami, the influence of the Islamists is still limited in that area.[10] To a great extent, these militant groups are largely hostile to the mainstream Islamists such as the Muslim Brotherhood and Jamaa't-e Islami, which are considered to be heretical and conformist.

However, with little doubt, Deobandism, in its radical version, has played the most significant role in stimulating the militant groups both politically and ideologically. In this sense, they are Neo-Fundamentalists or Talibanists. The majority of leaders and members of the militant forces, similar to those of the Taliban, have been trained in Deobandi madrasas, but also to a lesser extent in Ahl-e Hadith madrasas, which act under the umbrella of *Wafaq Al Madaris Salafia*. Some even have a Wahhabi educational background.[11]

Networks of radical Deobandi institutions have played an important role in supporting and promoting the radical jihadist activities in the whole region. A culture of suicide has also been established in Pakistan and Afghanistan, and now it seems to be an integrated part of radical jihad. The same networks of institutions, particularly Deobandi madrasas which act under the umbrella of *Wafaq Al Madris Al Arabia* madrasa networks in Pakistan, have expanded into south-eastern Iran, especially in Sistan and Baluchistan.

Deobandi madrasas in the subcontinent have been the main source of inspiration for the moulvis – Baluchistan's religious authorities – since the 1920s.[12] However, it is a simplistic idea to presume that the Deobandi networks are the same and have remained static over time.[13] Large sections of Deobandis are still traditional, quietest, and conservative. They are reluctant to join or support radical political activities or to challenge the existing political establishments.[14]

Most militant Deobandis in Pakistan started their sectarian activities in the 1980s and, to a large extent, emerged as a reaction to Shia radicals inspired by Ayatollah Khomeini and the Iranian Revolution of 1979. Since then, militant Deobandis such as *Sepah-e-Sahabah-e Pakistan, Lashkar-e Janguhi, Jaish-e-Mohammed,* and more recently the Pakistani Taliban; have been the most important sources of inspiration for anti-Shia political groups in south-eastern Iran. To a lesser extent, so have Pakistan's *Ahl-e- Hadithi* forces of *Lashkar-e-Tayyaba* (now known as *Jamaat-ud-Dawa*).During jihad in Afghanistan in the 1980s, through the networks of madrasas in Pakistan or through direct contacts with jihadist organisations in Pakistan, Baluch jihadists from Iranian Baluchistan had participated in jihad in Afghanistan. For this purpose, they received military training, funds and other facilities – mainly provided by Saudi Arabia and distributed by jihadist organisations in association with the Inter-Services Intelligence (ISI) agency in Pakistan.

There is no precise figure for the number of Baluch or Iranian Sunni jihadists who were killed in Afghanistan, but possibly dozens of them were killed during the jihad against the Soviets. For example, from Baluchistan, Abdolrabb-e Syedzadeh and Musa Damani, who were seminary students in Pakistan, were killed.[15] When the mujahidin took power in Afghanistan, many Iranian Sunni activists either stayed in Pakistan to organise their political activities from there, or they returned to Sistan and Baluchistan, Iran, where they initiated and led new brands of radical activities with clearer political ambitions. They also maintained communication with wider networks in Pakistan and Afghanistan.

The emergence of the Taliban in the 1990s strengthened the position of radical Deobandis and gave them a clearer political perspective. The Afghani Taliban added, to the political objectives of the previously sectarian Deobandis, an ambiguous vision of the Islamic Emirate. While violence and sectarian activities characterised the Taliban and their Deobandi allies as brutal forces, there is no evidence to suggest that there were any suicide bombings by either the radical Deobandis or the Taliban before US-led NATO attacks on Afghanistan in 2001. The new circumstances, even from the early 1990s, had influenced the Sunni Muslims in Sistan and Baluchistan, where clashes with the Shia authorities had become quite tense.

Through Deobandi networks of moulvis and madrasas, the image of the Taliban as being 'true' Muslims was widespread in south-eastern Iran. Sympathy with the Taliban grew among Sunnis in Sistan and Baluchistan, and also in the provinces of Khorasan. According to some observers, some groups or individuals often collected donations in many Sunni mosques for the support of jihad in Afghanistan. Some Baluch moulvis, in many cases, have admired and idealised jihadist suicide attacks in Afghanistan, Palestine, Chechnya, and Iraq. In this way, they have persuaded young religious Baluch to join the jihad.

Therefore, the Baluch militant jihadists developed immediate connections with radical groups in Pakistan and Afghanistan. The Taliban, *Sepah-e Sahabeh Pakistan*, *Lashkar-e Jhangvi*, and *Sepah-e Mohammed* were possibly the main sources of inspiration or experience for anti-Shia political groups in the eastern and south-eastern parts of Iran. These groups included the "Abu Salman" (Abdul Monem) group, *Hezab al-Forqan*, and "*Lashkar-e Rasool Ullah*". However, the global Salafi jihadists, in connection with Abu-Monem group, also had a strong presence.

4.2 Is there a connection between local Sunni radical groups and global jihadists?

The most significant militant Sunni groups in Iranian Baluchistan can be identified, in chronological order, as: *The Monem Group*, *Hezb-e al-Forqan* (HF), *Sepah-e Rasulullah* (SR), *Jondollah* (JA), *Sepah-e Sahaba-Iran* (SSI), *Jaish ul-Husain* (Army of Husain), *Jaish-ul-Adl* (Army of Justice), *Harkat-e Ansar-e Iran* (HAI), and *Jaish-e Nasr* (JN) (Army of Victory). With the exception of JA, there is no comprehensive and reliable, declassified information about these militant groups. Thus, despite the use of carefully-selected sources, which are publicly available, confirmation of the following information is not possible. These groups, in one way or another, have had connections with radical groups such as *Sepah-e Sahabah* and *Lashkar-e Jhangvi* in Pakistan and also with the Taliban in Afghanistan and Pakistan, but their connection with al-Qaeda networks and now ISIS remains a matter of speculation. Meanwhile, they have neither rejected them nor have they expressed open allegiance to them. All of these groups have been involved in violent armed activities against the Iranian regime and against Shia Muslims.

Jondollah, which later became the most formidable jihadist group in Sistan and Baluchistan, consistently denied a relationship with al-Qaeda and the Taliban—but they never condemned their global activities. Kamal Narui, spokeperson of Jondollah, said in an interview that "there are many differences between us and al-Qaeda in means and objectives. We are a moderate Islamic movement [of people] who struggle for achieving freedom for [the] Sunni community and Iranian Baluchistan while al-Qaeda has international objectives".[16] This means they had no criticism of al-Qaeda and explained their differences in terms of local (near) versus global (far) strategies.

Al-Zawahiri, now the leader of al-Qaeda, in his message on 22 February 2009, praised the Baluch for their jihadi activities. Dr. al-Zawahiri, in his message to "the growing jihadist awakening [in] the Arabian Peninsula in general and in Yemen in particular", said:

> Don't be less than your brothers in the defiant Pashtun and Baluch tribes who aided Allah and His Messenger and made America and the Crusaders dizzy in Afghanistan and Pakistan... Be helpers of Allah, and don't be helpers of America. Be helpers of Allah, and don't be helpers of Ali Abdullah Salih, the agent of the Crusaders[.] [A]nd be a help and support to your brothers the Mujahideen[,] and don't be a support to the Crusaders and their campaign which kills the Muslims in Afghanistan, Iraq and Palestine.[17]

This statement may be taken as evidence strongly suggesting that there are Sunni Baluch militants closely working with al-Qaeda networks. However, it is not clear who these militant groups or individuals are and where they are based. The Baluch mentioned by al-Zawahiri can include not only the militant groups in south-eastern Iran but also the militant Sunni Baluch in Afghanistan and Pakistan. In the Pakistani part of Baluchistan, militant Baluch and Brahui Sunnis affiliated to Sepah-e Sahabah Pakistan, Lashkar-e Janguhi, and the Pakistani Taliban have been rapidly growing in number and activity.

To clarify the complexity of these connections, now we look at the development of the earlier jihadist organisations in eastern and south-eastern Iran.

Abdul Monem Group

The Abdul Monem ('Abu Salman' or 'Yusef') group was a shadowy organization believed to be one of the earliest militant Sunni jihadist groups which emerged in the area under the leadership of the person for whom it is named: Abdul Monem.[18] The significance of this militant group can be seen in its four main features. First, this was an anti-Shia group which started by attacking the most important Shia shrine in Iran. Second, it had connections with international jihadist networks which were not clearly known as al-Qaeda at the time. Third, this may be the first Salafi jihadist group that started its operation inside Iranian borders. Fourth, it is also very likely that they had close connections with *Sepah-e Sahabeh Pakistan* (and later *Lashkr-e Jhangvi*, also in Pakistan).[19]

The global dimensions of this activity are related to the strong possibility that Ramzi Ahmed Yousef had an active role in implementation and planning of this operation. Ramzi Yousef and his younger brother Abdul Monem (also called Abdul Monem Arish or Abu Salman) were involved in detonating explosives at the Imam Reza Shrine, the most prominent Shia shrine in Iran, in Mashhad on 26 June 1994.[20] In this attack, 26 people were killed and over 200 were injured. Sunni radicals tried to justify this attack by framing it as revenge for the destruction of the Sunni Sheikh Faiz Mosque in 1993.[21]

At that time, the Iranian government, under the presidency of Hashemi Rafsanjani, placed responsibility for this attack on the Mojahedin Khalq-Iran organisation, possibly for political reasons. At the same time, the government security forces arrested a number of Baluch Sunni activists in Sistan and Baluchistan. Some of these detainees had connections with small Islamist groups which were sympathetic to the Muslim Brotherhood or Jama'at-e Islami.

Ramzi Yousef (also called 'Abdul Basit Balochi' or 'Mahmoud Kareem', alias 'Ramzi Ahmed Yousef') is the infamous global jihadist who detonated explosives at the World Trade Centre in New York a year earlier, on 26 February 1993. In July 1993, Ramzi Yousuf, in cooperation with Sepah-e Sahabah Pakistan, attempted to kill Prime Minister Benazir Bhutto[22]. Ramzi Yousef was arrested in Pakistan in 1995 and was extradited to the USA.[23]

However, many other members of Ramzi Yousef's family continued their jihadist activities, at the regional and global level. The most prominent member of this extraordinary family was Sheikh Khaled Mohammad. Sheikh Khaled Mohammad, who has been considered as the principal architect of 9/11 attacks, is the uncle of Ramzi Yousef. It is believed that Sheikh Mohammad's three brothers, Zahed, Abed and Aref, were also involved in jihad in Afghanistan.[24] Sheikh Mohammad was arrested in Rawalpindi, Pakistan on 1 March 2003 and, like Ramzi Yousef, was sent to the USA.[25]

Masrab Arochi, mentioned as a nephew of Sheikh Khaled Mohammed, and also being a jihadist militant, was arrested in June 2004 in Karachi.[26] Masrab Arochi is likely to be the same Abdul Monem mentioned previously. It was revealed by Pakistani police that Arochi, along with 8 others, was receiving training in South Waziristan.[27] This is approximately the same time when Abdolmalek Rigi began to establish the Iranian Jondollah. It is believed that Abdolmalek Rigi was also in Waziristan, but there is no evidence of any connection between Abdolmalek Rigi and Arochi.

Because these high-ranking al-Qaeda strategists originate from Sistan and Baluchistan, they are highly respected by radical religious activists in south-eastern Iran. They are originally from Kishkour-Sarbaz in Iranian Baluchistan, close to the Pakistani border. They had emigrated from Baluchistan to Kuwait, where they spent their youth and where they adopted a radical jihadist approach.

Due to their ethnic affiliation, this family has been a source of pride not just for jihadist religious groups but also for some secular ethnic Baluch nationalists. Some nationalists argue that they have enhanced the reputation of Baluchistan and the Baluch, and so deserve to be regarded as heroes. As a mark of respect, these nationalists refer to them by their first names as "Yousef" and "Khaled". There are other Baluch nationalists who, although rejecting the nature of their activities, consider their talents as proof that the Baluch have the capacity and potential to create their own successful, independent state.

There are also some secular nationalists who completely reject the idea by arguing that militant jihadists are not Baluch, and that the Baluch are naturally against such kinds of religious atrocities. From the nationalist point of view, some others consider these strategists purely as nationalists and deny their jihadist approach.

From the evidence provided, it is not very difficult to show some connections between the Abu Monem group and the other global jihadist groups mentioned above. The Monem Group's connections with subsequent jihadist groups in Baluchistan remain obscure. But it is very likely that the leaders of Hezb al-Forqan and Sepah-e Rasullalh had some sort of connection with them.

Hezb-e al-Forqan (HF)

This group is also known as the al-Forqan Party or Sazman-e Hezb-e Ahl-e Sonnat-e Iran. This group was founded and led by Moulvi Abdoljalil Qanbarzahi (also called Abu Shahid or

Moulvi Salhulddin) in the second half of the 1990s.

Moulvi Qanbarzahi, who had very little secular education, started his religious education in the Deobandi Madrasa of Darul-Ulum in Zahedan. Later on, he went to Pakistan to continue his education and training in other madrasas such as Badrul Ulum Madrasa in Rahimyarkhan and others in Multan and Kohat. He finally attended Darul Ulum Karachi, one of the most prestigious Deobandi madrasas in Pakistan. In Pakistan, he joined Sazman-e Mojahedin-e Ahl-e Sunnat-e Iran which had been established by Moulvi Abdolmalek Mollazadeh and a few other Iranian Sunni Moulvis and seminary students.

This organisation pursued an anti-Shia approach, but in general it was a moderate organisation in keeping with mujahidin groups in Afghanistan. They had no clear programme for armed jihad against the Iranian government. This organisation published a newsletter called "Azan-e Mojahed" in Pakistan. Moulvi Abdolmalek Mollazadeh was killed in an act of terrorism, one possibly perpetrated by Iranian security forces in Karachi. Moulvi Habibullah Husainbor, who was another activist and a founder of this organization, was arrested when he went to Iran. After being released, he was kept under surveillance—but then, he was mysteriously disappeared. His relatives and friends believe that he was kidnapped by Iranian security forces.

According to Moulvi Qanbarzahi's biography, written by Moulvi Ebrahim Safizadeh, Qanbarzahi then went to Afghanistan and took part in the jihad as a commander of forces fighting against the Russians in Lugar.[28] After the Russian forces withdrew from Afghanistan, Moulvi Qanbarzahi – now an experienced jihadist – returned to Iran.

Qanbarzahi settled in Noukchah and Chah Zard-e Domak, a village around Zahedan, and started teaching in a madrasa. He preached jihad there and then also established a new madrasa. In the meantime, he trained his students to join jihad. He established *Hezb-e al-Forqan* (HF) with the participation of his students Abdolqader Abdollahzahi (Omarshah) and Abdulshakoor Shahbakhsh. HF emerged as an armed jihadist group influenced by the Taliban and al-Qaeda. This group moved to Nimroz province, Afghanistan, and started to develop a close relationship with the Taliban.

Supported by the Taliban, Hezb-e al-Forqan spread their activities along the borders of Afghanistan and Iran by building further contacts with Sunni jihadists from Khorasan. HF also expanded their activities in Herat, Qandahar, and Helmand; and established a base in Kuh-e Malek, Helmand. While they were sporadically penetrating the border and organizing skirmishes against Iranian security forces, they focused mainly on supporting the Taliban in Afghanistan. Possibly because of being tied to conservative and traditional perspectives regarding the use of technology (much as the earlier Taliban were), HF was not keen on using television and global satellites and the internet as ways to publicise their operations efficiently.

When HF was very much involved in supporting the Taliban or possibly identifying Shia in Afghanistan, the Taliban captured Mazar-e Sharif and attacked the Diplomatic Premises of Iran (the Iranian embassy) and killed nine of the Iranian diplomatic staff, including a reporter.[29] Whether HF was involved in this massacre, or not remains unclear, but it is very likely that they had cheered the massacre perpetrated by the Taliban in which the diplomatic chief, Naser Rigi – a Sunni Baluch from Zahedan – was also killed. When HF was active in Herat, al-Zarqawi was also present in the area. And he had also met with the brother of Khalid Sheikh Mohammad.[30] But it is not very clear if there was any connection between al-Zarqawi and members of al-Forqan on the one hand, and any connection between al-Forqan and Sheikh Mohammad's jihadist relatives on the other. However, after the US invasion of Afghanistan, al-Zarqawi escaped through the Zahedan route, and later stayed with his Iranian Sunni friends – particularly Ansar-al Islam – in Kurdistan.[31]

As a result of NATO's heavy bombardment of Afghanistan, HF's base in Koh-e Malek, Helmand, was destroyed. According to Moulvi Safizadeh, about 40 members of HF were killed and many were injured, but Moulvi Qanbarzahi survived.[32] Since then, HF has not been able to recover enough to act as an important force. Some of their members eventually split or joined JA, which would become the most formidable jihadist group in south-eastern Iran.

The deaths of Moulvi Qanbarzahi and Hamzah Sarwani, Qanbarzahi's close colleague, were announced by al-Forqan's spokesperson Ali Haidar on 21 March 2012. It was not clear where, how, and by whom Moulvi Qanbarzahi was killed.[33] In a short biography written by Moulvi Safizadeh, there is no detail about the relationship of HF with Taliban and al-Qaeda. It has been claimed that Moulvi Qanbarzahi had a tremendous influence on the other Baluch jihadists such as the leader of Sepah-e Rasulallah, Moulabakhsh Derakhshan; and also the leader of *Jondollah*, Abdolmalek Rigi.

Sepah-e Rasulullah

This group is also known as the Army of the Prophet, or *Sazeman-e- Mobarezan-e Sepah-e- Rasulullah* (SR), or *Lashkar-e Rasullallh*. It was founded by Moulabkhsh Derakhshan in the 1990s. Derakhshan was from Rask, a town very close to the area where Khalid Sheikh Mohammad's family came from. Derkhshan, after being involved in an honour killing, escaped to Pakistan; and there, he established connections with radical and sectarian Sunnis. It is likely that he had developed a relationship with *Sepah-e Sahabah-e Pakistan* and then *Lashkar-e*

Jhangvi (Army of the Prophet's Companions) as well as with the Taliban and Salafi groups. In this context, he was influenced by groups who were spreading hatred against Shia and Barelavis and were involved in killing Shia and Sufi supporters in Pakistan. These conflicts were also rapidly spreading in Baluchistan as well. Moulabakhsh Derakhshan, at some point, came in contact with Mullah Kamalkhan Salahzahi, who had become famous for heavy clashes with Iranian security forces in Gornag.

Armian observes that Kamalkhan Salahzahi (Mullah), who was born in 1954, was a resident of Gornag, a small village between Sarbaz and Iranshahr.[34] Iranian security forces attacked the village in November 1999 to arrest Kamal Khan Salahzahi, who was accused of being a drug trafficker. In the armed clashes which ensued, a considerable number of security forces were killed. It was reported that security forces later ruined the whole village. Salahzahi denied any connection with drug traffickers and viewed himself as a social activist who sought justice and fairness in Baluchistan.[35]

It is very likely that SR cooperated closely with Moulvi Qanbarzahi and then HF to support jihadists, particularly al-Qaeda members, to cross Iran's borders with Pakistan and Afghanistan.[36] When the Allied forces invaded Afghanistan in 2001, al-Qaeda networks came under heavy attack. The routes through Pakistan became very risky for Arab militants. South-eastern Iran appeared to be the safest route for radical Arabs to escape to the Gulf countries and also to Iraq. After Moulabakhsh Derakhshan was killed by Iranian security forces, his brother Wahed Bakhsh Derkhsahan became the group's leader. Later on this group announced that they had joined JA under the leadership of Abdolmalek Rigi. Since there is no written evidence about the activities of this group, it is difficult to clarify its strategy beyond what is speculated here. Derakhshan's activities had much influence on Abdolmalek Rigi, who had left SR and few years later founded Jondollah.[37]

Abdolrauf Rigi, a founding member of Jondollah, had expressed great respect for all these groups and their leaders and said that Jondollah had a very strong connection with al-Forqan.

Therefore it can be concluded that, the south-eastern area of Iran, which is adjacent to Pakistan and Afghanistan, has been the most fertile ground for the emergence of radical jihadists and ethno-religious groups. The Iranian Shia regime's treatment of the Sunnis as second-class citizens has been an important internal factor in alienating the Sunnis and creating a basis for radicalism to grow in the area.

These radical groups have not been homogeneous in terms of their ideological sources, political strategies, and methods of action. They have been influenced by radical Deobandis on the one hand, and Wahhabi-Salafists on the other. However, most of them have focused on the near enemy. Some groups like al-Forqan have pursued a regional strategy and supported the Taliban in Afghanistan. Nearly all of them, including the most popular groups such as Jondollah and, to some extent, Jondollah's main successor, Jaish-e Adl, have been anti-Shia. They have also effectively used cross-border ethnic and religious networks to increase their support, facilitate their plans, organise their attacks inside Iran, and increase the level of security for their members and organisations.

The recent emergence of the Islamic State (ISIS) in Syria and Iraq has increased the level of security concerns in this area and has put an enormous amount of pressure on President Rouhani's government to undertake some reformist measures. Containing the disenfranchised Sunnis within local political governance has been seen by governmental advisers as a necessary solution. However, the most conservative Shia radicals – who control key areas of power, both nationally and locally – resist against any reform in this respect.

From mid-2004, Jondollah, and then its successor Jaish-e Adl, emerged as the most influential ethno-religious Sunni jihadist group in Iran. Thus, the next part of this section will explain Jondollah's activities and to some extent, those of Jaish-e Adl. But it will also briefly look at some other smaller groups, which emerged after the Iranian Islamic regime's 2010 arrest and subsequent execution of Abdolmalek Rigi, Jondollah's leader.

Jondollah has been a key organisation, so this section helps us to gain further insight into the ideology and strategies of other groups which emerged after the death of Abdolmalek Rigi.

4.3 Jihadism and ethnic nationalism

Emergence of Jondollah (Jundallah—Army of God)

Jondollah (Jundallah—Army of God) is also known as 'The Popular Resistance Movement of Iran' (The Iranian People's Resistance Movement). It was established by Abdolmalek Rigi, and it started an armed struggle in south-eastern Iran around 2004. Jondollah (JA) emerged as the most formidable violent ethnic-religious militant force in the area's recent history. It captured global media attention by demonstrating the beheading of prisoners in the earlier stage of its activities, and then by introducing suicide bombing into conflicts.[38]

Jondollah, similar to al-Zarqawi's operations in Iraq, used suicide attacks to cause colossal damage and mass killing among security forces and deliberately indiscriminate massacre of civilians in Shia places of worship (see Appendix 2). Targeting Shia along with their sacred places and religious identities was a clear manifestation of hatred and resentment.

Jondollah carried out its first suicide car bombing in Sistan and Baluchistan province on 29 December 2008. This suicide attack targeted an Iranian security forces base in the town of Saravan. It was carried out by Abdulgafoor Rigi, a teenage brother of Jondollah's Abdolmalek Rigi (see Appendix 3), not only to show JA's ability and create fear among the security forces, but also to propagate its leader's highly emotional appeal to dedication and sacrifice.[39]

Abdolmalek Rigi grew up in Zahedan, the capital city of Sistan and Baluchistan. Zahedan is quite close to both the Pakistani and Afghani borders. Some mere miles away from Zahedan is Rabat, a tri-border spot between Iran, Pakistan, and Afghanistan notorious as a hub for big-league drug traffickers and arms traders.[40] Zahedan, which was previously called Dozdap (Dozzap), is a new city which emerged in the 1930s and has since grown rapidly, particularly after the 1970s. Now it is home to over 600,000 people. Its population consists, in large part, of Baluch migrants who came from the rural areas of other parts of Sistan and Baluchistan; immigrants from other parts of Iran; and now, a large number of Afghans. Many of the Baluch immigrants have been nomadic and semi-nomadic tribal people. Particularly so are the Rigi, Narui, Esmailzahi (Shah Bakhsh), Yarahmadzahi (Shah Nawazi), and others who used to live in the surrounding areas of Zahedan, in a region known as Sarhad.

Trading and public-sector employment are the main sources of income in the province. Considering the geographically strategic position of Zahedan, it has also been a popular route of international drug traffickers and big-time smugglers of luxury items, popular consumer goods, and fuel—as well as human trafficking between Iran and neighbouring countries. In the context of endemic unemployment among the local people, there are a huge number of Baluch in Zahedan who live off of the trading of smuggled goods, either by having their kiosks and shops located in Zahedan itself; or by transporting goods and people across borders or between Zahedan and other cities, particularly through Chahbahar Port, which benefits from its status as a Free Zone trading area.

A considerable number of Jondollah members and some other militant groups' members, are mainly from the area of Zahedan, and are likely to have strong nomadic-tribal roots; and an experience of clashing with the notoriously corrupt and violent security forces. Abdolmalek Rigi, who had lost his brother at an early stage, during clashes with security forces, also from an early age, started trading smuggled goods and engaging in human trafficking. During this time, he joined SR. Then, as an ambitious jihadist, Abdolmalek Rigi split from SR and, as a talib (seminary student), entered a Deobandi madrasa of A'in–ululum located in Gosht in the Saravan District. But soon, he was pushed to leave (or perhaps was even expelled from) the madrasa by Moulvi Mohammad Yousuf Husainpoor, its head, because of the tensions and risks he caused. Being politically-oriented, he went to Pakistan and entered either Jamia Farooqia or Bennuri, or possibly both (they are well-known Deobandi madrasas in Karachi).[41]

For Rigi, as for many other jihadists, madrasas were not only covers or safe houses, but also appropriate places for identifying and recruiting jihadists; as well as centers important for gaining religious prestige and the title of Moulvi (a clerical title in the sub-continent of India). Most importantly, many madrasas in Pakistan were used as the safest contact points for current and potential jihadists. Being in Pakistan for a few years, Rigi had gained plenty of experience and possibly military training in Waziristan and other places.

It seems that Rigi, after a few years of gaining training and wider contacts in Pakistan – particularly during the turbulent years of the first half of the 2000s – had become more sceptical about joining "global jihad", so he had decided to localise his strategy by returning to Iranian Baluchistan and establishing a new militant jihadist organisation there. Around 2004-2005, he founded his own political organisation with his other companions and an older brother, Moulvi Abdolrauf Rigi, a Deobandi Sunni cleric. Abdolrauf Rigi was a cleric who was teaching staff in a madrasa in Nahook, a village in Saravan district. The founding members included Haji Mohammad Zaher (who later, for a short while, became Jondollah's leader), and Nosrati Nahooki (who would later signed an announcements on behalf of Mohammad Zaher).[42]

Jondollah succeeded in persuading many other radical jihadists and also religious nationalists in south-eastern Iran to join and strengthen their radical activities against the security forces of the Iranian Shia regime. Pursuing a strategy of localisation and of highlighting Sunni Muslim issues, especially in Baluchistan, attracted the attention of ethnic nationalists as well. Baluch ethnic nationalists living abroad, particularly those in Europe and the USA, used communications facilities to spread JA's issues worldwide; but this also pushed JA to pay some attention to the Baluch's ethnic issues. The hybrid religious-ethnic ideology of JA gained widespread support among both ethnic and religious radicals; but JA always denied the presence of any nationalist-ethnic approaches in their Islamic ideology.

Apart from a number of other massive attacks on security forces, JA carried out 5 suicide attacks in total. Three of the 5 were carried out in Shia places of worship. In these operations, 7 suicide attackers were involved. Many of them were seminary students and had little secular education.

Figure 4-1 Photos of Saifulrahman Chahbahari and Hesan Khashi—suicide attackers in Chah Bahar (Jondollah)

In spite of many institutional and cultural links that the previous radical groups had developed with Global jihadists in the area, there is no evidence of jihadist suicide bombings in Iran before JA's suicide attacks. Despite Jondollah's rhetoric, all suicide attacks carried out by them remained limited to local areas in Iranian Baluchistan rather than being carried out anywhere else in Iran. However, JA actively used cross-border networks, particularly in Pakistan and Afghanistan, to facilitate the attacks and find safe shelters for their operatives.

Religious and ethnic rhetoric in Jondollah's political strategy

Ideologically, Jondollah has not been homogeneous. To a great extent, that is due to the nature of the alliance Jondollah was based on. This is an important factor in explaining the existing inconsistencies in Jondollah's policies. Ethnic and religious elements are both obvious parts of Jondollah's ideology; however, they are not cohesively interconnected.

The amalgamation of religious rhetoric with ethnic nationalism makes it quite difficult to clearly define Jondollah's ideological incentives, political strategies, and ultimate objectives. The lack of a coherent strategy is a reason behind all vacillations, ambiguities and contradictions which have appeared, sometimes in very unexpected ways, in Jondollah's statements. The ambiguities and inconsistencies can even be seen in the identity of the organisation's own name, as it has appeared under different names.[43]

Religious and ethnic values are expressed in Jondollah's objectives in an assorted, 'mixed-message', and ambiguous manner. For example, Delawar Baluch (a then-pseudonym used, at the time, by Movlvi Abdolrauf Rigi, brother of the Leader and one of the founding members) has presented both ethnic and religious objectives side by side. As one of the most religious figures in Jondullah, he argued that Jondollah defends "the oppressed nation of the Baluch and Iranian Sunni community" and confronts "Shia fascists in Iran...and...the Baluch martyrs shed their blood to defend the Islamic land of the Baluchistan" in a simultaneous quest for "power and [out of] respect of the Baluch Muslim nation and in defence of the religion and the Quran and the mosques and people and honour". This is the blood which "destroys the infidels"—"today's Baluchistan (Sunni Baluch) has risen up with an identity of Islam and faith to dedicate its children to a glorious land for world Islam".[44]

Ideologically, Abdulrauf Rigi closely followed Abdolmalek Rigi's anti-Shia approach. In an announcement by the 'Association of Jondollah's Ulamas [scholars]' in which Abdulrauf Rigi had a leading role, much effort was made to prove that 'Shias are non-believers' and that therefore, shedding their blood as occupiers is legitimate.[45]

At the same time, Jondollah – in an approach similar to that of many other jihadist groups – attempted to distance itself ideologically from the secular nationalists by heavily appealing to Islamic symbols, Quranic verses, and *ahadith* (traditions) to define their distinctive religious identity.

Religious symbols, for instance, are reflected in emblems used by Jondollah.

Jondollah Mujahedin in Baluchistan(Mojehed website: https://m0jahed. wordpress.com/page/19/

Figure 4-2 Jondollah's Mujahedin

Jaish- al Adl Mujadidin (Mojehed website: https://m0jahed. wordpress.com/page/19/

Figure 4-3 Jaish al_Adl Mujahedin

Jondollah's earlier emblem had been a Saudi-style featuring of the *shahadah* creed, "there is no God apart from the Allah and his prophet is Mohammed". Under this motto, the name of Jondollah was written in such a way that the flag is seen to be carried by Jondollah. In a more recent emblem, the name of Jondollah is seen (as part of a global force?) as a forceful hand (force), inspired by a book (the Quran) and carrying a gun. But besides the presence of the Quran, no other distinctively Islamic motto is clearly seen. There is also no mention of either the Baluch or Baluchistan, and there is no sign of either Baluchi traditions or symbols (see Figure 1).

Jondollah and homeland

After the arrest of Abdolmalek Rigi, Moulvi Abdolrauf Rigi gained a key role in Jondollah and continued to formulate an Islamic identity for Jondollah. Abdolraufr Rigi endeavoured to justify attacks on non-Sunnis by claiming they were non-nationalist, while frequently using the concepts of homeland and national identity to support the attacks. He gave examples of the Taliban in Afghanistan and Palestinians in Palestine, along with what the Deobandis did in India against the British occupiers, to prove that the principle of using the concepts of 'ethnicity' and 'homeland' to mobilize attacks against Shias in Baluchistan has nothing to do with any nationalistic approach.[46]

To justify Jondollah's attacks on non-Sunni "outsiders" in Baluchistan, Abdolrauf Rigi believes that they are "like Israeli citizens" who "support invaders and infidels" in the "occupied lands".[47] So according to Abdolrauf Rigi, ordinary Israelis are considered as collaborators of the Israeli government and occupiers of the Islamic lands (Palestine). He believes this is somehow a basis for justification of the killing of all Jewish people in Israel by jihadists, and that likewise, the killing of the non-Sunni outsiders, particularly Shias in Baluchistan, is likewise somehow justifiable.[48]

These indicate that Jondollah ideologically, in the view of Moulvi Abdolrauf Rigi, suggested that Shia are "Infidels" who have occupied Sunni Islamic lands in Iran such as "Kurdistan, Turkmen Sahra, and Arabistan [Khuzestan]". In a religious decree (*fatwa*), as was shown earlier, much effort was made to establish this sectarian idea that Shias are infidels and that it is therefore supposedly legitimate to massacre them.

They support their arguments by "*fatwas*" issued by well-known Deobandi moulvis in Pakistan such as Maulana Salimullah Khan (head of Jamia Farooqia) and Maulana Rasheed Ahmad Ludhianvi (president of JUI-F Punjab).[49] From such *fatwas*, Jondollah draws the conclusion that its activities have no connection whatsoever with using nationalism/ethnicity to gain national power, but that it is about jihad against non-Muslim invaders who have occupied Baluchistan as an Islamic land—a holy territory. From this point of view, the mere presence of ordinary Shia civilians – no matter how quietist, peaceful, or well-intentioned they are – is considered to be an act of occupation.

This line of argument was even more clearly expressed on online comments made by Saeed (a pseudonym), who strongly affiliated himself with Jondollah. Saeed argued that "Being a Baluch has never been a source of pride for Jondollah, since Jondollah has been proud of Islam and Islamic figures". He continued that titles like 'Baluch' or 'Arab' are just labels used for the sake of encouragement and mobilization of people as the Prophet himself had done. He suggested that we:

> Believe that our Islamic lands have been occupied by Safavid (Shias). Baluchistan, Kurdistan, and Turkmen Sahra are [...] Islamic lands which have been occupied by Safavid [as] infidels who have played a role in the

occupation of the Islamic lands and [who] support occupiers, like Shias who live in Baluchistan, [who themselves] are occupiers. Therefore, in the same way as they have targeted our ordinary people and killed them, we can target them.

Saeed believes that the "infidel Shias" were brought in by Shia regimes to occupy the Muslim (Sunni) lands. For this reason, Saeed and Abdolrauf Rigi do not mention non-Sunni ethnic groups in Iran such as Turks because they are Shia.[50]

There are some other areas, such as language and territory, in which members of Jondollah have defined their identity differently from what secular nationalists have done. There is an element of de-territorialisation in Jondollah's argument, because as a defender of Sunnis in Iran, all Sunnis are not bound within territorially- and ethnically-defined units like 'Kurdistan' or 'Kurdish'. Radical Sunnis in Khorasan who are Farsi speakers do not consider themselves 'Fars' in ethnic terms. They have much influence among Sunnis in Baluchistan. And they share with other radical Muslims the view that over-emphasis of 'Baluch' and 'Baluchistan' as divisive ethnic issues is against Islamic values and the need for Ummah-related solidarity across ethnic divides. The Baluchi language, for the Baluch Nationalists, is a key issue for defining their identity; while it is not the same for Jondollah.[51]

Nearly all jihadist songs which have been released by Jondollah on YouTube are in Arabic or Dari/Persian and are related to jihadist movements in Afghanistan, Pakistan, and Arab countries. Only a few songs are in Baluchi, but even these songs have jihadist content, rather than strictly ethnic-related features. By contrast, it would be unthinkable for the secular Baluch ethnic nationalists to broadcast their own national songs in languages other than Baluchi.[52] (See appendix 4).

In this case, the "fundamentalist" tendency has been to lean strongly towards

justification of the purification of Islamic territory, by means of a so-called 'cleansing'. To them, this 'cleansing' means erasing from the land 'those' people (along with their identities) who are seen as being apostates or non-believers. In this case, Jondollah particularly focuses their attention on Shia and Sistanis (Zabolis).[53]

Anti-Shia and anti-Sistani

Jondollah, according to some of their supporters, used the term 'Baluch' as a label rather than as an identity. Jondollah attacked 'Shias' as being "religious-occupiers", rather than as an ethnic group with a "Fars" (Persian-speaker) identity, as the Baluch secular ethnic nationalists usually do. Jondollah's immediate targets of criticism and attack were their neighbours, Shia Sistanis, who are present and more visible in Baluchistan than are any other Shia groups. As Shias, Jondollah calls them "Sabaei", "Rafezi" (rafida), "Majus" (zartostraian), and "blasphemous infidel Zabolis".[54]

In response to hard-line Shia groups, Jondollah used strong emotional appeals to preach hatred and intolerance regarding "Zabolis" and also "non-natives" or non-Sunnis in Baluchistan. Jondollah very frequently used provocatively incendiary phrases such as "Zaboli occupiers" who have spread throughout Baluchistan like "ants and locusts" and who control the "land and the wealth" of Baluchistan. Shia Sistanis were named as being "knavish" ('bisharaf', which carries a strong connotation in the Persian language), "fleers", "criminal Zabolis", and "mercenary puppets of the regime".[55]

This anti-Sistani approach was well-received by many Baluch ethnic nationalists, who also considered Sistanis as the immediate ('near') "Persian" force competing with them over resources in Sistan and Baluchistan.

In a very-rapidly-proliferating network of weblogs by Jondollah and its supporters, there began appearing language brimming full with venomous hatred, swearing, and extremely rude, underhanded, and offensive insults levelled against the honour of Sistanis. But it should be noticed that the extremist Shia, through their unrestricted and professionally-made weblogs, attack their Sunni opponents with equal viciousness. They attack Jondollah, Abdolmalek Rigi, Sunnis, and the Baluch. Since this article is not about the Shia radicals, we do not allocate further space to them. Suffice to say that these tensions indicate the escalation of a sense of sectarian hatred, which has been dangerously spreading among the public with support from the radical political groups, both from Shias and Sunnis in Sistan and Baluchistan province. These local confrontations also reflect severe competition between the local communities for limited resources.

Jondollah has frequently urged young people to attack and kill Zabolis and Shias and non-natives in Baluchistan. For example, in an announcement regarding "martyrs", they wrote:

> While the Movement [Jondollah] expresses its condolences to the families of the martyrs whose children have been executed as innocent and victims, it warns all non- natives in Baluchistan to be ready for death. The Movement does not allow any non-native to live in Baluchistan[;] and Jondollah orders the young Baluch not to hesitate in killing any non-native[s] and Zabolis. The movement will offer prizes, to the young people, for killing non-natives. The young people should know that if non-natives were not in Baluchistan, this Government could not exist. So if we want to survive, we should free Baluchistan from occupation. So we should attack non-natives. Non-natives both from the public or

the armed forces will be under attack. Of course, Jondollah's new policy is to target the non-native civilians, as [they are] the main cause of our nation misfortune.[56]

The statements quoted show that Jondollah did not hesitate to applaud ethnic cleansing, saying that "Zabolis' crimes have caused [the] Baluch to thirst for their blood" and then they continued to say that Zabolis:

> created a volcano which can erupt at any moment and destroy the race of Zabolis and lead to a racial, ethnic and religious war in Baluchistan. This will only result in [the] complete destruction of Zabolis [...] you should [well] know that Baluchistan's flame will spread all over Iran[;] and the [scent] of a bloodier war than East Timor and Bosnia Herzegovina is [seen] from the land of Baluchistan.[57]

On the one hand, Jondollah and their supporting networks used weblogs to preach hatred and intolerance. This creates an extremely dangerous situation. On the other hand, speaking from the position of being a minority group, they were criticising the Islamic regime for real violations of the human rights of minorities. On a number of occasions, they have announced that they were committed to human rights. But at the same time, on such occasions they have vigorously violated human rights and seen Shias and Sistanis as "infidels" to be punished and killed. On the grounds of their human rights having been violated by the Iranian regime, they were trying to justify their own extremist form of retaliation through reciprocal violation of human rights.[58]

A political solution?

Jondollah's inconsistent, general statements about their objectives have been used as a basis for many different interpretations of what constitutes the best course of action, as has been seen among nationalists on the one hand and radical religious groups on the other.

Kamal Narui, the first spokesperson for Jondollah, places some emphasis on ethnic aspects of their objectives. He explains that the objectives were about gaining the rights of: "Iran's oppressed nations, the Sunni community, and the Baluch nation". However, by cutting across ethnics and religious boundaries both in Baluchistan and in all other parts of Iran, he also made Jondollah's objectives appear vague (at least to his audience) and even contradictory (though these contradictions and the vague rhetoric may reflect a deliberate policy of devising different statements for different audiences). He says:

> We as Baluch Sunnis want to stop oppression and achieve the rights of all Iranian ethnic peoples under a federal System, local governments [emirates or provincialities] in areas of Baluchistan, Kurdistan and Arabistan [Khuzistan, and either most or part of Hormozgan and Bushehr].[59]

Narui's statements seemingly moved towards very close alignment with the projects suggested by non-separatist secular nationalists. However, Narui ignored non-Sunni ethnic groups such as Turks and others. And he did not clearly explain how an ethnically-based "emirate" would meet the religious needs of the Sunni community in the whole of Iran (for example in Khurasan, where many Sunnis are geographically less concentrated than they are in Sistan and Baluchistan). Narui's statements, to some extent, were inconsistent with what Abdulrauf

Rigi (the second spokesperson of Jondollah after the death of Abdolmalek Rigi) suggested. Abdolrauf Rigi, who put further emphasis on what he viewed to be the Islamic character of their objectives, had said:

> The Jondollah Movement is an Islamic movement to defend the oppressed Sunni Baluch people against invasions and oppressions imposed by the polytheists and infidel Shias. And it wants to achieve respect and freedom for the Sunni people in regional and local governments ruled according to Sunni religious instructions.[60]

In this religious project [in which] the Shias are seen as infidels, it is not clear what sort of position the majority Shia would have in an 'emirate'-based Iran and what would happen to a large population of Shias and secularists (including the Baluch) already settled in Sunni areas such as Sistan and Baluchistan. More importantly, what relationships would Islamic Sunni "emirates" develop with each other if established in the middle of what they call an 'infidel' state? What would be the role of a state they consider to be "infidel"? How could these "dar al-Islam" islands regulate their relationship with an imagined Sunni Ummah?

While it is apparent that some secular ethnic nationalists support Jondollah by focusing on the ethnic side of the organization's objectives, the religious militant groups have focused on the religious-Islamic dimensions of those objectives. Even so, however, the Baluch secular ethnic nationalists have hardly adopted an overtly critical approach towards Jondollah. Somewhat ironically, it has been the religious leaders who have been the ones to mount the strongest opposition to Jondollah to date. Both moderate and hardliner clerics have boldly criticised Jondollah for its "distortion" of Islamic ideas and its appeal to nationalism, homeland, and ethnicity, etc. In the following section, debates on ethnic identity and homeland among the religious groups will be explained in more detail.

▌ Internal criticisms of Jondollah and ethnic identity

Jondollah has been criticised, from two Sunni religious points of view, by different figures. These critics can be broadly categorised within two different approaches. Firstly, a spectrum of traditionalists, quietists, and pragmatist moulvis (ulama) has presented a moderate approach. Secondly, global-oriented opponents have, comparatively, presented a more consistently anti-ethnic and anti-nationalist approach.

Firstly, the moderate critics are mainly concerned with maintaining the current balance of power in the area. So as to decrease the pressures imposed by the government and minimize the risk of inter-ethnic and intra-ethnic tensions, they distance themselves from the extremely violent actions of Jondollah. Most of these figures are Deobandi quietists. Many of them, deep down inside, may even share Jondollah's anti-Shia approach. But they do not agree with Jondollah's harsh tactics of indiscriminate killings and attacks against Shia religious institutions.

This spectrum of moulvis is represented by a moderate figure, Moulvi Abdolhamid Esmailzahi, who is the leader of a Grand Sunni mosque in Zahedan. He is supported by some other prominent traditional Deobandis from an older generation such as Moulvi Mohammad Yousuf Husainpoor and Moulvi Abdolrahman Chahbahari. Moulvi Abdolhamid has not only criticised Jondollah but has also supported the reformists in Iran and criticised conservative governments for their harsh policies and lack of flexibility regarding, or recognition of, the rights of the Baluch as Sunni and as an ethnic minority.[61]

The leadership of Jondollah, cautiously but clearly, rejected Moulvi Abdolhamid's criticisms of their actions.

Instead, they urged him to instead focus his attention on criticising the Islamic regime for their many "killings, executions[,] and destruction[s] of mosques".[62] In support of Jondollah, some nationalists such as Karim Baluch (an ethnic nationalist in Europe) have also criticised Moulvi Abdolhamid. In a Baluchi article, he even expressed admiration for a suicide attacker of Jondollah's, Hafiz Abdolkhaleq Mullazahi. While he regarded Shias as "fascists, frantic and mad",[63] he described this suicide bombing which targeted Shias and their place of worship as an attack on the "nest of outsider insects" in their "safest place".

The second approach seems to have an implicitly global Islamist tendency, although there is no explicit evidence to show their affiliation with the global jihadists. In the area, they are less influential and less outspoken than those who hold to the first approach. While they criticise "Safavid" Shiaism and the Islamic Republic of Iran, they are cautious regarding whether to consider the Shia as infidels; and they do not agree with violent attacks on Shia civilians. To some extent, this approach borrows ideas from Yousuf Qarzawi, a prominent scholar close to the Muslim Brotherhood and Turkish Islamists. But at the same time, supporters of this approach find themselves, to some extent, in alliance with the traditionalist 'local-first' approach. And in the same way, they blame Jondollah's activities and ideas as unacceptable, unwise, nationalistic, or even un-Islamic.

They believe that Jondollah's violent activities have led to more repression and pressure on Sunnis rather than less. They also argue that Jondollah lacks a true Islamic identity, and that for this reason, it has misinterpreted and twisted Islamic ideas regarding the nature of nationalism. For example, Abdolwahed Rigi (a pseudonym), who admires radical global jihadists, from a religious perspective, wrote that in Baluchistan:

Unfortunately, "Jondollah" as a movement lacked a recognisable identity. Jondollah's various announcements have been very simplistic and lacked [...] adequate preparation. This small group sometimes regards itself as religious for defending the rights of the Sunnis in Iran and sometimes regards itself as an ethnic group for defending the rights of the Baluch people. It may be an ethnic religious group which defends the rights of the Sunnis in Baluchistan. Of course, the spirit of tribalism, as being [from the] Rigi [tribe], also exists in this approach.

In form, Jondollah's announcements appear similar to those of global jihad movements. In substance, however, Jondollah's militant operations have proven that they lack any kind of Islamic identity. It also became clear that this group only uses religion as a propaganda tool to recruit more members. Possibly the teenagers associated with this group [...] [may] have good religious intentions, but [...] [they lack necessary] knowledge of Sharia and [the teachings of Islam]. Jondollah [is] absolutely [not backed by the teachings of any prominent] religious authorities [or by] the Ulama [as a whole].[64]

In support of Abdolwahed Rigi's comments, Moinul Din Gamshadzahi" (a pseudonym) argues that:

When tension and oppression dominate life in Baluchistan, when the Baluch are under tyrannical pressure and suffer from discrimination and humiliation, and when the people are in the mood for uprising and disobedience, if Jondollah changes their Arabic [n]ame to "Soldiers of the

Baluch", undoubtedly they will gradually become a strong movement. In that case, at least, their "Persian Killing" mission can be justified by *jahelya* (ignorance) of nationalism.[65]

Both writers and critics (Ghamshadzahi and Rigi) of Jondullah use some familiar concepts employed by Islamists to reject nationalism as a parochial ethnic issue and as a form of Jahiliyya. They defend jihad as a universal struggle for the achievement of grand objectives which transcend petty local issues and small squabbles over ethnic divides.[66] They have also supported Moulvi Abdolhamid in criticising Jondollah for using unnecessary violence against ordinary people and places of worship. As the statements show, these global jihadist supporters are particularly ideologically inconsistent.

In reply to Abdolwahed Rigi, Abdolrauf Rigi – arguing in favour of violence – quoted the Quranic verse stating that "when you face those who are blasphemous, behead them to shed their blood". This was further explained in support of Abdolrauf Rigi by a commentator called Mowahhed (pseudonym). Mowahhed believes that a critique should be "scientific" and regards Gamshadzahi's and Abdolwahed Rigi's ideas as being emotional, and explains that "neither [the] beheading of soldiers nor the beheading of those who [are fulfilling their nationally-compulsory] 2 years of service, is wrong". Then he asks, was not it true that "under the command of the Prophet, the men of Bani Qariza were beheaded like sheep?" Then he continues that on the basis of sharia, this critique is scientific and that it is legitimate to behead infidels, including Shias—but that for the sake of expediency, taking into account the prevailing political considerations and conditions, it may be better to kill the Shia leadership rather than to kill ordinary people.[67]

This logic was strongly reflected in the songs that Jondollah used to incite violence and hatred among its supporters. For example, in the video clip 11 in Arabic with Persian footnotes, it is said 'We are the same people who built their forts with the skulls next to the plunder brought from the land of the oppressors. This is the only word [message], the word [message] of the sword until the wicked convert into truthful [people].'[68]

In response to respond to these critics, Moulvi Abdolrauf Rigi has presented the ideology and objectives of Jondollah in this way:

> The Jondollah movement [lies] between two extremist approaches. Secular extremists who write every day against Jondollah [ask] why the members of Jondollah are Muslim and [why they are] supporting religion. Another extremist approach includes some religious figures who consider Jondollah's position on the issues of [the] oppressed Baluch and violation of the rights of the Baluch as polytheism, and they issue fatwas in this regard.[69]

In this sense, Jondollah is ideologically defined as something between secular nationalism and jihadism. Killing Shias and preaching sectarian activities was not seen as extremism by Abdolrauf Rigi. At the same time, Rigi implicitly admired global jihadists without mentioning any particular groups or figures. So is there any clear connection between Jondollah and al-Qaeda networks?

▓ A connection between Jondollah and al-Qaeda?

As discussed in earlier parts of this section, a connection between the radical groups and al-Qaeda is not very clear; and none of them have openly expressed their allegiance to Bin Laden or al-Zawahiri. By contrast, connections with the Taliban and with radical Deobandi sectarian groups such as

Sepah-e Sahabeh and Lashkar-e Jhangvi are very likely. While the United States, European Union, and UN Security Council regarded Jondollah as a terrorist group, Jondollah, at least prior to the capture of Abdolmalek Rigi by the Iranian security forces, never openly criticised the US and other western countries. Some analysts even argued that the US security forces had actively supported Jondollah.[70] When Rigi was captured, Jondollah accused the American, British, and Israeli intelligence services of cooperating with Iranian security forces in capturing Abdolmalek Rigi.[71] Jondollah had sent open letters to the UN and to Saudi Arabia's king explaining the condition of Sunnis in Iran, so as to get support. Sometimes in sympathy with (the mainly Shia) Mujahedin-e Khalq-e Iran, they condemned the IRI for attacking Ashraf Camp in Iraq.[72] In other cases, they harshly attacked IRI's policy of "criminal interference" in Bahrain and asked the world's other Muslim countries, Arab ones in particular, to support Jondollah.[73] Jondollah also asked suicide attackers from Arab and other Muslim countries to join Jondollah. Jondollah also remained silent about the US and NATO's invasion of Afghanistan and Iraq. In spite of a lack of evidence to suggest that Jondollah was ever criticised by either the Taliban or al-Qaeda, the evidence provided above raises this question: How could the Taliban or al-Qaeda trust Jondollah?

Jondollah had frequently made use of Palestinian suicide attacks on ordinary Israeli citizens as examples to justify their own attacks on ordinary Shia mourners as so-called "occupiers" of Islamic Baluchistan. However, the leaks from CIA as revealed by Mark Perry (2012)[74] seemed to indicate that the Israelis, under a 'false flag', had developed connections with JA.

Crisis in JA and emergence of Jaishe al-Adl

After the capture of Abdolmalek Rigi by Iranian security forces on 23 February 2010 followed by his execution on

20 June 2010, it did not take more than six months until JA came under crisis. The reasons were not just the brutal and widespread arrests or the imprisonment and executions of JA members and their relatives by the Iranian regime. Contributing reasons were also the sectarian and brutal actions carried out by JA against civilians, particularly against Shia Muslims. While Iranian security forces and the courts had little to no commitment to follow just procedures of arrest and trial, JA was committing atrocities and spreading hatred against civilian Shia Muslims and Sistanis (Zabolis). Such atrocities did not exactly contribute to their popularity or endear them in the eyes of a large section of the public.

Taking action to cleanse certain areas of "spies" had a disastrous effect on Jondollah, because popular support for Jondollah was understandably very small. On the basis of allegations (whether true or false) of collaboration with Iranian security forces or of speaking out against Jondollah, JA threatened many Baluch families and even kidnapped and killed some people. Their enforcement actions happened within the context of Jondollah not having much popular support, despite their former claims to such support. Rather, they generated widespread hostilities with influential conservative and moderate Baluchistan Moulvis, including Moulvi Abdolhamid Ismailzahi as well as with some influential tribal figures who had witnessed members of their own tribe being publicly humiliated or killed by Jondollah.

After their last suicide attack in December 2010, there were hardly any important operations conducted by JA. In an announcement released to mourn Moulvi Abdoljalil Qanbarzahi's death in March 2012, Naser Nosrati Nahooki had signed off on behalf of Mohammad Zaher (the leader), who was reported to be travelling.[75] In one of its last announcements, published in August 2012, JA had rejected affiliation with two other jihadist groups, *Jaish ul-Husain* (JH) and *Harkat-e Ansar-e Iran* (HAI). JA even warned these groups not to use statements, pictures, or even the name of Abdolmalek Rigi on their sites (Jondollah 2012). This shows the extent to which uncertainty and disintegration has developed inside these radical groups in south-eastern Iran.

Figure 4-4 Hamza Saravani, attacker in Chahbahar (Ansar Fighters Movement 2012)

Some radical jihadist groups have emerged from the crisis that started in late 2010. These groups have included Sepah-e Sahaba-e Iran (Army of the Companions of the Prophet) (SSI), Jaish ul-Husain (Army of Husain), Harkat-e Ansar-e Iran (Movement of the Supporters in Iran) (HAI), and most importantly, Jaish-ul-Adl (Army of Justice) (JAD).

All these groups consider Abdolmalek Rigi as a great leader and an inspirational character; and they all use his pictures, video clips, and statements on their sites. They are small groups; but by using weblogs and social media, they have rapidly spread jihadist sectarian ideas and attracted supporters. All of them have identified themselves as armed Sunni jihadists fighting against the Shias and the Iranian Shia regime.

Harkat-e Ansar-e Iran (HAI) accepted responsibility for a suicide attempt in Chahbahar Port in south-eastern Iran. This operation, which targeted either a militia base (as HAI reported) or a mosque (as an Iranian news agency reported), happened in October 2012.[76] Whether this was a true suicide attack or not was unclear; but a 19-year-old man, called (by HAI) "Hamzae Saravani", during a clash with Iranian security forces, was killed while reportedly wearing an explosive vest. Following this attack, Yaser Maskotani introduced himself in an announcement as *Emir* of HAI, and referred to the attackers as followers of Abdolmalek Rigi.[77]

The leadership of Jondollah had rejected HAI simply as an "unknown" quantity and mere 'internet-based' group, with possible ties to foreign forces (perhaps they meant al-Qaeda or the Taliban); and kept silent about this operation. But the SSI sent a congratulatory message to HAI for this operation. HAI later merged with al-Forqan and formed Ansar al-Forqan.[78]

Among these post-Jondollah groups, *Sepah-e Saha-bah-e-Iran* (SSI) has been the oldest one. The formative SSI announced its founding, on 14 March 2011, through its "military branch".[79] The announcement was signed by a person called Commander Mohammad Baluch. SSI considers the group loyal to JA's ideas. Their name is very similar to *Sepah-e Sahabah-e Pakistan*, but they have not shown any affiliation with them. ISS has performed hardly any important operations in the area; but once, they claimed that they had been involved in the explosion of gas pipelines near Qom in central Iran. They have mainly focused on kidnapping and punishing Sunni Baluch who were labelled as traitors. For example, SSI has revealed in its September announcement that they have killed Nader Shahbakhsh, a local Sunni Baluch, on the basis of his alleged collaboration with Iranian intelligence agencies.[80] SSI has joined Jaish-e Adl (JAD).[81]

Jaish-e Adl (Jaish al-Adl) became the most popular group—a point which strengthened its claim of being the successor of JA.

Jaish-e Adl

Jaish-e Adl (Jaish al-Adl) (JAD), having absorbed the core commanders and many members of JA, has emerged as the strongest and most popular militant organisation after Jondollah. Salah-ul Din Farooqi was announced as JAD's leader, and Abdolrauf Rigi became its spokesperson. In reality, JAD was a restructured rebuild of Jondollah after the execution of Abdolmalek Rigi.

JAD has been very active, both in attacking security forces and (to some extent) intimidating Shia Zabolis along the Iranian-Pakistani border. JAD has not used suicide attacks; but it is not clear if they have abandoned this tactic due to strategic reasons or whether they lack volunteers willing to do so. To achieve their goals, as clearly illustrated on their websites, they have used children in training camps for military purposes.[82]

Jaishe Adl Adalat news

Figure 4-5 Military training of childern by Jaish al-Adl

Among the activities which have been ascribed to JAD was the assassination of a Sunni cleric, Moulvi Mostafa Jangizahi, in January 2012.[83] Jangizahi was a cleric who had criticised JA and was accused of having close ties with the Iranian security forces. He had previously been threatened by JA and had once even managed to escape from an attack targeting his house. Following this terrifying experience, two local Baluch clerics, Moulvi Fateh Mohammad Naqshbandi and his son Moulvi Abdolghaffar Naqshbandi, were arrested by Iranian security forces.[84] This arrest led to a protest in Rask, a town inside Iran, quite close to the Iranian-Pakistani border.

Since then, JAD has claimed involvement in many attacks on security posts and many killings of security forces within

Sistan and Baluchistan, especially along the Iranian-Pakistani border of Iran-Pakistan. Kidnapping, hostage taking, and punishment of opponents have all been frequently reported by *Jaish-e Adl*. Some of these attacks were considered as revenge attacks for the involvement of Iran in Syra. One such example is when Jaish-e Adl took 5 members of the Iranian border corps hostage in February 2014. JAD announced that the hostages would be freed if 50 members of Jaish-e Adl, 300 Sunni prisoners in Iran and Syria, and 50 Sunni women prisoners in Syria (who were presumed to be members of RGC) were released.[85] JAD later released four of them but announced that they had executed one of them.

JAD, as compared with its predecessor Jondollah, in general, has adopted a more moderate and quite softer approach towards Shias, and to some extent has moved further towards Baluch ethnic nationalism. However, JAD has threatened non-Baluch such as Zabolis (Shia residents of Sistan) to leave the Baluch/Sunni-dominated area or else otherwise to wait for the consequences. It is believed that the killing of several Zaboli teachers is related to JAD; however, they have not clearly accepted any responsibility for this event.[86] They have also adopted a softer approach towards moderate Sunni clerics.

Jaish-e Adl split into two factions, possibly in line with the ethnic-religious gaps which had already existed in Jondollah. A small faction, under the leadership of Moulvi Abdulrauf Rigi, emerged as a separate organisation calling itself *Jaish-e al Nassr*. It announced itself as being the true follower of Abdolmalek Rigi and Jondollah. Disputes between *Jaish al-Adl* and *Jaish al-Nasr* erupted into threats and intimidation, and finally led to the mysterious killing of Abdulrauf Rigi in Quetta in August 2014.[87]

4.4 Conclusion and consequences

Both politically and ideologically, the Islamic Republic of Iran has failed to pursue a clearly inclusive hegemonic policy of including Sunnis in its Shia-based alliance led by *Velayat-e Faqih*. Alienation of the Baluch Sunnis from the Iranian political system has been increasing since the Islamic revolution occurred in 1979. This has considerably weakened moral support for the Iranian Islamic Shia regime among Sunnis in Sistan and Baluchistan. Consequently, the regime heavily used coercion as an important source of control of the Sunni Baluch. While the government tended to further rely on local Shias (particularly some Sistani groups), polarisation of the communities along religious and ethnic lines widened the divide further. Entangled as it is with severe competition over the gaining of resources (particularly economic ones) and job opportunities, the conflicts between Sunnis and Shias and/or Baluch and Fars/Zabolis escalated to alarming levels.

The IRI's harsh policies created a fertile ground for the development of stronger links between many Sunni Baluch and Sunni fundamentalists in Pakistan, Afghanistan, and Arabic countries. This boosted sympathy with the global jihadists. This was also an ideal opportunity for the regional and international jihadists to spread their influence across borders and include Iranian Sunnis along the south-eastern border.

It was in this context that radical religious groups emerged in Iranian Baluchistan. By perpetrating devastating attacks on Iranian security forces and also by launching indiscriminative suicide attacks causing colossal damages in south-eastern Iran, Jondollah captured the attention of the international media more than any of the other groups in Iranian Baluchistan. Ideologically Jondollah was mainly (but not only) inspired by radical anti-Shia Deobandis in Pakistan. But at the same time, to a certain extent, Jondollah made an appeal to the Baluch as an ethnic group . This shaped Jondollah's politics as a hybrid approach with an ethno-religious nature.

Whatever the nature of the incentives and the sources of inspiration behind Jondollah's violent attacks, the consequences for community relations, particularly between the Baluch and Sistanis, have been devastating. However, the Sistani Shia hard-liners, with strong support from Tehran, caused further divisions and hatred. On many occasions, this situation brought the already fragile relations among local communities to a breaking point.

After the death of Abdolmalek Rigi, Jondollah fragmented to some extent, but they easily reorganised themselves under different names. The main group appeared as Jaish-e Adl and has been active in organising attacks against Iranian security forces along the border. Jaish-e Adl has adopted a relatively more developed ethnic approach than that of its predecessor, Jondollah; but it still acts as a jihadist group with a religious and political agenda.

With the escalation of violence, instability, and sense of insecurity, the expansion of activities is very unlikely to remain purely confined to militant Islamic forces alone. Taking into account the strong drug-taking and Kalashnikov-toting culture in this area, insecurity can easily extend in other directions and can strengthen connections with drug runners and arms mafias. It means that political and religious tensions are more likely to politicise and 'sanctify' all criminal activities in the area further, as similar to the result of analogous tensions within Afghanistan and Somalia.

However, local conditions in Baluchistan do not develop in isolation. So the continuity and severity of the conflicts are very much contingent on the changing circumstances relative to the relationship between Iran and the West. This is particularly true of the United States on the one hand and, on the other, relationships with regionally-located countries such as Pakistan, Afghanistan, and Syria as well as Gulf countries such as Iraq and, more importantly, Saudi Arabia.

Currently, apart from moderate religious authorities, there is simply no other credible alternative secularly political force. Not only are the nationalists weak and fragmented, but they have also further gravitated towards splintering into narrowly-defined ethnic factions. Ethnic nationalists are emotionally too fragile to resist against religious "fundamentalists", particularly if they are seen as being ethnically Baluch. Therefore, they lack a clear set of guidelines for building a credible alternative solution which is flexible enough to withstand radical, sectarian and "fundamentalist" groups by building a comparatively wider civic alliance. Given current conditions, where polarisation between Shias and Sunnis has already ratcheted up the tensions between the two communities, the area is at risk of even further escalation and more serious calamity. ISIS and al-Qaeda affiliates are searching for just this sort of insecurity, chaos, and societal polarisation—viewing the fault line of religious beliefs as fertile ground in which to plant roots and extend their networks. As was argued earlier, there is much sympathy for them both among the current radical ethnic-religious groups and among a sizeable section of the Sunni population.

References

Abdolmalek Rigi edam shod" [Abdolmalek Rigi was executed]. *BBC Persian.* 20 June 2010. 12 June 2011. <http://www.bbc.co.uk/persian/iran/2010/06/100619_u03-rigi-execution.shtml>.

"Abdul Basit Balochi (Mahmoud Kareem), alias Ramzi Ahmed Yousef". *Washington Post.* 12 Sept. 2007. 31 Dec. 2010 <http://www.washingtonpost.com/wp-dyn/content/article/2007/09/12/AR2007091201375.html>.

Ahuran News. Blog post 554. *Ahuran News* [blog]. Sept. 2010. 24 Jan. 2011. Formerly available at <http://ahoran2.blogspot.com/2010/09/blog-post_554.htm>.

Armian, Mohammad. "*Takhrib-e Gornag*" [Destruction of Gornag]. [Place of publication and publisher are unknown], 2000. 113.

Azane Mujahid. "Zendagani shahid Musa damani" [Life of martyr Musa Damani]. *Azane Mujahid* 16.4 1989 (1367 *hs*): 20-21.

Baluch, Karim. "Baluch-e hoon ham sohrent moulvi sahib!" [Baluch blood also runs red, sir!]. *Taftanna* [blog]. 9 Khordad 1388 *hs* [May 2009]. 23 Aug. 2011 <http://taftanna.blogspot.com/2009/05/blog-post_7730.html>.

"Bazdasht-e yek Irani be Zann-e talash baray-e hamleh-e entehari dar Afghanistan" [Arrest of an Iranian on Suspicion of (Involvement in a) Suicide attack in Afghanistan]. 15 June 2011. *BBC Persian.* 28 June 2011 <http://www.bbc.co.uk/persian/afghanistan/2011/06/110615_k01_iranian_arrest.shtml>.

Best, Shaun. "Liquid Terrorism: Altruistic Fundamentalism in the Context of Liquid Modernity". *Sociology* 44.4 (2010): 678-694.

Charles River Editors. *The Islamic State of Iraq and Syria:*

The History of ISIS/ISIL. Marson Gate: CreateSpace, 2014.

Cockburn, Patrick. *The Rise of Islamic State: ISIS and the New Sunni Revolution*. London: Verso, 2014.

Delawar, Baluch. "Khoon-e shahidan enqelab miafrinad" [The blood of martyrs generates revolution]. *Taftan News Agency* [blog]. 24 May 2010. 21 Sept. 2011 <http://taptan313.blogspot.com/2010/05/blog-post_6853.html>.

—. "Yadi az alem shahid, mobarez-e enqelabi Hafez Salahuldin-e syedi sarbazi" [In memory of revolutionary martyr Hafez Salahuldin-e Syedi Sarbazi]. Jan. 2010. روالد [Brave] [blog]. 21 Sept. 2011 <http://delaavar33.blogspot.com>.

Doostdar-e shohadai Jondollah [Jondollah's lovers of the martyrs]. دوستدار شهدای جندالله ایران [blog]. 2011-2012. 18 Sept. 2011; 10 Jan. 2013 <http://www.shohada111.blogspot.com>.

Doshoki, Abdolsattar. "Haqayeq-e zaendagi-e Abdolmalek Rigi az souod ta soqut" [The Facts of Abdolmalek-e Rigi's Life from Rise to Fall]. *Sardamdar*. 23 June 2010. 20 Feb. 2011 <http://www.sardamdar.com/2010/06/blog-post_28.html>.

Esmailzahi, Abdolhamid. "[Moulana Abdolhamid:] Hades-e tororisti-e pishin ra beshedat mahkoom mikonim" [Moulana Abdolhamid: We strongly condemn the terrorist incident in Pishin]. *Sunni News*. 2010. 23 Nov. 2011. Formerly available at <http://old.Sunni-news.net/?p=8321>.

"'Eteraz-e bipasokh" be jolougiri az eqameh nemaz-e Eid-e Fetr-e ahl-e sonnat dar Tehran' [Unanswered protest regarding the stoppage (cancellation) of the Eid Fetr prayer in Tehran]. *BBC Persian*. 14 Sept. 2010. 10 Sept. 2015 <http://www.bbc.co.uk/persian/iran/2010/09/100914_l38_iran_moulaviabdullhamid_protest.shtml>.

"Eteraz-e Moulvi Abdolhamid-e be jolougiry az bargozari nemaz-e eid ahl-e sonnat" [Objection of Moulvi Abdol-

hamid Regarding the Cancellation of Sunni Eid prayers].
BBC. 30 Aug. 2011. 12 Apr. 2016 <http //www.bbc.co.uk/
persian/iran/2011/08/110830_l39_moulavi-abdulhamid_
fitr-prayers.shtml>.

Farooqi, Asif. "Profile: Lashkar-e-Jhangvi". *BBC World Service.* 11 Jan. 2013. 15 Jan. 2016 <http://www.bbc.co.uk/
news/world-asia-20982987>.

Gamshadzahi, Moinuldin. "Jondollah namidanad chetour
yakh mikhorand" [Jondollah does not know how to 'eat
ice']. *Sunni.rr.nu.* 21 Dec. 2010. 15 Jan. 2011. Formerly
available at <http://Sunni.rr.nu/fa/articles.aspx?select-
ed_article_no=12856>.

Gerges, Fawz A. *The Far Enemy: Why Jihad Went Global?*
Cambridge: Cambridge UP, 2005.

—. "Islamic State: Can its savagery be explained?" *BBC World
Service.* 9 Sept. 2014. 5 Dec. 2015 <http://www.bbc.co.uk/
news/world-middle-east-29123528>.

GlobalSecurity.org. "Khalid Sheikh Mohammed". *GlobalSe-
curity.org.* 2011. 10 May 2012 <http://www.globalsecurity.
org/military/world/para/ksm.htm>.

Google Images. JAD weblog images of children used in JAD
camps. Search <https://images.google.com> for "جیش عدل
.و آموزش نظامی بچه ها".

Hall, Stuart. "The Question of Cultural Identity". Ed. Stuart
Hall and Paul de Gay. *Modernity and Its Future.* Cambridge: Polity Press, 1992.

Harkat-e Ansar-e Iran (Ansar Fighters Movement). "Elamyeh
Jadid Harkat Ansar-e Iran mabni bar amalyat-e estoon 1
Chahbahar" [New Announcement of Harkat-e Ansar-e
Iran about Thunder-1 Operations in Chahbahar]. *Harkat
e Ansar (Iran)* [blog]. 14 Oct. 2012. 14 Oct. 2012 <http://
ansariran.blogspot.co.uk/2012/10/1.html>.

—. Shaheed Hamza [photograph]. *Harkat e Ansar (Iran)*

[blog]. 28 Mehr 1391 *hs* [19 Oct. 2012]. Nov. 2012 <http://ansariran.blogspot.co.uk/2012/10/blog-post_561.html>.

—. "Beyanyeh ea'lan-e mojudyat-e Harkat-e Ansar-e Iran" [Statement announcing the foundation of the Ansar movement in Iran]. *Harkat e Ansar (Iran)* [blog]. June 2012. 2 Oct. 2012 <http://ansariran.blogspot.co.uk/2012/06/blog-post.html>.

Harrison, S. Selig. *In Afghanistan's Shadow: Baluch Nationalism and Soviet Temptations*. New York: Carnegie Endowment for International Peace, 1981.

Haven, Paul. "Pakistan ambush led to a wide terror sweep which turned up suspects and key intelligence". *Associated Press* (cit. in *Boston Globe*). 7 Aug. 2004. 12 Apr. 2016 < http://archive.boston.com/news/nation/articles/2004/08/07/pakistan_ambush_led_to_wide_terror_sweep_turned_up_suspects_and_key_intelligence>.

Hegghammer, Thomas. "Jihadi-Salafi or revolutionaries? On religion and politics in the study of militant Islamism". Ed. Roel Meijer. *Global Salafism; Islam's new religious movement*. London: Hurst 2009, 244-266.

Hersh, M. Seymour. "Preparing the Battlefield: The Bush administration steps up its secret moves against Iran". *The New Yorker*. 7 July 2008. 12 Apr. 2016 <http://www.newyorker.com/magazine/2008/07/07/preparing-the-battlefield>.

Hezb-ul Forqan. Ettelaeih ettehad-e mujahedin-e hezb-e al-Forqan wa harkat al-Ansar" [Announcement of alliance between Hizb al-Forqan mujahidin and Harkat al-Ansar]. *Hezbul Furqan* [blog]. 11 Dey 1392 *hs* [1 Jan. 2014]. 12 Dec. 2015 <http://hezbulfurqan.blogspot.co.uk/2014/01/blog-post.html>.

International Crisis Group. "Pakistan: The militant jihadi

challenge". *Asia Report* 164. 13 Mar. 2009. 12 Jan. 12 <http://www.crisisgroup.org/~/media/Files/asia/south-asia/pakistan/164_pakistan___the_militant_jihadi_challenge.pdf>.

—. "Unfulfilled Promises: Pakistan's Failure to Tackle Extremism". *Asia Report* 73. 16 Jan. 2004. 12 Apr. 2016 <http://www.crisisgroup.org/en/regions/asia/south-asia/pakistan/073-unfulfilled-promises-pakistans-failure-to-tackle-extremism.aspx>.

Islamic Republic of Iran. Constitution. Approved 24 Oct. 1979. Enforced from 3 Dec. 1979. Amended 28 July 1989. *Iran Online.* Accessed 10 Oct. 2015 <http://www.iranonline.com/iran/iran-info/government/constitution-2.html>.

Jaish al-Adl. *Jaish ul-Adl* [Army of Justice] [blog]. 2014. 2 Oct. 2014 <http://jaishuladl.blogspot.co.uk>.

Jaishe al-Adl. "Elamye sazeman-e Jaish al-Adl; shahdat-e Abdulrauf Rigi ra be khanawadeh an amir-e bozrguar wa mellat-e baluchistan we ahle-sonnat-e aziz tasliat miguim" [Announcement of Jaishe al-Adl organisation: We express our condolences regarding the martyrdom of Abdulrau]. *Edaalat News* [blog]. 28 Aug. 2014. 15 Nov. 2014 <http://edaalatnews.blogspot.co.uk>.

"Jiashe al-Adl Khastar-e Azadi-ye 300 zendani sunni dar moqabel azadi 5 marzban-e zendani shod" [Jaish-e Adl wanted 300 Sunni prisoners to be released in a deal for releasing 5 prisoners of the Iranian Border Corps]. *Al-Arabiya.* 14 Feb. 2014. 18 Dec. 2015. Formerly available at <http://farsi.alarabiya.net/fa/iran/2014/02/14>.

Jaish al-Husain. "Beyanyeh-e Ealane mojodyat-e Jaish al-Husain (RA) dar Baluchistan" [Statement declaring the existence of Jaish al-Hussain (RA) in Baluchistan]. *Sunni News.* 12 July 2011. 2 Oct. 2012 <http://sunninews.org/

FA/articles.asp>.

Jamia Farooqia Karachi. *Farooqia*. 2010. 27 Dec. 2011
    <http://farooqia.com/jamia.php>.

Jondollah. 40 of Jondollah's video clips. *YouTube*. 10 June
    2013 <http://www.youtube.com/user/taftaanbaloch/vid-
    eos>.

—. "Abdolbaset Rigi" [video]. Linked from " شهدای جندالله ایران
    جان شهیدعبدالباسط)) " [Iranian Jundallah martyrs (Shaheed
    Abdolbaset Jan) Islam] [video]. *YouTube*. 31 Jul. 2010. 12
    Apr. 2016. Formerly available at <http://www.youtube.
    com/watch?v=WnBeVDpN4_s&feature=related>.

—. "Amliyate Fatholmobin 2" [Fatholmobin 2 Operations]
    [video]. *YouTube*. 16 Apr. 2009. 9 Oct. 2011. Formerly
    available at <http://www.youtube.com/user/taftaanba-
    loch#p/u/25/DJW_vjjW_Y8>.

—. "Amliyate Fatholmobin 11" [Fatholmobin 11 Operations]
    [video]. *YouTube*. 22 Apr. 2009. 9 Sept. 2011. Formerly
    available at <http://www.youtube.com/user/taftaanba-
    loch#p/u/16/gxs1KVRN3_w>.

—. "Etelaeiyeh-e jonbesh dar barh e'dam-e se jawan-e baluch
    wa bigonah" [Announcement: The Movement executed
    three young and innocent Baloch in Zahedan]. آنتي زابلي
    [Anti Zaboli] [blog]. 9 Khordad 1388 *hs* [May 2009]. 24
    Jan. 2011 <http://antizavabol.blogspot.com/2009/05/
    blog-post_5911.html>.

—. "Ashraf Camp Mujahedin-e Khalq-e Iran". *Baloch United
    Front*. n.d. 12 Apr. 2016 <http://www.balochunitedfront.
    org/articles/Farsi/jond_ashraf_1.htm>.

—. "Beyanyeh majma-e Olamay-e Jonbesh-e Jondollah dar
    Pasokh be Fatway-e Siasi Akhir dar Baluchistan" [The
    Annoucement of the Association of Jondollah Move-
    ment's Religious Authorities in response to the Recent
    Political Fatwas in Baluchistan]. *Junbish* [blog]. 3 June

2009. 11 Jan. 2010. Formerly available at <http://junbish.
blogspot.com/2009/06/blog-post_3149.html>.

—. "Beyanyeh majma-e Olamay-e Jonbesh-e moqavemat dar
Pasokh kasani ke jihad ra enkar mikonand" [The An-
nouncement of the Association of Jodullah Movement'
Religious Authorities in Response to the People who
Reject Jihad]. *Rigi News Agency* [blog]. 7 July 2010. 16
Sept. 2010 <http://riginews.blogspot.com/2010/07/blog-
post_2872.html>.

—. "Etelayeh jonbesh-e moqavemat jondollah baray shahadat-e sarvar-e mojahedan va rahbar-e enqelabi Amir
Abdolmalek" [Press Release of the Resistance Movement
of Jondollah regarding the Leader of the Mujahidin and
Leader of the Revolution, Abdolmalek]. 20 June 2010. *De-
zak News Agency* [blog]. 8 Oct. 2011 <http://dezaknews4.
blogspot.com/2010/06/blog-post_20.html>.

—. "Etellaieh jadid-e jonbesh: Amaliat-e esteshhadi-e Zahedan" [New Press Coverage of the Movement on Suicide
operations in Zahedan]. 29 May 2009. *Taftanna* [blog]. 25
Aug. 2011 <http://taftanna.blogspot.com/2009/05/blog-
post_2945.html>.

—. "Ettelaei jadid dar maured-e eterafat-e dicte-ei-e jawanan-e mazloom" [New Press Coverage on the Pressured
(Forced) Confession(s) of the Oppressed Young Peo-
ple]. *Junbish* [blog]. 3 June 2009. 12 July 2010. Formerly
available at <http://junbish.blogspot.com/2009/07/blog-
post_03.html>.

—. "Ettelaiye jonbeshe moqawemat khetab be jawanan-e Baluchistan" [Jondollah's announcement to the young people
in Baluchistan]. *Baloch News Agency* [blog]. 30 May 2009.
21 Sept. 2011 <http://www.balochna.blogspot.com>. Site
has moved to <http://www.bbalochna.blogspot.com>.

—. "Ettelaiyeh Jadid-e jonbesh moqavemat nasbe sokhangui jadid" [New spokesman (Abdul Rauf Rigi) appointed for the Jundallah Resistance Movement]. 28 Tir 1389 *hs* [19 July 2010]. *Taftan News Agency* [blog]. 29 July 2010 <http://taptan313.blogspot.com/2010/07/blog-post_5482.html>.

—. "Ettelaye Jonbesh-e Moqawemat dar moured-e eterazat-e khiabani-e mardom" [A Press Release of the Resistance Movement regarding (the) People's Street Protests]. *Taptaan* [blog]. 16 June 2009. 10 Jan. 2010 <http://taptaan. blogspot.com/2009/06/blog-post_4563.html>.

—. "Ettelaye Jonbesh Moqavemat Mardomi Iran (Jondollah)" [(Iranian Jondollah Movement)]. *shahinb.wordpress. com* [blog]. 18 Dec. 2010. 17 Oct. 2011 <http://shaheinb. wordpress.com /2010/12/page/7>.

—. "Ettelayeh Jadid-e Jonbeshe-e Moqavemat-e Jondollah, Iran be dkhalathaye mojremaneh khod dar keshvarhay-e Arabi payan dahad" [A new announcement by the Resistance Movement of Jondollah: Iran should stop its criminal interference with the internal affairs of Arab countries]. جنبش مقاومت مردمی ایران جنداله [People's Resistance Movement of Iranian Jundullah] [blog]. 2 Apr. 2011. 25 Aug. 2011 <http://jonbesh-mardom.blogspot.com>.

—. "Film-e amalyatte- esteshhadi zahedan 2" [Film of the sucide operation Zahedan-2] [video]. 10 Oct. 2009. *YouTube.* 7 Oct. 2011 <http://www.youtube.com/user/tafta-anbaloch#p/u/10/-iBZpPQGG3M>.

—. "Jondollah (Nanu Jund Allah)" [We are Jondollah (song] [Mohammadi Saravani-related video]. *YouTube.* n.d. 12 Aug. 2013. Formerly available at <http://www.youtube. com/watch?v=ZzryYv9tb5U>.

—. "Namehei sar goshadeh az rahbar-e Jonbesh-e Moqavemat-e Jondollah abdolmalek-e Baluch be rahbare nezam-e valayat-e faqih-e Iran Ali Khamaneei" [An open letter from the leader of Jondollah Resistance Movement to Iran's supreme leader Ali Khamenei]. *Sunni News.* 17 Dec. 2009. 2 Oct. 2011 <http://sunni-news.org/ar/articles.aspx?selected_article_no=1917>.

—. "Pasokh be bianat Moulvi Abdolhamid emam joma' ahlesunnat-e zahedan" [A reply to Moulvi Abdolhamid, Friday prayer leader of the Sunnis in Zahedan]. *Baloch News Agency* [blog]. 29 May 2009. 20 July 2009 <http:// balochna.blogspot.com/2009/05/blog-post_4389.html>.

—. "Payame rahbar-e Jonbesh moqavemat dar pasokh- be sazeman-e melal wa shoray-e amnyat wa groohay-e hoquq-e bashari" [Response of the Leader of the the Resistance Movement to the UN, the Security Council, and Human Rights groups]. *Ostomaan.* 11 Nov. 2009. 28 Aug. 2011 <http://www.ostomaan.org/articles/84/4426>.

Keddie, R. Nikki. *Modern Iran: Roots and Results of Revolution.* New Haven: Yale UP, 2006. 332.

Khomeini, Ruhollah. *KaLam-I Imam: Melli Grayee (daftr-I Yazdahom: Az Byanat va Ealamiyeh haye Imam Khomeini az sale 1341 ta 1361)* [Imam's speeches: Nationalism (Eleventh section: Speeches and announcements from 1341-1361 *hs* (ca. 1962-1982))]. Tehran: Entesharat-I Amir Kabir, 1362h [ca. 1983].

—. *Vilayat-i faqih: Hukumat-I Islami* [Vilayat-e Faqih: Islamic Government]. Tehran: Entesharat-e Amir Kabir, 1978.

Kohlmann, Evan. 'NEFA Foundation: New Zawahiri audio – "From Kabul to Mogadishu"'. *Counterterrorism.* 22 Feb. 2009. 10 Oct. 2011. Formerly available at <http://counterterrorismblog.org/2009/02/nefa_foundation_new_zawahiri_a.php>.

"Koshtar diplomathay-e Irani in Mazar-e Sharif az zabanetanha shahed" [The Massacre of Iranian Diplomats in Mazar-e Sharif, (as) told by the only surviving witness].

Quds Online. 18 Mordad 1390 *hs* [9 Aug. 2011]. 14 Dec. 2014 <http://www.qudsonline.ir/detail/News/4638>.

Madani, Ahmed Hasan (Maulana). *Composite Nationalism and Islam.* 1938. Trans. Mohammad Anwar Hussain and Hasan Imam. Manohar Publishers, 2005.

Mojahed, "Jondollah military commander conveys a message of condolence on Qanbarzahi's martyrdom." *M0jahed-- The most recent news of the Mujahideen of Islam* 29 Mar. 2012, 10 Oct. 2012 <http://m0jahed.wordpress.com>.

"Moqam-e qazaye Iran: madarek-e ertebat-e Jondollah va Pakistan be Pakistan tahvil shod" [An Iranian Judicial Authority: The Evidence regarding Jondollah and Pakistan was submitted to Pakistan]. 9 Dec. 2009. *BBC Persian.* 23 Feb. 2010. <http://www.bbc.co.uk/persian/iran/2009/12/091216_he_Baluchestan_pakistan.shtml>.

Mortimer, Edward. Introduction. *People, Nation, and State: The Meaning of Ethnicity and Nationalism.* Ed. Edward Mortimer and Robert Fine. London: I.B. Tauris Publishers, 1999. vii-xvii.

"Moulwi Abdoljalil-e QanbarZahi rahbar-e sazeman-e hezb-e al-Forqan koshteh shod" [Moulwi Abdoljalil Qanbarzahi, the leader of the al-Forqan Organisation, has been killed]. *Sunni News.* 22 Mar. 2012. 10 Oct. 2014 <http://sunni-news.net/fa/articles.aspx?selected_article_no=21517>.

"Na arami dar shahr-e Rask-e ostan-e Sistan wa Baluchistan" [Unrest in Rask City in Sistan and Baluchistan]. *BBC Persian.* 16 May 2012. 15 Dec. 2014 <http://www.bbc.co.uk/persian/iran/2012/05/120516_l39_rask_baluchestan_unrest.shtml>.

Naqavi, A[li]. M[uhammad]. *Islam and Natiionalism.* Trans. Alaedin. Pazargadi. Tehran: Organization of Islamic Culture and Religion, 1988.

Narui, Kamal. Interview. *Sunni.rr.nu.* 2010. 29 Dec. 2010. Formerly available at <http://Sunni.rr.nu/fa/articles.aspx-?selected_article_no=5101>.

—. "Sokhanguy-e jondollah pardeh az moameleh penha-ny-e dastigiri-e Rigi bardasht" [Jondollah's spokeperson revealed secret deals regarding the arrest of Rigi]. Mar. 2010. *Taftan 313* [blog]. 10 Jan. 2013 <http://taftan313. blogspot.co.uk/2010/03/blog-p>.

Nimrooz. Feb. 1944.

Noraiee, Hoshang (Ayub Husainbor). "Change and continuity: Power and religion in Iranian Baluchistan". *The Baloch and Others: Linguistic, Historical, and Socio-Political Perspectives on Pluralism in Baluchistan.* Ed. Carina Jahani, Agnes Korn, and P. Titus. Weisbaden, Germany: Reichert Verlag, 2008.

—. "Globalization and Islam: Modernity, Diversity and Identities". *Globalisation, Religion, and Development.* Ed. Farhang Morady and Sirier Ismail. Istanbul: IJOPEC Publication, 2011: 39-62.

—. "Jedal-e Bain-e Jaish-e Adl wa Jaish-e Nasr: jehad baray Khods, jehad baray mellat, jehad baray-e qodrat" [Conflicts between Jaishe Adl and Jaishe Nasr: Jihad for God, Jihad for the Nation, Jihad for Power?]. *Taptan.* 16 Aug. 2014. 20 Sept. 2014 <http://www.taptan.com/?p=129>.

—. "Khavaremyaneh wa kashmakesh bain-e Iran wa Arabestan-e Saudi" [The Middle East and Clashes between Iran and Saudi Arabia]. 2011. *Taptan.* 17 Nov. 2014 <www. taptan.com/?page_id=84>.

—. "Proseh-e Tadavom and Taghier dar Mazhab dar Baluchistan-e Iran dar Qarn-e Akhir: Az Sunnathay-e mohalli wa sufianeh ta Deobandism-e radical wa syasi" [The process of continuity and change in religion within Iranian Baluchistan during the last century: From local traditions…to radical political Deobandism]. *Taptan.* 2011. 10 Nov. 2014 <http://www.taptan.com/?page_id=82>.

—. "Review of Zaeef's Autobiograpy *My Life With the Taliban*". *Academia.edu.* 2014. 10 Nov. 2014 <http://www.academia.edu/8740651/A_review_of_Zaeefs_Autobiography_My_Life_With_Taliban>.

—. "Sunni Militants in Iran: Activities, Ideological Sources and Political Strategies". *International Research Journal of Social Science* 4.3 (Mar. 2015): 79-87 <http://www.isca.in/IJSS/Archive/v4/i3/14.ISCA-IRJSS-2014-331.pdf>.

—. "Torror-e moulvi Abdolrauf-e Rigi kare kist?" [Who has killed Moulvi Abdolrauf Rigi?] *Taptan.* 29 Aug. 2014. 10 Jan. 2016<http://www.taptan.com/?paged=2&lang=fa>.

"Pakistan Rigi ra azad kardeh bud" [Pakistan had Released Rigi]. 9 Nov. 2009. *BBC Persian.* 23 Feb. 2010 <http://www.bbc.co.uk/persian/iran/2009/11/091105_ba-iran-pakistan-rigi.shtml>.

'Pakistan seizes "al-Qaeda gang"'. *BBC World Service.* 13 June 2004. 10 July 2015 <http://news.bbc.co.uk/1/hi/world/south_asia/3803321.stm>.

PediaView. "Khalid Sheikh Mohammed". *PediaView.* 2011a. 13 May 2012 <https://pediaview.com/openpedia/Khalid_Sheikh_Mohammed>.

PediaView. "Ramzi Ahmed Yousef". *PediaView.* 2011b. 17 Sept. 2011 <http://pediaview.com/openpedia/Ramzi_Ahmed_Yousef>.

Perry, Mark. "False Flag". *Foreign Policy.* 13 Jan. 2012. 4 Sept. 2012 <http://foreignpolicy.com/2012/01/13/false-flag>.

Peters, Gretchen. *Seeds of Terror: How Drugs, Thugs, and Crime Are Reshaping the Afghan War.* New York: Macmillan, 2009.

Portal-e Sistan wa Baluchistan. "Simay-e Sistan wa Baluchistan" [Features of Sistan and Baluchistan Province].

Portal-e Sistan wa Baluchistan. n.d. 10 Jan. 2016 <http://www.sbportal.ir/fa/aboutostan>.

Rashid, Ahmed. *Taliban: The Power of Militant Islam in Afghanistan and Beyond*, 2nd ed. London: I.B. Tauris, 2010.

—. *Taliban: The story of the Afghan Warlords.* Basingstoke: Pan Books, 2001.

Rigi, Abdolrauf. "Eshkalat-e matlab-e aqay-e Doshoki" [Mistakes in Mr. Doshoki's Article]. *Taftan News Agency* [blog]. 7 Tir 1389 *hs* [28 June 2010]. 28 Aug. 2010 <http://taptan313.blogspot.com/2010/06/blog-post_7799.html>.

—. "Jawab-e Abdulrauf-e Rigi Uzu-e Majma'-e ulamay-e Jonbesh-e Moqavemat Jondollah wa sokhangvi Rasmi-e Jonbesh be Abdolwahed-e Rigi" [The response of Abdolrauf Rigi, member of the Association of Clerical Authorities of the Resistance Movement of Jondollah and official spokesperson of Jondollah, to Abdolwahed Rigi]. *Sunni News.* 18 Dec. 2010. 29 Dec. 2010. Formerly available at <http://sunni.rr.nu/fa/articles.aspx?selected_article_no=12815>.

Rigi, Abdolwahed. "Jundollah: hwyatt-e nashonakhteh" [Jundollah: unknown identity]. *Ostomaan.* 18 Dec. 2010. 2 Oct. 2012 <http://www.ostomaan.org/articles/A7/7754>.

Rigi, Bashirahmad. "Nagoftehayee az zendagi Abdolmalek-e Rigi" [Untold stories about Abdolmalek Rigi]. *Jame Jam Online.* 23 Khordad 1389 *hs* [13 June 2010]. 15 Sept. 2011 <http://www.jamejamonline.ir/newstext.aspx?newsnum=100883064833>..

Sadr, Mohammad. "Hamkary-e Iran wa Amerika alih-e Daesh momken ast" [Mohammad Sadr: Cooperation between Iran and the US regarding ISIS is possible]. 11 Aug. 2014 (20 Mordad 1393 *hs*). 13 Aug. 2014 <http://www.bbc.co.uk/persian/iran/2014/08/140811_l12_iran_isis_iran_us_cooperation_iraq.shtml>.

Safizadeh, Ebrahim. "Biography-e Shahid moulvi Abdoljalil-e Qanbarzahi" [Biography of the martyr Moulvi Abdol-jalil-e Qanbarzahi]. ""خاطرات مولوی ابراهیم صفی زاده"" [Memories of Moulvi Ebrahim Safizadeh] [blog]. April 2012. 2 Oct. 2012. Formerly available at <http://safizadah.blogspot.co.uk/2012/04/blog-post.html>.

Salahzahi, Kamalkhan. "ملا کمال" [Mullah Kamalkhan] [video]. *YouTube*. 23 Apr. 2009. 10 July 2011 <http://www.youtube.com/watch?v=1oeP7QKFoKo>.

—. "Mullah [KamalKhan Salahzahi]" [video]. *Taftan TV. YouTube*. 12 Nov. 2010. 7 Oct. 2011 <http://www.youtube.com/watch?v=7sdohVNzhmM>.

Sepah-e Sahabah-e-Iran. "فعالیت شاخه نظامی سپاه صحابه ایران واحد بلوچستان" [The military wing of SSP's activities in Balochistan]. *Sepah-e Sahaba* [blog]. 23 Esfand 1389 *hs* [14 Mar. 2011]. 2 Oct. 2012 <http://www.sepah-esahaba.blogspot.co.uk/2011/03/blog-post.html>.

—. "Yeki az Mozdooran-e rezim bewasil mojahedin koshteh shod" [One of the regime's mercenaries killed by Mujahideen]. *Sepah-e Sahaba* [blog]. 21 Sept. 2012. 2 Oct. 2012 <http://ssiran.wordpress.com/2012/09>.

—. "Ettehad wa hambastagy-e Sepah-e Sahbeh Iran with Sazeman-e Jaish al-Adl" [Alliance and Solidarity of Sepah-e Sahabeh Iran with Jaish al Adl Organisation]. *Sepahe Sahabae Iran* [blog]. 25 Farvardin 1394 *hs* [14 Apr. 2015]. 19 Dec. 2015 <http://www.ss-iran.blogspot.co.uk>.

"Sipah-e Sahaba Pakistan, Lashkar-e-Jhangvi, Bin Laden, & Ramzi Yousef". *South Asia Analysis*. 2002. 31 Dec. 2010. Formerly available at <http://www.southasiaanalysis.org/%5Cpapers5%5Cpaper484.html>.

Shaheed, Ahmed. "March 2016 report of the Special Rapporteur on the situation of human rights in the Islamic

Republic of Iran". United Nations: Human Rights Council. 10 Mar. 2016. 24 Mar. 2016 <http://shaheedoniran. org/english/dr-shaheeds-work/march-2016-report-of-the-special-rapporteur-on-the-situation-of-human-rights-in-the-islamic-republic-of-iran>.

Shaheed, Ahmed. "October 2011 report of the Special Rapporteur on the situation of human rights in the Islamic Republic of Iran". United Nations: General Assembly. 23 Sept. 2011. 24 Mar. 2016 <http://shaheedoniran.org/english/dr-shaheeds-work/latest-reports/report-of-the-special-rapporteur-to-the-un-general-assembly-dr-ahmed-shaheed-2011>.

"Tazahorat-e Karachi dar eatraz be eadam-e Abdolmalek-e Rigi" [Protests in Karachi over the Execution of Abdolmalek Rigi]. *BBC Persian.* 24 June 2010. 24 Aug. 2011 <http://www.bbc.co.uk/persian/iran/2010/06/100624_l03_rigi_karachi.shtml>.

"Torror-e emam Jomaeh Rask dar ostan-e sistan wa Baluchistan" [Terror of Friday prayers Imam of Rask in Sistan and Baluchistan]. *BBC Persian.* 21 Jan. 2012. 10 Dec. 2014 <http://www.bbc.co.uk/persian/iran/2012/01/120121_l31>.

"Vazarat-e Ettellat-e Iran: Abdolmalek-e Rigi dastgir shod" [Iranian Intelligence Ministry: Abolmalek Rigi Arrested]. *BBC Persian.* 23 Feb. 2010. 12 Sept. 2016 <http://www.bbc.co.uk/persian/iran/2010/02/100223_l03_rigi_arrest.shtml>.

Weiss, Michael and Hassan Hassan. *ISIS: Inside the Army of Terror.* New York: Regan Arts, 2015.

Younesi, Ali. "Doulat Natawanest be aqqalyathay-e qawmi wa mazhabi ostandari wa vazarat bedahad" [The Government offers Ministerial and Provincial Governorship to the Religious and Ethnic Minorities]. *BBC Persian.* 13 Azar 1392 *hs*) [4 Dec. 2013]. 12 Aug. 2014 <http://www. bbc.co.uk/persian/iran/2013/12/131204_l39_younesi_minorities_appointments.shtml>.

Zambelis, Chris. "Balochi Nationalists Intensify Violent Rebellion in Iran". *Terrorism Monitor* 7.3 (9 Feb. 2009). 21 Sept. 2011 <http://www.jamestown.org/programs/gta/single/?tx_ttnews[tt_news]=34479>.

Endnotes

1 Ali Younesi, "Doulat Natawanest be aqqalyathay-e qawmi wa mazhabi ostandari wa vazarat bedahad" [The Government offers Ministerial and Provincial Governorship to the Religious and Ethnic Minorities], *BBC Persian* 13 Azar 1392 *hs*) [4 Dec. 2013], 12 Aug. 2014 <http://www.bbc. co.uk/persian/iran/2013/12/131204_l39_younesi_minorities_appoint-ments.shtml>.

2 Portal-e Sistan wa Baluchistan, "Simay-e Sistan wa Baluchistan" [Features of Sistan and Baluchistan Province], *Portal-e Sistan wa Baluchistan* n.d., 10 Jan. 2016 <http://www.sbportal.ir/fa/aboutostan>.

3 See p. 259 of Thomas Hegghammer, "Jihadi-Salafi or revolutionaries? On religion and politics in the study of militant Islamism", ed. Roel Meijer, *Global Salafism; Islam's new religious movement* (London: Hurst 2009) 244-266.

4 Hoshang Noraiee, "Sunni Militants in Iran: Activities, Ideological Sources and Political Strategies", *International Research Journal of Social Science* 4.3 (Mar. 2015): 79-87 <http://www.isca.in/IJSS/Archive/v4/i3/14. ISCA-IRJSS-2014-331.pdf>.

5 See p. 113 of Patrick Cockburn, *The Rise of Islamic State: ISIS and the New Sunni Revolution* (London: Verso, 2014).

6 Cockburn 120-121.

7 Fawz A. Gerges, *The Far Enemy: Why Jihad Went Global?* (Cambridge: Cambridge UP, 2005). —. "Islamic State: Can its savagery be explained?" *BBC World Service* 9 Sept. 2014, 5 Dec. 2015 <http://www.bbc.co.uk/ news/world-middle-east-29123528>.

8 International Crisis Group, "Pakistan: The militant jihadi challenge", *Asia Report* 164 13 Mar. 2009, 12 Jan. 12 <http://www.crisisgroup.org/~/ media/Files/asia/south-asia/pakistan/164_pakistan___the_militant_ji-hadi_challenge.pdf>.

9 More recently, Afghani officials reported that they had arrested an Iranian suicide bomber from Zahedan. They have not identified the person as being a Baluch. However, the bomber is very likely to be a Sunni, possibly a Baluch Sunni. See "Bazdasht-e yek Irani be Zann-e talash baray-e hamleh-e entehari dar Afghanistan" [Arrest of an Iranian on Suspicion of (Involvement in a) Suicide attack in Afghanistan], *BBC Persian* 15 June 2011, 28 June 2011 <http://www.bbc.co.uk/persian/afghanistan/2011/06/110615_k01_iranian_arrest.shtml>.

10 See pp. 199-201 of Olivier Roy, "Has Islamism a future in Afghanistan?" *Fundamentalism Reborn? Afghanistan and the Taliban*, ed. William Maley (London: Hurst, 2001) 199-201.

11 Ahmed Rashid, *Taliban: The Power of Militant Islam in Afghanistan and Beyond*, 2nd ed. (London: I.B. Tauris, 2010).

12 Hoshang Noraiee, "Change and continuity: Power and religion in Iranian Baluchistan", *The Baloch and Others: Linguistic, Historical, and Socio-Political Perspectives on Pluralism in Baluchistan*, ed. Carina Jahani, Agnes Korn, and P. Titus (Weisbaden, Germany: Reichert Verlag, 2008).

13 Hoshang Noraiee, "Globalization and Islam: Modernity, Diversity and Identities", *Globalisation, Religion, and Development*, ed. Farhang Morady and Sirier Ismail (Istanbul: IJOPEC Publication, 2011) 39-62.

14 Hoshang Noraiee, "Proseh-e Tadavom and Taghier dar Mazhab dar Baluchistan-e Iran dar Qarn-e Akhir: Az Sunnathay-e mohalli wa sufianeh ta Deobandism-e radical wa syasi" [The process of continuity and change in religion within Iranian Baluchistan during the last century: From local traditions...to radical political Deobandism], *Taptan* 2011, 10 Nov. 2014 <http://www.taptan.com/?page_id=82>.

15 21 See p. 21 of Azane Mujahid, "Zendagani shahid Musa damani" [Life of martyr Musa Damani], *Azane Mujahid* 16.4 1989 (1367 *hs*): 20-21..

16 Kamal Narui, Interview, *Sunni.rr.nu* 2010, 29 Dec. 2010, formerly available at <http://Sunni.rr.nu/fa/articles.aspx?selected_article_no=5101>.

17 Evan Kohlmann, 'NEFA Foundation: New Zawahiri audio – "From Kabul to Mogadishu"', *Counterterrorism* 22 Feb. 2009, 10 Oct. 2011, formerly available at <http://counterterrorismblog.org/2009/02/nefa_foundation_new_zawahiri_a.php>.

18 Abdolwahed Rigi, "Jundollah: hwyatt-e nashonakhteh" [Jundollah: unknown identity], *Ostomaan* 18 Dec. 2010, 2 Oct. 2012 <http://www.ostomaan.org/articles/A7/7754>.

19 Asif Farooqi, "Profile: Lashkar-e-Jhangvi", *BBC World Service* 11 Jan. 2013, 15 Jan. 2016 <http://www.bbc.co.uk/news/world-asia-20982987>.

20 Abdolwahed Rigi (2010).

21 "Abdul Basit Balochi (Mahmoud Kareem), alias Ramzi Ahmed Yousef", *Washington Post* 12 Sept. 2007, 31 Dec. 2010 <http://www.washington-post.com/wp-dyn/content/article/2007/09/12/AR2007091201375.html>. See also PediaView, "Ramzi Ahmed Yousef", *PediaView* 2011b, 17 Sept. 2011 <http://pediaview.com/openpedia/Ramzi_Ahmed_Yousef>.

22 "Abdul Basit Baloch..." (2007). Also consulted: Sipah-e Sahaba Pakistan, Lashkar-e-Jhangvi, Bin Laden, & Ramzi Yousef", *South Asia Analysis* 2002, 31 Dec. 2010, formerly available at <http://www.southasiaanalysis.org/%5Cpapers5%5Cpaper484.html>. According to Raman, an Indian writer and retired official referenced in the article, there was a network of activists connected to Sepah-e Sahabah Pakistan and Ramzi Yousef in Lyari, in Karachi. Abdul Shakoor is mentioned as a person closely connected with Ramzi Yousef. He suggests that "Besides Shakoor, investigators believed that Abdul Wahab, owner of Junaid Bakery in the Lyari area of Karachi and the unit in charge of the Sipah Sahaba Pakistan in Chakiwarah, a neighbourhood of Karachi, was another close associate of Ramzi Yousef. Raids to arrest Abdul Wahab in Karachi remained unsuccessful". Raman also talks about 'Lashkar-e- Jhangvi's Naeem Bukhari as [being] the ring leader of the group that also included "three Yemeni-Baluch" ([the] father [being] Yemeni and [the] mother [being] Baloch) who took part in [journalist Daniel] Pearl's kidnapping, his murder[,] and [the] disposal of his body parts.'

23 PediaView (2011b).

24 PediaView, "Khalid Sheikh Mohammed", *PediaView* 2011a, 13 May 2012 <https://pediaview.com/openpedia/Khalid_Sheikh_Mohammed>.

25 GlobalSecurity.org, "Khalid Sheikh Mohammed", *GlobalSecurity.org* 2011, 10 May 2012 <http://www.globalsecurity.org/military/world/para/ksm.htm>.

26 'Pakistan seizes "al-Qaeda gang"', *BBC World Service* 13 June 2004, 10 July 2015 <http://news.bbc.co.uk/1/hi/world/south_asia/3803321.stm>.

27 According to some reports, Masrab Arochi, a nephew of Khalid Sheikh Mohammad's and also the cousin of Ramzi Yousef, was arrested by Pakistani security forces in Karachi in 2004 ('Pakistan seizes "al-Qaeda gang"' 2004).

Arochi was arrested with two others, named Atta-ul-Rahman and Shahzad Bajwa, each of whom had, in 2003, trained in an al-Qaeda training camp located in Shakai, Waziristan. Rahman and Bajawa were considered to be member of a group called Jondollah in Pakistan. This is approximately the same time as Abdolmalek Rigi established Iranian

Jondollah. See Paul Haven, "Pakistan ambush led to a wide terror sweep which turned up suspects and key intelligence", *Associated Press* (cit. in *Boston Globe*) 7 Aug. 2004, 12 Apr. 2016 < http://archive.boston.com/ news/nation/articles/2004/08/07/pakistan_ambush_led_to_wide_terror_sweep_turned_up_suspects_and_key_intelligence>. Moreover, it is believed that Abdolmalek Rigi was also in Waziristan. However, it should be noted that there is no hard evidence explicitly pointing towards any connection between Abdolmalek Rigi and the other three men or between the Iranian and Pakistani Jondollahs.

28 Ebrahim Safizadeh, "Biography-e Shahid moulvi Abdoljalil-e Qanbarzahi" [Biography of the martyr Moulvi Abdoljalil-e Qanbarzahi], "خاطرات مولوی ابراهیم صفی زاده" [Memories of Moulvi Ebrahim Safizadeh] [blog] Apr. 2012, 2 Oct. 2012, formerly available at <http://safizadah.blogspot. co.uk/2012/04/blog-post.html>.

29 "کشتار دیپلمات های ایرانی در مزار شریف از زبان تنها شاهد" [Koshtar diplomathay-e Irani az zabanetanha shed] [The Massacre of Iranian Diplomats in Mazar-e Sharif, (as) told by the only surviving witness], *Quds Online* 18 Mordad 1390 *hs* [9 Aug. 2011], 14 Dec. 2014 <http://www.qudsonline.ir/ detail/News/4638>.

30 It remains unclear precisely who this brother of Khalid Sheikh Mohammad was, but it is likely that it was in this way that al-Zarqawi had established himself with jihadists related to Baluchistan from the early 1990s. See p. 6 of Michael Weiss and Hassan Hassan, *ISIS: Inside the Army of Terror* (New York: Regan Arts, 2015).

31 Charles River Editors, *The Islamic State of Iraq and Syria: The History of ISIS/ISIL* (Marson Gate: CreateSpace, 2014). See also Weiss and Hassan (2015).

see also Wiess and Hassan 2015

32 Safizadeh (2012).

33 "Moulwi Abdoljalil-e QanbarZahi rahbar-e sazeman-e hezb-e al-Forqan koshteh shod" [Moulwi Abdoljalil Qanbarzahi, the leader of the al-Forqan Organisation, has been killed], *Sunni News* 22 Mar. 2012, 10 Oct. 2014 <http://sunni-news.net/fa/articles.aspx?selected_article_ no=21517>.

34Kamalkhan Salahzahi, "ملا کمال" [Mullah Kamal] [video], *YouTube* 23 Apr. 2009, 10 July 2011 <http://www.youtube.com/watch?v=1oeP7QK-FoKo>.

—. "Mullah [Kamal Khan]" [video], *Taftan TV, YouTube* 12 Nov. 2010, 7 Oct. 2011 <http://www.youtube.com/watch?v=7sdohVNzhmM>.

35 Mohammad Armian, "Takhrib-e Gornag" [Destruction of Gornag]

(place of publication and publisher are unknown, 2000) 113.

36 Abdolsattar Doshoki, "Haqayeq-e zaendagi-e Abdolmalek Rigi az souod ta soqut" [The Facts of Abdolmalek-e Rigi's Life from Rise to Fall], *Sardamdar* 23 June 2010, 20 Feb. 2011 <http://www.sardamdar. com/2010/06/blog-post_28.html>.

37 Abdolrauf Rigi, "Eshkalat-e matlab-e aqay-e Doshoki" [Mistakes in Mr. Doshoki's Article]. *Taftan News Agency* [blog], 7 Tir 1389 *hs* [28 June 2010], 28 Aug. 2010 <http://taftan313.blogspot.com/2010/06/blog-post_7799.html>.

38 According to reporting by the IRNA, an official Iranian news agency, between 2005 and mid 2010 Jondollah had killed 152 people and had injured 320 people, both from the security forces and from the public. However, the actual figure may be considerably higher than what has been officially reported. See "Abdolmalek Rigi edam shod" [Abdolmalek Rigi was executed], *BBC Persian* 20 June 2010, 12 June 2011 <http://www. bbc.co.uk/persian/iran/2010/06/100619_u03-rigi-execution.shtml>.

39 Some interesting points can be made regarding the handwritten note left by the suicide bomber. The message is in Farsi, and contains some spelling mistakes. It is emotional and simple; and it contains nothing about Baluch, Baluchistan, nationalism, freedom, the land, or even jihad. It is very much about a lay person willing to be remembered by his peers and to be praised by them as was the case with other heroic martyrs, and to be rewarded by God and the Prophet by their taking him to paradise as he leaves this 'cursed' world. It idealizes martyrdom and inviting others to do the same. He brings his letter to end with a poem – a 'robaey' (a quatrain composed of two distiches) – by a famous Sufi, Khwajah Abdullah Ansari of Herat.

40 Gretchen Peters, *Seeds of Terror: How Drugs, Thugs, and Crime Are Reshaping the Afghan War* (New York: Macmillan, 2009).

41 Abdolrauf Rigi, "Jawab-e Abdulrauf-e Rigi Uzu-e Majma'-e ulamay-e Jonbesh-e Moqavemat Jondollah wa sokhangvi Rasmi-e Jonbesh be Abdolwahed-e Rigi" [The response of Abdolrauf Rigi, member of the Association of Clerical Authorities of the Resistance Movement of Jondollah and official spokesperson of Jondollah, to Abdolwahed Rigi], *Sunni News* 18 Dec. 2010, 29 Dec. 2010, formerly available at <http://sunni.rr.nu/fa/articles.aspx?selected_article_no=12815>.

42 Abdolrauf Rigi (18 Dec. 2010).

43 Initially, they had chosen the title "Jondollah" (God's Army) as an expression of Arabic religious organisational identity. But later, they changed it to the secular name of "Iranian Popular Resistance Move-

ment" (IPRM). Yet in their announcements, they have never abandoned the name of Jondollah. They have remained very inconsistent in using either one or the other as their identification. Since then, they have always used Jondollah, whether in or out of brackets, next to IPRM. Sometimes, they have simply used "Popular Resistant Movement" without mentioning Iran. At other times, they have used the name "Popular Resistance Movement of Jondollah" or "Popular Resistance Movement—Jondollah". This lack of consistency can be seen in both Arabic and Persian announcements. At the same time, a point which should be noticed is that they have not used either Baluchistan or Baluch in their organisational identity; and in many places, they have dropped "Iran" as well.

44 Delawar, Baluch, "Khoon-e shahidan enqelab miafrinad" [The blood of martyrs generates revolution], *Taftan News Agency* [blog] 24 May 2010, 21 Sept. 2011 <http://taptan313.blogspot.com/2010/05/blog-post_6853.html>.

45 See Jondollah, "Bayanyeh majma-e Olamay-e Jonbesh-e moqavemat dar Pasokh kasani ke jihad ra enkar mikonand" [The Announcement of the Association of Jodullah Movement' Religious Authorities in Response to the People who Reject Jihad], *Rigi News Agency* [blog] 7 July 2010, 16 Sept. 2010 <http://riginews.blogspot.com/2010/07/blog-post_2872.html>.

46 Abdolrauf Rigi (29 Dec. 2010).

47 Jondollah has sometimes used the term 'Shia outsiders' or just the more generalized 'outsiders'. But since Jondollah has clearly considered the support of Sunnis in Iran as an especially important objective, it can be said that by referring to 'outsiders' or 'occupiers', Jondollah merely means Shias in general, and Zabolis in particular, in Baluchistan.

48 Abdolrauf Rigi (29 Dec. 2010).

49 See Jondollah (7 July 2010). But it should be noted that even in this respect, Jondollah has not been consistent because there are some cases where they had supported the revolutionary movement of young Iranians in Tehran and other cities against the Iranian Islamic Republic. See Jondollah, "Ettelaye Jonbesh-e Moqawemat dar moured-e eterazat-e khiabani-e mardom" [A Press Release of the Resistance Movement regarding (the) People's Street Protests], *Taptaan* [blog] 16 June 2009, 10 Jan. 2010 <http://taptaan.blogspot.com/2009/06/blog-post_4563.html>. Also, in an announcement supporting Mojahedin Khalaq-e Iran, they condemned an attack on the Ashraf Base in Iraq. See Jondollah, "Ashraf Camp Mujahedin-e Khalq-e Iran", *Baloch United Front* n.d., 12 Apr. 2016 <http://www.balochunitedfront.org/articles/Farsi/jond_ashraf_1.htm>.

50 Jondollah, "Beyanyeh majma-e Olamay-e Jonbesh-e Jondollah dar Pa-sokh be Fatway-e Siasi Akhir dar Baluchistan" [The Annoucement of the Association of Jondollah Movement's Religious Authorities in response to the Recent Political Fatwas in Baluchistan], *Junbish* [blog] 3 June 2009, 11 Jan. 2010, formerly available at <http://junbish.blogspot.com/2009/06/blog-post_3149.html>.

See also Jondollah, "Ettelaei jadid dar maured-e eterafat-e dicte-ei-e jawanan-e mazloom" [New Press Coverage on the Pressured (Forced) Confession(s) of the Oppressed Young People], *Junbish* [blog] 3 June 2009, 12 July 2010, formerly available at <http://junbish.blogspot.com/2009/07/blog-post_03.html>.

51 Islamic groups in Baluchistan have hardly put up a peep of protest against the government's oppressive policies against the Baluchi language. By contrast, the secular ethnic nationalists have decidedly expressed their own concerns about this problem. At issue is a vaguely-worded article (Article 15) in the Constitution which technically grants some freedom to ethnic peoples including the use of their own language in schools or in media. However, the Iranian government has never facilitated the conditions necessary for them to actually use their language. They have even severely punished the cultural-language activists, claiming different reasons for doing so. The government has only broadcast Baluchi for a very few short hours on official local radio and television outlets. Article 15 specifies: "The official language and script of Iran, the lingua franca of its people, is Persian. Official documents, correspondence, and texts, as well as text-books, must be in this language and script. However, the use of regional and tribal languages in the press and mass media, as well as for teaching of their literature in schools, is allowed in addition to Persian". See the online text: Islamic Republic of Iran, Constitution, approved 24 Oct. 1979, enforced from 3 Dec. 1979, amended 28 July 1989, *Iran Online*, accessed 10 Oct. 2015 <http://www.iranonline.com/iran/iran-info/government/constitution-2.html>.

52 Jondollah, "Jondollah (Nanu Jund Allah)" [We are Jondollah] [video], *YouTube* n.d., 12 Aug. 2013, formerly available at <http://www.youtube.com/watch?v=ZzryYv9tb5U>.

53 Zabol is the main city in Sistan. The same name is also used for the whole Sistani area. But nowadays, for many Baluch, the term 'Zaboli' has become a derogatory word, much as the nomen 'Baluch' has become for many Sistanis.

54 Jondollah, "Ettelaeih Jonbesh, e'dam se jawan Baluch wa bigonah dar Zahedan" [Announcement of the Movement (Jondollah) on execution

on three young and innocent Baloch (by Iranian Regime) in Zahedan], آنتي زابلي [Anti Zaboli] [blog] 9 Khordad 1388 *hs* [May 2009], 24 Jan. 2011 <http://antizavabol.blogspot.com/2009/05/blog-post_5911.html>.

55 Ibid.

56 Ibid. Also see "Ettelaiye jonbeshe moqawemat khetab be jawanan-e Baluchistan" [The message of the Resistance Movement(Jondollah)to the young people in Baluchistan], *Baloch News Agency* [blog] 30 May 2009, 21 Sept. 2011 <http://www.balochna.blogspot.com>. Site has moved to <http://www.bbalochna.blogspot.com>.

57 "Namehei sar goshadeh az rahbar-e Jonbesh-e Moqavemat-e Jondollah abdolmalek-e Baluch be rahbare nezam-e valayat-e faqih-e Iran Ali Khamaneei" [Open letter of Abdolmalek Rigi the leader of Resistence Movement of Jondollah to the leader of regime of valayat-e faqih Ali Khamenei], *Sunni News* 17 Dec. 2009, 2 Oct. 2011 <http://sunni-news. org/ar/articles.aspx?selected_article_no=1917>.

58 Jondollah, "Payame rahbar-e Jonbesh moqavemat dar pasokh- be sazeman-e melal wa shoray-e amnyat wa groohay-e hoquq-e bashari" [Response of the Leader of the the Resistance Movement to the UN, the Security Council, and Human Rights groups], *Ostomaan* 11 Nov. 2009, 28 Aug. 2011 <http://www.ostomaan.org/articles/84/4426>.

59 Narui (2010).

60 Abdolrauf Rigi (29 Dec. 2010).

61 Abdolhamid Esmailzahi, "[Moulana Abdolhamid:] Hades-e tororisti-e pishin ra beshedat mahkoom mikonim" [Moulana Abdolhamid: We strongly condemn the terrorist incident in Pishin], *Sunni News* 2010, 23 Nov. 2011, formerly available at <http://old.Sunni-news.net/?p=8321>.

62 Jondollah, "Pasokh be bianat Moulvi Abdolhamid emam joma' ahle-sunnat-e zahedan" [A reply to Moulvi Abdolhamid, Friday prayer leader of the Sunnis in Zahedan], *Baloch News Agency* [blog] 29 May 2009, 20 July 2009 <http://balochna.blogspot.com/2009/05/blog-post_4389.html>.

63 Karim Baluch, "Baluch-e hoon ham sohrent moulvi sahib!" [Baluch blood also runs red, sir!], *Taftanna* [blog] 9 Khordad 1388 *hs* [May 2009], 23 Aug. 2011 <http://taftanna.blogspot.com/2009/05/blog-post_7730. html>.

64 Online comments regarding Abdolwahed Rigi (2010).

65 Moinuldin Gamshadzahi, "Jondollah namidanad chetour yakh mikhorand" [Jondollah does not know how to 'eat ice'], *Sunni.rr.nu* 21 Dec. 2010, 15 Jan. 2011, formerly available at <http://Sunni.rr.nu/fa/articles. aspx?selected_article_no=12856>. On the same page of the site, some interesting comments had been posted:-A commentator, going by the

pseudonym of Syed, believes that the "nationalism" ('qawmgrayee'—ethnic approach) of Jondollah's approach has caused mujahidin to distance themselves from Jondollah.

-Another commentator, going by the pseudonym of Abdullah, said that "if Jondollah does not put aside the flag of nationalism, [its continued usage] is considered as an invitation for "jahelya" (ignorance/polytheism) and in that case, [those of] Jondollah's people who are killed go to hell.

-On the basis of a hadith, a commentator added that "Whoever becomes angry under a grey or unclear flag and invites people on the basis of fanaticism and nationalism or [who] becomes angry and fight[s], to support a tribe or an ethnic[ity], his war is based on jahelya (polytheism)"

-In a more supportive way, another person (also called Abdullah) comments that there "should be animosity against infidels[;] and [the] hearts of Muslims should be full of hatred, animosity[,] and resentment against all infidels" (Abdolrauf Rigi, 29 Dec. 2010).

66 These critics' comments were published on *Sunni Online News*, which is a popular Sunni website. The critics were themselves criticised by supporters of Jondollah; and after a short while, the comments were removed from the website. The writers were accused of being agents of the Islamic Republic of Iran. While it seemed that *Sunni Online News* was not sure about the credibility of these writers, and Abdolrauf Rigi attacked them only on the basis of their interpretation of Islamic traditions, it did not challenge them on the credibility of their knowledge.

67 Online comments posted to (the formerly available) Gamshadzahi (2010).

68 Jondollah, "Amliyate Fatholmobin 11" [Fatholmobin 11 Operations] [video], *YouTube* 22 Apr. 2009, 9 Sept. 2011, formerly available at <http://www.youtube.com/user/taftaanbaloch#p/u/16/gxs1KVRN3_w>.

69 Abdolrauf Rigi (29 Dec. 2010).

70 M. Seymour Hersh, "Preparing the Battlefield: The Bush administration steps up its secret moves against Iran", *The New Yorker* 7 July 2008, 12 Apr. 2016 <http://www.newyorker.com/magazine/2008/07/07/preparing-the-battlefield>.

Bashirahmad Rigi, a Rigi tribal leader who was serving as mediator relative to the Iranian security forces, has also mentioned that Abdolmalek Rigi had been proudly boasting of all the support he had received from the US. See Bashirahmad Rigi, "Nagoftehayee az zendagi Abdolmalek-e Rigi" [Untold stories about Abdolmalek Rigi], *Jame Jam Online* 23 Khordad 1389 *hs* [13 June 2010], 15 Sept. 2011 <http://www.jamejamonline.ir/newstext.aspx?newsnum=100883064833>.

71 See Kamal Narui, "Sokhanguy-e jondollah pardeh az moameleh pen-

hany-e dastigiri-e Rigi bardasht [Jondollah's spokeperson revealed the secret deals about arrest of Rigi]." March 210. *Taftan Blogspot.* 10 January 2013. < http://taftan313.blogspot.co.uk/2010/03/blog-p>.
72 Jondollah (n.d.), "Ashraf Camp Mujahedin-e Khalq-e Iran". http:// www.balochunitedfront.org/articles/Farsi/jond_ashraf_1.htm
73 Jondollah, "Ettelayeh Jadid-e Jonbeshe-e Moqavemat-e Jondollah, Iran be dkhalathaye mojremaneh khod dar keshvarhay-e Arabi payan dahad" [A new announcement by the Resistance Movement of Jondollah: Iran should stop its criminal interference with the internal affairs of Arab countries], جنبش مقاومت مردمي ايران جندالله [People's Resistance Movement of Iranian Jundullah] [blog] 2 Apr. 2011, 25 Aug. 2011 <http://jonbesh-mar-dom.blogspot.com>.
74 Mark Perry, "False Flag", *Foreign Policy* 13 Jan. 2012, 4 Sept. 2012 <http://foreignpolicy.com/2012/01/13/false-flag>.
75 Mojahed, "Jondollah military commander conveys a message of condolence on Qanbarzahi's martyrdom." *M0jahed--The most recent news of the Mujahideen of Islam* 29 Mar. 2012, 10 Oct. 2012 <http://m0jahed.wordpress.com>.
76 Harkat-e Ansar-e Iran (Ansar Fighters Movement), "Elamyeh Jadid Harkat Ansar-e Iran mabni bar amalyat-e estoon 1 Chahbahar" [New Announcement of Harkat-e Ansar-e Iran about Thunder-1 Operations in Chahbahar], *Harkat e Ansar* (Iran) [blog] 14 Oct. 2012, 14 Oct. 2012 <http://ansariran.blogspot.co.uk/2012/10/1.html>.
77 Shaheed Hamza [photograph], *Harkat e Ansar (Iran)* [blog] 28 Mehr 1391 *hs* [19 Oct. 2012], Nov. 2012 <http://ansariran.blogspot. co.uk/2012/10/blog-post_561.html>.
78 Hezb-ul Forqan. Ettelaeih ettehad-e mujahedin-e hezb-e al-Forqan wa harkat al-Ansar" [Announcement of alliance between Hizb al-Forqan mujahidin and Harkat al-Ansar]. *Hezbul Furqan* [blog] 11 Dey 1392 *hs* [1 Jan. 2014], 12 Dec. 2015 <http://hezbulfurqan.blogspot.co.uk/2014/01/blog-post.html>.
79 Sepah-e Sahabah-e-Iran, "فعاليت شاخه نظامی سپاه صحابه ايران واحد بلوچستان" [The military wing of SSP's activities in Balochistan], *Sepah-Sahaba* [blog] 23 Esfand 1389 *hs* [14 Mar. 2011], 2 Oct. 2012 <http://www. sepah-sahaba.blogspot.co.uk/2011/03/blog-post.html>.
80 Sepah-e Sahabah-e-Iran, "Yeki az Mozdooran-e rezim bewasil mojahedin koshteh shod" [One of the regime's mercenaries killed by Mujahideen], "حركت مبارزين سپاه صحابه ايران" [Companions of SS-Iran Militants] [blog] 21 Sept. 2012, 2 Oct. 2012 <http://ssiran.wordpress.com/2012/09>.
81Sepah-e Sahabeh Iran, "Ettehad wa hambastagy-e Sepah-e Sahbeh Iran with Sazeman-e Jaish al-Adl" [Alliance and Solidarity of Sepah-e Sahabeh Iran with Jaish al Adl Organisation], *Sepahe Sahabae Iran* [blog]

25 Farvardin 1394 *hs* [14 Apr. 2015], 19 Dec. 2015 <http://www.ss-iran.blogspot.co.uk>.

82 *Google Images*, JAD weblog images of children used in JAD camps; search https://images.google.com for "جیش عدل و آموزش نظامی بچه ها".

83 "Torror-e emam Jomaeh Rask dar ostan-e sistan wa Baluchistan" [Terror Imam of Friday prayers of Rask in Sistan and Baluchistan], *BBC Persian* 21 Jan. 2012, 10 Dec. 2014 <http://www.bbc.co.uk/persian/iran/2012/01/120121_l31>.

84 "Na arami dar shahr-e Rask-e ostan-e Sistan wa Baluchistan" [Unrest in Rask City in Sistan and Baluchistan], *BBC Persian* 16 May 2012, 15 Dec. 2014 <http://www.bbc.co.uk/persian/iran/2012/05/120516_l39_rask_baluchestan_unrest.shtml>.

85 "Jiashe al-Adl Khastar-e Azadi-ye 300 zendani sunni dar moqabel azadi 5 marzban-e zendani shod" [Jaish-e Adl wanted 300 Sunni prisoners to be released in a deal for releasing 5 prisoners of the Iranian Border Corps], *Al-Arabiya* 14 Feb. 2014, 18 Dec. 2015, formerly available at <http://farsi.alarabiya.net/fa/iran/2014/02/14>.

86 Hoshang Noraiee (Ayub Husainbor), "Jedal-e Bain-e Jaish-e Adl wa Jaish-e Nasr: jehad baray Khods, jehad baray mellat, jehad baray-e qodrat" [Conflicts between Jaishe Adl and Jaishe Nasr: Jihad for God, Jihad for the Nation, Jihad for Power?], *Taptan* 16 Aug. 2014, 20 Sept. 2014 <http://www.taptan.com/?p=129>.

87 Hoshang Noraiee (Ayub Husainbor), "Torror-e moulvi Abdolrauf-e Rigi Kar Kist?" [Who has killed Moulvi Abdolrauf Rigi?] *Taptan* 29 Aug. 2014, 10 Jan. 2016<http://www.taptan.com/?paged=2&lang=fa>. See also Jaishe al-Adl, "Elamye sazeman-e Jaish al-Adl; shahdat-e Abdulrauf Rigi ra be khanawadeh an amir-e bozrguar wa mellat-e baluchistan we ahle-sonnat-e aziz tasliat miguim" [Announcement of Jaishe al-Adl organisation: We express our condolences regarding the martyrdom of Abdulrau], *Edaalat News* [blog] 28 Aug. 2014, 15 Nov. 2014 <http://edaalatnews.blogspot.co.uk>.

CONCLUSION

Currently, the ISIS phenomenon is the dominant issue in global and regional political security. ISIS inherited the most hardline of al-Qaeda traditions, those introduced by Abu Musa'ab al-Zarqawi. Al-Zarqawi even challenged mainstream al-Qaeda leaders particularly al-Zawahiri, but he never abandoned al-Qaeda as the mother organisation. However, for about four years, al-Zarqawi's tradition became more under the control of al-Qaeda; and it also suffered from the successful attacks of the Anbar Awakening movement supported by the US. After the death of Omar al-Baghdadi, his successor Abu Bakr al-Baghdadi not only continued al-Zarqawi's tradition but after a while even entered into open conflict with al-Zawahiri and mainstream al-Qaeda. This led to bloody rivalries and the worldwide split between al-Qaeda and ISIS, which had established the Islamic State (IS) and announced Abubakr al-Baghdadi as caliph.

The extremist anti-Shia elements of al-Zarqawi's ideology remained particularly important to the caliph but within the context of his much greater ambition to expand the caliphate and control the areas conquered with an iron fist. The principles of compromise and building of alliances with other Islamic and jihadist groups (as al-Qaeda had done) nearly came to an end—and all alliances became limited to those who had pledged *bayat* (paying homage and allegiance) to the caliph.

The dimensions of the conflicts have, in their depth and breadth, reached both regional and global levels. ISIS has been challenging Salafi jihadists in Syria and Iraq and some other parts of the world. Furthermore, ISIS has also challenged the Taliban inside Afghanistan. And it has posed a serious threat to the IRI and the Shia population in all other parts of the world, as well as to the rulers of countries with majority-Sunni populations.

This disarray in the jihadists' camp was clear by ISIS's ferocious attacks, including suicide attacks, against other (fellow) jihadist groups such as Jibhat al-Nosrah, Ahrar al-Sham, and Jaish Islam, in Syria. These rivalries have not been limited to the conflict zones in Syria and Iraq, but instead have spread to all other parts of the world including to other countries in the Middle East, North Africa, Central Asia, and South Asia.

In spite of all these inter-jihadist feuds, ISIS emerged, with even greater strength, as a worldwide organisation with far more power and the ability to carry out widespread actions nearly all over the globe. ISIS more successfully combined the two strategies of 'near enemy' and 'far enemy'. While it territorialised its efforts by building a caliphate, it did not abandon its flexibility to retreat, attack, and planning for conquering territory on different fronts and in different directions.

Since the emergence of ISIS, the activities of other jihadists such as Jibhat al-Nosrah and virtually all al-Qaeda affiliates' activities have been either ignored or obscured by the media, and the main focus has been placed on ISIS. This may give enough space for al-Qaeda to strengthen their capacities for later, when ISIS may have been weakened or defeated in Syria and Iraq. To build up their network of alliances, al-Qaeda has tried to develop its relationships with other Sunni groups while avoiding ISIS-type sectarian confrontations.

Similar to al-Qaeda, ISIS has openly and vigorously challenged all other rulers, particularly in Sunni dominant countries, as apostate. Even Saudi Arabia's rulers have been one of their important targets. But the dimensions of this threat are far more serious for countries with a large Shia population, especially if that population is dominant. In this regard, in ISIS's view, IRI has a 'special place' in being not only a Shia theocratic regime but also the main supporters of Shias in Iraq, Syria, Lebanon, and Bahrain along with Houthis in Yemen. Furthermore, Iran has directly organised and sent Shia jihadists to fight with Salafi jihadists in Syria and Iraq.

After the Iran-Iraq war, ISIS is, in reality, the biggest challenge IRI has faced from the outside, although there are some certain ideological elements in IRI, which are similar to all other radical jihadists including ISIS. IRI's radical Islamism as presented by Khomeini and now Khamenei is, to a great extent, close to what radical jihadists, particularly Sayyid Qutb, had presented in Egypt. However, in contrast to Qutb, Khomeini pursued a cleric-oriented approach. For instance, he gave the highest and most determining positions to clerics, particularly *valy-e faqih*. The holding of such a position was not a necessity for Qutb, who had criticised the role of priests and rabbis as polytheism and the rule of men by men. Khomeini hardly even trusted non-clerical Islamist leaders; and it was possibly for this reason that he did not want to talk about increasing their authority. However, Khomeini's successor, Ayatollah Khamenei, the current leader of IRI, has shown great respect for the legacy of Qutb and has translated some of his books into Persian. Qutb, as a radical Muslim ideologue, had not had an anti-Shia tendency; while ironically, Salafists who derived much inspiration from Qutb's ideas tended to adopt very strong anti-Shia positions.

It is not very strange that if anti-Shia rhetoric is taken out of Salafist jihadist literature, in many respects they become quite similar to Khomeini's or Khamenei's ideas. In terms of political exercises, IRI has pursued discriminative policies towards all minorities, even Sunnis. It has been brutally supressing minorities and non-compliant opponents, and it has a long record of the killing and torturing of political prisoners; but it is also true that IRI has not pursued a policy of televised beheadings or the capturing and market-place selling of minorities. In spite of all this, IRI has planted the seeds of a deep-seated sense of alienation and despair among the Sunnis, many of whom may consider the case/cause of ISIS with a degree of sympathy.

ISIS's activities have quickly spread to other countries by building its organisations in regions surrounding Iran—not only close to the Iranian borders but also inside Iran itself, where the emergence of ISIS cells and alliances has been reported. In the context of threats imposed by Salafist jihadists, Iran has now moved across Eastern borders towards what had been its formidable enemy in the 1990s, the Taliban, to confront their common enemy: ISIS. This is easy to understand, as ISIS is the common enemy of both IRI and the Taliban.

As far as the Taliban is concerned, they themselves are quite a different force than ISIS. The Taliban has not developed a systematic body of literature clarifying their political ideology. However, in an ad hoc manner, they have cherry-picked some ideas from the Deobandi, who also tend to lack a political ideology as such. Some Deobandi branches have quite strong anti-Shia approaches. Their ideas have been mixed with the rural and ethnic-tribal codes of behaviour which existed among Pashtuns, shaped in part by the de-territorialised forces of Afghan refugees in Pakistan. There is no evidence to show that the Taliban have ambitions to act in the role of being a vanguard of 'true' Muslims for the spread or export of their ideas beyond Afghanistan into adjacent regions.

In operational terms, the Taliban have been a source of inspiration – as well as criticism – for many Salafist jihadists. They have been positively regarded in terms of their being brutal, motivated, and strong warriors. But they have also been criticised by many Salafist jihadists for being tribal, and have even been considered as nothing more than a mere "herd of cows" with un-Islamic manners and ideas. ISIS, which reflects the views of the hard-line critics, now directly challenges the Taliban in Afghanistan, where many bloody clashes between them have been reported.

Since Salafi jihadists' commitment to the ideological and

political purification of Islam seemingly has no limit, sectarian conflict between them is inevitable. This is possibly one of the most important factors which discredits and weakens them. But furthermore, wherever they have a chance to rule, economically they are unable to run a country with success in an era of globalization. This does not mean that they will immediately collapse. However, it will create disillusionment and dissatisfaction among the majority of those people who expect them to restructure society from a modern perspective and to provide prosperity and security. Even Iran, in a more flexible process incorporating both 'push' and 'pull', has managed to survive and, to a large extent, even adapt to international conditions. There is no prospect of a fundamental solution within the current political and ideological framework.

ISIS, in particular, may cause the emergence of more borders on the political map of the world and sow the seeds of further ethnic and religious conflicts outside the jihadist agenda. But Salafi jihadism is a conflict-ridden approach, which easily disturbs societies, destroys lives and resources, and dislocates large sections of the population – even Sunni Muslims and their clerics who adhere to non-Salafi schools.

Salafist jihadists have shown that they are not only aggressive but they also do not simply define their enemies on the basis of a strategy of either near or far enemy. This mean they are likely to remain as global jihadists, while they fight for and occupy territories. At the same time, the experience of the 'war on terror' clearly shows that there are no easy solutions for eradicating ISIS-type phenomena. Aggressive wars and the occupation of lands are (arguably) likely to create more problems and fuel the jihadists further. Further attention should be paid to socio-economic conditions as well as to political issues within the Middle Eastern countries. As far as regional politics are disrupted by rivalries between Sunni and Shia powers (particularly between Iran and Saudi Arabia), there will always be a fertile ground for radicals to emerge and justify their activities. Without abandoning sectarian policies by all parties in both Shia and Sunni countries, these countries will not be able to take genuine steps towards cooperating and eradicating discrimination and sectarian conflict. Yet the problem will not be solved without promoting a global approach.

The United Nations and other international players, instead of concentrating on trivial, ad hoc measures, should have a more fundamental policy of encouraging the regional powers towards more sustainable and profound cooperation based on participatory politics free from religiously-based and ethnic-based sectarian rivalries. At the same time, economic support should be in place to decrease the levels of deprivation and alienation in these countries and thus build stronger institutions of civil society.

Glossary

Ahrar al-Sham: a Salafist jihadist group in Syria. It had been in conflict with ISIS.

Al-Derar Mosque: a Medina mosque which was destroyed by Mohammad on the basis of the belief that it was a place of conspiracy by hypocritical Muslims.

Alim (pl. ulama): an Islamic scholar who is a person knowledgeable in religion. The term 'cleric' has, to some extent, the same meaning.

Al-Qaeda in Iraq (AQI): the first affiliate of al-Qaeda, AQI was established by al-Zarqawi. Later on, it became ISI, which became ISIS or ISIL, which then finally became IS (the Islamic State).

Al-Qaeda in the Arabian Peninsula (AQAP): this branch of al-Qaeda operates within Saudi Arabia and other neighbouring countries, particularly in Yemen.

Al-Shabab: a Somali jihadist group which is affiliated with al-Qaeda.

Al-Wala' Wal-bara': 'loyalty and disavowal'—an important principle among Salafists. The term means loyalty only to God, Islam, and Muslims – and disavowal of all other religions and their followers.

Amir al-Mu'menin ('Commander of [the] Muslims'): Commander of the Muslims. It is a title used principally for a caliph. In Sufi tradition caliph also may be used as a title.

Ansar al-Islam: a Salafist jihadist organization with a Kurdish connection. It was the first group sheltered al-Zarqawi in Iran and Iraq.

Ansar Bayt al-Maqdis: a jihadist Salafist group which operates in the Sinai Peninsula of Egypt and is connected with ISIS.

Bayat (Bay'at; Baia'at; Bia'ah): pledge of allegiance to an Islamic commander or leader.

Beda'ati: revisionist in nature; reformist according to orthodox Islamic principles. It refers to an ideology or a group. Traditionalist Sunni use it against Shias or other Islamic approaches like Jamaa't-e-Islami and Moududi.

Boko Haram: a jihadist group in Nigeria which has close connection with al-Qaeda.

Daesh: a name which has been used in Arabic and Farsi to refer to ISIL/ISIS – acronyms for the Islamic State of Iraq and the Levant/Syria (al-Sham) – and which is now used to refer to IS (the Islamic State).

Dar al-Kufr: home of the apostates. Its antonym is Dar al-Islam.

Dar al-Islam: abode/house/home of Muslims, where Sharia rules are enforced, and which should be defended and expanded by means of jihad.

Deobandi: a relatively new approach, originating from the Hanafi school of jurisprudence. Deobandi developed in the sub-continent of India in the mid-1850s.

Fatwa: a religious decree ordering the legitimatisation or de-legitimatisation of a certain action or behaviour. Fatwas are issued by an authority called a mujtahid or mufti.

Free Syrian Army: a moderate, armed anti-Assad army fighting the Syrian regime. It was formed by army officers who left the army to defend the protesters. It has become weak and, to a large extent, has lost ground to the Salafist jihadists.

Hadith (pl. Ahadith): traditions which are attributed to Mohammad's behaviour and sayings.

Hezbollahis: individuals or groups related to Hezbollah. In Iran it has been widely used for the extremist Shias, and it is almost correspondent to Shia jihadists.

IRI: The Islamic Republic of Iran. As a theocratic state, it was established in 1979-1980 by Ayatollah Khomeini.

ISAF (International Security Assistance Force): NATO's International Security Force in Afghanistan.

ISI (Islamic State of Iraq): the name, before the formation of ISIS, of the group which became ISIS.

Jebhat al-Nusra: the affiliate of al-Qaeda in Syria. Although it has clashed with ISIS, it has developed good relationships with other Salafist jihadists.

Jaish-e Adl (JAD): an ethnic religious jihadist group involved in armed struggle in the southeastern Iranian province of Sistan and Baluchistan. It is the main successor of Jondollah.

Jihad: struggle or holy war. Two types of jihad have been defined: jihad akbar (great struggle) and jihad asghar (small struggle). The first type relates to the comparatively greater challenge of self-improvement and spiritual warfare while the second type regards the comparatively lesser challenge of battle in the field of physical combat.

Jihadists (Jihadis): people who, or organisations which, enforce jihad; in this case, particularly those who wage war against people or states who are seen as apostates.

Jondollah/Jondallh ('Army of God'): also known as 'The Popular Resistance Movement of Iran' and the: a jihadist ethno-religious group which emerged under the leadership of Abdolmalik Rigi, in southeastern Iran in the mid-2000s. It has adopted a very anti-Shia approach.

Kafir (Kuffar): non-believer. The term includes those who are believed to be non-Muslims or who are viewed as not being 'real' Muslims. For some jihadists, the concept includes Shias along with Christians and Jews. To be 'kafir in belief' is viewed as a more sinful state than to be merely 'kafir in practice' by making mistakes.

Khurasan Group (Khorasan): an al-Qaeda affiliate which is known for organising international operations.

Lashkar-e Tayyiba (LeT): an armed group of al-Hadithi (Salafists in the subcontinent) in Pakistan. Its activities, to a large extent, are related to violent attacks on India and support of the Kashmiri cause in the Kashmir conflict. There is a belief that it has a close relationship with Pakistan's intelligence services (ISI).

Laskar-e Jhangvi: a radical Deobandi sectarian group in Pakistan. Technically, it was separated off from Sepah-e Sahabeh Pakistan (SSP). However, there is a belief that it is the armed branch of SSP. It is very anti-Shia and anti-Sufi.

Mahdi: Islamic messiah. It refers to a man who comes to save the world and spread Justice and the Islamic faith against all evils.

Mojahid (Mujahed or Mujahid; pl. Mujahidin, Mujahedin, or Mojahedeen): holy warrior, or someone who struggles to fulfil certain aspects of jihad in its wider sense.

Moshrek: apostate—though more precisely, the term means 'polytheist'. Shias and Sufis, for Salafist jihadists, are also considered to be 'moshrek'. Its antonym is *tawhid* (monotheism).

Moulvi: a title used in the subcontinent of India particularly in Pakistan, India and now in south-eastern Iran (similar to the use of 'sheikh' in Arabic counties), to refer to clerics or ulama.

Murttad: 'renegade'—meaning a Muslim who converts to another religion.

Rafida: a rejectionist, it is mainly used by Salafists, Wahhabis, and radical Deobandis as a derogatory slur against Shias.

RGC (Revolutionary Guard Corps; Sepah-e Pasdaran Inqelabe Islami-e Iran: a highly-powerful revolutionary army established after the 1979 Iranian Revolution. The traditional army still exists, but it remains under the shadow of the RGC.

Sahwa Movement: the Anbar Awakening movement which emerged, in the Anbar province of Iraq, to combat al-Qaeda. With the mobilization of tribes, to a large extent it succeeded in defeating al-Qaeda.

Salafiyya (Salafisim): a conservative reformist school in Islam, related to those who believe that Muslims should only imitate the first three generations (Salaf-e Saleh) of Islam and should only rely on the Quran and the Hadith rather than on the laws suggested by other principle jurists founded 4 main Sunni schools. For this reason, they are called 'non-imitators'.

Salafist (Salafi): those who believe in Salafism and who typically do not follow other schools of jurisprudence like Hanafi, Maleki, Hanbali, or Shafaei.

Sepah-e Qods (Quds): Quds Corps is the Iranian cross-border branch of the RGC.

Sepah-e Sahabeh Iran ('The Iranian Army of the Prophet's Companion'): this is a jihadist organisation which had operated in Sistan and Baluchistan but has now joined Jaish-e Adl.

Sepah-e Sahabah Pakistan ('The Pakistani Army of the Prophet's Companion'): a radical Deobandi jihadist organisation in Pakistan. Lashkar-e Jhangvi is the armed force which some view as the armed wing of its parent organization, the SSP, due to how closely it operates in conjunction with the SSP.

Sharia (Shariah): Islamic law. Sharia has been interpreted and implemented in different ways, both moderate and harsh.

Shia Islam: an important branch of Islam. Shia Islam, in certain points, differs from Sunni Islam, particularly in relation to the successors of Mohammad. They believe that the legitimate successor of Mohammad was Ali and that only his descendants have the right to inherit or to be considered for the sacred position of Imam. While there are many different sub-branches of Shia Islam, Twelver Shias (meaning those who believe in there being a series of 12 Imams) are comparatively more numerous and are now in power in Iran. The majority of Shias in Iran, Iraq, and Lebanon are 'Twelvers'.

Sunna: Islamic tradition, which refers to the behaviour and sayings of Mohammad, the companions of Mohammad, or Imams.

Sunni Islam (Ahl-e Sunnat): the comparatively larger branch of Islam. Sunni Islam is also subdivided into different branches with regards to types of jurisprudence. Its main schools of jurisprudence are Hanafi, Maleki, Shafaei and Hanbali. Over the course of history, each has sprouted sub-branches. For example, Wahhabism has grown from Hanbalism, while Deobandism has branched off from Hanafi. The followers of these branches are seen as 'imitators' (meaning 'followers') because they follow a certain juritical authority. All Sunnis believe that the rightful successors of Mohammad were the 4 rightly-guided caliphs: Abu Bakr, Omar, Othman, and Ali.

Takfir: excommunication. It is also a religious authorisation which, by considering some person in question to be apostate, allows for their blood to be shed. A takfirist (takfiri) refers to a person or an organisation who believes in the validity of declarations of takfir against others.

Taliban: Afghan jihadists who emerged and seized power under the leadership of Mullah Omar in the context of post-mujahidin chaos, rivalries, and insecurity.

TTP (Tahrik-e Taliban Pakistan): Pakistan's Taliban Movement. Although inspired by and connected to the Taliban in Afghanistan, the TTP does not openly act as a branch of Afghanistan's Taliban. The TTP is mainly active among the Pakistani Pashtun.

Ummah: all Muslims. The ummah is considered to be an integrated community rather than as a non-unified conglomerate of divisions according to race, language class, or nationality.

Velayat: a division in Islamic administration similar to a province or an emirate.

Velayat-e Faqih: a system of Shia Islamic government which is led by a Supreme Leader. The term means that a powerful leader should be a highly-ranked cleric. However, all Shia clerics do not agree with this form of governance, which is mainly defined and enforced by Ayatollah Khomeini.

Valy-e Faqih: among Shia, the Valy-e Faqih is a Supreme Leader with the requisite clerical legitimacy necessary to guide an Islamic state. Khomeini was the first Valy-e Faqih. He was then succeeded by Ayatollah Ali Khamenei.

Wahhabi: followers of Mohammad ibn Abd al-Wahhab, who emerged in Saudi Arabia in 18th century. It is a hard-line version of Hanbalism which is close to Salafism. This is a very anti-Shia approach. It is dominant in Saudi Arabia and has been successful in spreading its radical ideas among many other Muslims all over the world.

Yazidis: Yazidis are Kurdish and settled in North Iraq. They are seen as an ethnic-religious community with an ancient religion, different from Islam or Zoroastrian. The community suffered in Sinjar from ISIS brutal attacks.

Appendices

Appendix 1

Executive Summary [of the Open Letter to al-Baghdadi, signed by 126 Islamic scholars (seconded by 49 subsequent signatories) from different countries]:[1]

1. It is forbidden in Islam to issue fatwas without all the necessary learning requirements. Even then fatwas must follow Islamic legal theory as defined in the Classical texts. It is also forbidden to cite a portion of a verse from the Qur'an—or part of a verse—to derive a ruling without looking at everything that the Qur'an and Hadith teach related to that matter. In other words, there are strict subjective and objective prerequisites for fatwas, and one cannot 'cherrypick' Qur'anic verses for legal arguments without considering the entire Qur'an and Hadith.

2. It is forbidden in Islam to issue legal rulings about anything without mastery of the Arabic language.

3. It is forbidden in Islam to oversimplify Shari'ah matters and ignore established Islamic sciences.

4. It is permissible in Islam [for scholars] to differ on any matter, except those fundamentals of religion that all Muslims must know.

5. It is forbidden in Islam to ignore the reality of contemporary times when deriving legal rulings.

6. It is forbidden in Islam to kill the innocent.

7. It is forbidden in Islam to kill emissaries, ambassadors, and diplomats; hence it is forbidden to kill journalists and aid workers.

8. Jihad in Islam is defensive war. It is not permissible without the right cause, the right purpose and without the right rules of conduct.

9. It is forbidden in Islam to declare people non-Muslim unless he (or she) openly declares disbelief.

10. It is forbidden in Islam to harm or mistreat—in any way—Christians or any 'People of the Scripture'.

11. It is obligatory to consider Yazidis as People of the Scripture.

12. The re-introduction of slavery is forbidden in Islam. It was abolished by universal consensus.

13. It is forbidden in Islam to force people to convert.

14. It is forbidden in Islam to deny women their rights.

15. It is forbidden in Islam to deny children their rights.

16. It is forbidden in Islam to enact legal punishments (hudud) without following the correct procedures that ensure justice and mercy.

17. It is forbidden in Islam to torture people.

18. It is forbidden in Islam to disfigure the dead.

19. It is forbidden in Islam to attribute evil acts to God.

20. It is forbidden in Islam to destroy the graves and shrines of Prophets and Companions.

21. Armed insurrection is forbidden in Islam for any reason other than clear disbelief by the ruler and not allowing people to pray.

22. It is forbidden in Islam to declare a caliphate without consensus from all Muslims.

23. Loyalty to one's nation is permissible in Islam.

24. After the death of the Prophet, Islam does not require anyone to emigrate anywhere.

Appendix 2: A list of major attacks by Jondollah[2]

In 2005, when Ahmadinejad, the Iranian president, was visiting Baluchistan, his convey was attacked and a member of the presidential bodyguard was killed.

In March 2006, the Tasooki Attack occurred in which over 20 people, including some high-ranking officials, were killed while others were taken hostage.

In February 2007, as result of a car bomb and gunfire targeted a convoy of the Revolutionary Guards in Zahedan in which at least 18 members of the Revolutionary Guards were killed.

On 13-19 August 2007, Jondollah militants kidnapped 21 truck drivers near Chahbahar and took them to Pakistan. Later, Pakistani forces succeeded to freed the hostages from Jondollah's forces inside Pakistan.

On June 2008, Jondollah abducted 16 low-ranking security forces. One of them was released, but 15 of them were killed.

On 29 December 2008, Jondollah conducted its first suicide attack in which a car bomb was driven into a security forces compound in Saravan. It was reported that four people were killed

On 25 January 2009, 12 Iranian security forces were killed in an attack by Jondollah near Saravan.

On 28 May 2009, a bomb was exploded in a place of worship for Shias in Zahedan, when mourners were engaged in a religious ceremony. As result of this attack, 25 people were killed and 125 people were injured.

On 18 October 2009, 42 people were killed in a suicide bombing in the Pishin in south-eastern Sistan-Baluchistan province. At least 6 officers of Iran's elite Revolutionary Guard – including the deputy commander of the Revolutionary Guard's ground force, General Noor Ali Shooshtari, and the Revolutionary Guard's chief provincial commander, Rajab Ali – were killed in this gathering.

On 23 February 2010, Abdolmalek Rigi was arrested.

On 20 June 2010, Abdolmalek Rigi was executed.

On 16 July 2010 (shortly followingAbdolmalek's execution), 27 people were killed as a result of 2 suicide bombings at the Shia Grand Mosque in Zahedan. These were conducted under the leadership of Haji Mohammad Zaher. It is believed that several members of the Revolutionary Guard were also killed.

On 14 December 2010, in a suicide bombing of Shia worshippers participating in a mourning ceremony near a mosque in Chah Bahar, at least 39 people were killed.

Appendix 3: Suicide letter by Abdolghafoor Rigi to his colleagues (written a day before his suicide attack).[3]

بسم الله الرحمن الرحیم

با سلام ودرود فراوان بر حضرت مصطفی(ص)و اصحاب جلیل القدرش وسلام و درود فراوان بر آن شیرمردان وشیر زنان وآن طفلان معصومی که با خون پاک خود درخت اسلام را آبیاری کردند وسلام درود فراوان به صداقت ابوبکر صدیق(رض) وحیای عثمان(رض) وشجاعت ودلیری حیدر کرار(رض) وسلام ودرود فراوان به آن عزیزانی که تکبیر گویان به بالای دار رفتند وآن عزیزانی که با اخلاص جام شهادت را در ایرانشهر نوشیدند وشهدای گران قدر کوهون وشهدای پیرسوران هم جمله حاجی محمود جان(رح) که با رفتنش عرصه دنیا را بر من وشما تنگ کرد وسلام به شما عزیزان محترم و دوستان عزیز ما چند روزی را در جمع همدیگر گذراندیم اگر در این وقت کوتاه اما طولانی شوخی کردیم که موجب ناراحتی شما شده است اول از الله وبعد از شما دوستان عزیز معافی می طلبم امیدوارم حق خودتان را فقط به خاطر رضای الله(ج) معاف کنید وبه امید روزی که حق مظلوم از ظالم گرفته شود و در سراسر دنیا حکومت الله الله(ج) وسیرت حضرت محمد(ص) و عدل حضرت عمر(رض) نافذ شود وآن روز نزدیک است که صبح پیروزی بدمد اگر چه آن وقت که این نامه را می خوانید من در جمع شما نیستم یا بلکه در این دنیا نیستم این یقین را دارم که وعده الله(ج) حق است وجای من در فردوس اعلی است

که شما با ایمان واخلاص ویقین بر وعدهای الله(ج)بر پیش من بیایید ومن تا آن لحظه انتظار شما را می کشم واین را یقین دارم که الله(ج) خون شهیدان را ضایع نمی کند او این ظالمان را نابود می کند واین را بدانید که چراغ ظالم تا آخر نمی سوزد اگر سوزد شبی به والله(ج) دیگر نمی سوزد

و در آخر همه شما را دوست دارم

وهمیشه برای شما دعا می کنم وشما برای مغفرت من هم دعا کنید تا الله(ج) مرا مورد عفو ومغفرت خود قرار دهد وشهادتم را قبول کند

آن کس که تو را شناسد جان را چه کند

زن وبچه اهل وعیال خانمان را چه کند

دیوانه کنی و دو جهانش بخشی

آخی یا رب دیوانه ای تو دو جهان را چه کند

از طرف عبدالغفور ریگی به همگی دوستان به امید روزی که شما را در جایی بهتری از این دنیای ملعون یعنی فردوس اعلی ملاقات کنم

خداحافظ خداحافظ خداحافظ

بسم الله الرحمن الرحیم

English translation of Abdolghafoor Rigi's letter:

In the name of God,

With abundant greetings to the prophet Mohammad (peace be upon him) and his glorious companions, [I write]. And many greetings to and much chanting for those courageous men and women mrtyrs and innocent babies who have irrigated the tree of Islam with their own holy blood. And abundant greetings and praise [to] the sincerity of the truthful Abu Bakr (God's satisfaction be upon him) and the justice of Omar Farooq and the honour of Othman and the bravery of Haidar Karrar [Ali] (God's satisfaction be upon him). And abundant greetings and praise to those dear people who were hanged while they were chanting "The God is great". And also [greetings] to those dear people who drank from the cup of martyrdom in Iranshahr. And greetings to [the] highly respected martyrs of KohVan and [the] martyrs of Pir Swaran, particularly Haji Mohammad Jan (The God's mercy be upon him) who left me and you in a smaller world, full of sorrows, by his passing. And greetings to my dear, well-respected friends: we spent some days together. If, during this short time [together] [(if only it had been] for a long[er] period [of time)] [?], we [may have] joked [in ways] which have caused you [to be] upset, first I apologise to The God and then to you, my dear friends. And I hope that you [will] forgive me only for [the] sake of The Almighty God's satisfaction and hope for a day when the oppressors are punished for violating the rights of the oppressed. And [with] The Almighty God's rule and the prophet Mohammad's (peace be upon him) sharia and [that of] Omar (may God be satisfied with him), justice will be enforced. And that day is close [at hand, now] that the dawn of victory starts. However, when you read this letter, I will not be in your meeting [place] and possibly I will not be in this world. I am certain that the promise of The God (Almighty) is right and [that] my place is in heaven, and I am expecting that day......And you [–] with faith, purity, and belief in God's promises [–] come to me, and I will wait for you until that moment; and I am sure that God doesn't waste the blood of the martyrs. God will destroy these oppressors—and you should know this: that the candlelight of [the] oppressors will not burn forever, [even] if it burns for a night—but [I] swear to God that it does not anymore.

And [now,] at [the end—to the] last, I love all of you

And I always pray for you and you also pray for me to be forgiven in the hope that God forgives me and accepts my martyrdom.

One who knows you (God), he does not need this life
He has no need for children, family, or wife
You make him passionate for both worlds
Those who become frenzied for you don't need both worlds
From Abdolhafoor Rigi to all friends—and:

I leave you and this life with the hope that I will meet you
in a better place—
one that is a magnificent paradise rather than in this
cursed world
[The letter ends with a 'Robaey' poem (a quatrain composed of two distiches) from a famous Sufi, Khwajah Abdullah Ansari of Herat.]

Appendix 4: A song used by Jondollah

In this YouTube video clip, the first song is in Persian (while Abdolmalek is embracing Abdolghaffor, and later when Abdolghafoor says goodbye to his mother):

(1)
How sweet is to die with faith
To die for an eternal friend
How good is to die entrenched in truth
To die under the shade of the Quran
Repeat (1)
How good is, like [Abubakr Sediq the Great,
To die truly in the [true] path of faith
How good is, like Omar in the sanct-
-tuary, to die in the house of The Forgiver
Repeat (1)
How good is, like Osman the [O]ppressed,
[For one] to die while reading the Quran
How good is, like Ali in the mosque,
To die by sword-strokes of unworthy men
...

Then they perform collective [p]rayer under [the] leadership of a person [who] seems to be Abdolmalek Rigi.

Then Abdolmalek Rigi is seen [to] raise [his] hands to [the] sky—praying to God while crying and asking God to curse, kill, and destroy the enemies.

The last section is an Arabic song in admiration of God. [4]

INDEX